Football's Blackest Hole

Football's Blackest Hole

A Fan's Perspective

CRAIG PARKER

Frog, Ltd.
Berkeley, California

Published by Frog, Ltd.

Frog, Ltd. books are distributed by
North Atlantic Books
P.O. Box 12327
Berkeley, California 94712

Cover and book design by Suzanne Albertson

Printed in Canada

North Atlantic Books' publications are available through most bookstores. For further information, call 800-337-2665 or visit our website at www.northatlanticbooks.com.

Substantial discounts on bulk quantities are available to corporations, professional associations, and other organizations. For details and discount information, contact our special sales department.

Library of Congress Cataloging-in-Publication Data

Parker, Craig, 1954–
    Football's blackest hole : a fan's perspective / by Craig Parker.
        p. cm.
    ISBN 1-58394-092-8 (pbk.)
    1. Oakland Raiders (Football team) 2. Football fans—United States.
I. Title.
gv956.o24p37 2003
796.332'64'0979494—dc21

2003014751
CIP

1 2 3 4 5 6 7 8 9 TRANSCON 08 07 06 05 04 03

To
My wife, Denise, for love
My daughter, Sarah, for family

ACKNOWLEDGEMENTS

Matt Coyle (Editor); Steve Eason; Tim Del Rosario; Shelton Hochstedler; Jim Apukka; Mike Sando; Patty Bergman; Rob Rivera; Jason Creasman; Gary Russell; Bob Carroll; Eric Shadinger; Michael Lambirth; Todd Olsen; Crystal Lentz; Mike Boysun; Don Marquez; Robert Kerns; Alex Chavez; Dan Postle; Allynn Czomba; Griz Jones; Bob Sanderson; Denise Lariviere; Jeff Aaron; Mark Parker; Andy Dinocola; Max Vekich; Marty Chorba; Sarah Kelley; Richard Grossinger; Mark Del Secco; Zach Glazer; Christopher Pyle; Bruce Bradford; Victoria Wischnesky; Jim Sagona; Joe Campo; Joe Richmond; Ron Riesterer; Judy Sherrill; Michael Maysonet; Major Stephanie Holcombe; Max Rattie; Scott Boe.

TABLE OF CONTENTS

CHAPTER FOUR
2002: First Quarter 93

CHAPTER FIVE
2002: Second Quarter 129

CHAPTER SIX
2002: Third Quarter 157

George Kimball

Over a quarter of a century has passed, but I'll never forget the look on Pete Rozelle's face the day he had to present the Vince Lombardi Trophy for the first time. The late NFL commissioner looked a lot like a guy who'd eaten some bad mushrooms, and Al didn't look much better. He was so overwhelmed by the moment that when, a few minutes later, I offered him my outstretched hand, he shook it and earnestly told me "congratulations."

Craig Parker hasn't forgotten the first time *he* met the Prince of Darkness, either. He and some buddies had driven down to the Raiders' complex in El Segundo, and when they spotted Al Davis they rushed over to talk some football. That particular conversation came to an abrupt conclusion when the budding author attempted to bum $50 off the Managing General Partner.

When the publisher asked me last spring if I'd be interested in introducing a book written by a card-carrying citizen of Raider Nation, a few questions leapt immediately to mind.

"Is it typed," I wondered, "or is it written in crayon?"

The second question concerned the author.

"Does he have a bone through his nose?" I asked.

"And just in case I DON'T like the book, does he know where I live?"

A few days before Super Bowl XXXVII in San Diego, I was in the process of writing a column tweaking Raider fans. That same day my boxing buddy Al Bernstein, who was doing his Las Vegas radio show from the NFL media center in San Diego, invited me on. It seemed a perfect opportunity to try out some of my Black Hole material, so I threw out line after line. Bernstein was rolling in the aisle, laughing so hard he couldn't keep his headset on. What I hadn't apperceived was that the Vegas station also beamed straight into Southern California, where there remains a residue of Raider loyalists. By the time I got off the air several of them had phoned in. Several, I was warned, had asked for my home address.

I'd forecast on the air that day that the Raider fans would start arriving in San Diego as soon as they made bail.

The profusion of pious types throughout the National Football League, you see, always gives rise to an interesting question come Super Bowl time: If both rosters are replete with born-again players, you find yourself wondering, which team is God supposed to root for?

My own supposition has always been that God had better things to do than worry about who wins the Super Bowl, but in the instance of the game which was going to be played at QualComm Stadium last January, we were presented with a more interesting theological phenomenon.

Super Bowl XXXVII may have marked, I supposed, the first time in the history of the event in which *Satan* had an active rooting interest.

Seriously, folks, you could approach a man on the street in any one of a hundred cities and ask the question: 'What is Lucifer's favorite football team?', and a hundred out of a hundred responses would be: "The Raiders, you idiot."

Besides, if ever evidence existed that God did actually care enough about who wins a football game to intervene, it took place on January 19, 2001, in a snowstorm in Foxboro, Massachusetts.

Craig Parker commemorates the events of that evening in the pages of this book by noting that "the urine on referee Walt Coleman's Depends drawers was barely dry before Al Davis began making plans for the 2002 Oakland Raiders football season."

I'd tell Parker to get over it, but I know he won't. While even New England fans recognize that Coleman's call was based on a stupid rule, they prefer to regard it as a 26-years-too-late makeup call for that flag Ben Dreith threw when Ray Hamilton hit Snake Stabler in that 1976 playoff game.

In the case of the Super Bowl just passed, the Buccaneers might not have sold their souls to the Devil to get to the Super Bowl, but they did the next best thing by sending a bunch of draft choices as compensation to Al Davis, who was, the best we can tell, Beelzebub's emissary on earth.

"Sure, Al's teams had been to Super Bowls before, but that was before the toothless, Darth Raider, studded dog-collar and body-odor element took over the stands," I wrote. "Back in the old days when you mentioned The Black Hole, you were probably talking about John Matuszak's armpit. Now Raider fans all look like John Matuszak in face paint, and root for common lowlifes like Bill Romanowski and Sebastian Janikowski."

In the pages of *Football's Blackest Hole,* Parker quotes Cliff Branch ("If you wanted to be a hippie or a Hell's Angel, that was fine as long as you played Raiders football," along with the Raiders credo as expressed by Ted (The Mad Stork) Hendricks:

"There were only two rules: Number One: Show up on Sunday ready to play. Number Two: Stay out of jail. Oh ... and Number two's not all that important."

Romo's locker, by the way, is commonly stocked with more pills than your neighborhood pharmacy. After he famously spit in the face of San Francisco's J.J. Stokes in a Monday Night game a few years ago, 49er Garrison Hearst described the Raider-in-the-making as "a racist dope pusher."

Janikowski, whom Parker describes as "The Polish Sausage," sometimes seems more like a walking Polish joke, a fellow so unremittingly stupid that a couple of years ago he became the only man other than Nick Nolte to give himself an overdose of the date-rape drug GHB. According to a police report, Janikowski collapsed on the floor of the Sno-Drift Bar on the October, 2001, night in question, cutting his face and requiring five stitches.

But then Al Davis has always prided himself by stocking his rosters with the bottom feeders of the NFL scrap heap. Although last year's edition of the Raiders was unusual in that as far as we can tell it didn't include a single convicted rapist, the team's fans could often compensate for that oversight.

A few hours before kickoff at the 2003 AFC Championship Game

I saw a woman wandering the mezzanine wearing a skimpy black t-shirt that read "Fuck You If You Hate The Raiders." This particular damsel had her ten-year-old son in tow. Somebody, presumably the mother, had spiked the poor kid's hair and painted it black and silver.

Two dozen of the Raiders' more enthusiastic supporters were detained by the local constabulary after celebrating the team's 41–24 win in that night's AFC championship game by trashing several blocks of downtown Oakland, torching an auto repair shop, and overturning several cars.

You couldn't help but wonder what they might have done if the Raiders had *lost,* but the city fathers were unlikely to spend much time worrying about it, since they were all on their way to San Diego.

The way I figured it, after a lifetime of trying, Brown had finally made it to the big stage.

No, not Tim Brown. *Jerry* Brown. I was trying to picture the Mayor of Oakland in a dog collar.

Before any given Raiders game the stadium parking lot looks like a casting call for a remake of "The Road Warrior."

As Parker points out in the pages of "Football's Blackest Hole," "there are actually three separate and distinct tailgate parties"—the first starts the night before the game, the second when the Coliseum gates officially open at 8 am, and the third after the game. When the Patriots played their regular season game in Oakland that November, I witnessed this phenomenon firsthand, and wondered aloud how all these people had so much time on their hands.

"When you own a meth lab, you don't exactly have to keep regular hours," explained a Bay Area colleague.

Like most denizens of the Black Hole, Craig Parker would rather drive to games, but it would be misleading to suggest that Raider fans don't ever get on airplanes. Take the case of Charles Dawson Jones, who in 1990, despite no visible means of support, attended every Raiders game, home and away. Only after the security cameras were examined did it come to light that Jones had financed his devotion to the skull-and-crossbones by sticking up 24 Sacramento-area banks.

Parker would no doubt hold that the image of Raider fans today continues to suffer from the unfortunate Los Angeles experiment, which is true enough. Many of the more unwholesome trappings of Raiderhood were adopted during this historical interlude, when the toothless swarms from Oakland were joined by Angelinos who brought, if nothing else, superior weaponry to football games. (The Raiders were embraced as the favored team of the Crips *and* the Bloods.)

Parker, in any case, writes very well, has a sharp eye for detail, and remembers more than just about any sportswriter I could name.

Of course, his memory is almost necessarily selective. In his run-down of NFL rules changes (invariably promulgated, in his view, to penalize the Raiders), he recounts the time Lyle Alzado ripped the helmet off the head of the Jets' Chris Ward and threw it at him, an incident which directly led to the NFL changing its regulations to proscribe using an unworn helmet as a weapon.

Alas, Parker somehow missed the greatest Raider helmet-as-a-weapon story of all, which took place immediately following a play-off game at the L.A. Coliseum in January of 1986.

Pat Sullivan, whose father Billy owned the Patriots, had by then risen to the rank of general manager, but with the Patriots sniffing their first-ever Super Bowl appearance, he let his fan's emotions get the better of him that day. In possession of an 'Official' (all-access) NFL credential, he was patrolling the sidelines of the Coliseum during the waning moments of the game, unmercifully taunting the Raider defenders, and Howie Long in particular.

Long was curious, astonished that anyone in possession of an official credential would behave so unprofessionally, and as he came off the field after one series, got close enough to ask his tormentor, quite reasonably, I thought, "Who the fuck *are* you, anyway?"

"I own the Patriots," replied a grinning Sullivan.

Now, Howie is from Boston and even with the limited information at his disposal was quickly able to piece together the whole picture. He didn't miss a beat.

"Unless your Daddy died at halftime, you don't own anything

yet," Long told him.

So far as I know, that was the last Long saw of Sullivan that day, but as the defeated Raiders came trooping up the runway after the game, Matt Millen spotted Sullivan and recognized him as the guy who'd been jawing from the sidelines. Using the helmet he was carrying like a sledge, he lunged out and delivered a mighty blow to the head that drove Sullivan to his knees, and, once he was revived, to a local hospital for several stitches in his noggin.

The momentous occasion was captured by a photographer, and years later, Pat Sullivan asked Millen to inscribe the picture, which he did. Sullivan *fils* is now out of football and runs his own television production company. Matt Millen became the President of the Detroit Lions, in which position, we can happily report, he often behaves every bit as unprofessionally as Sullivan did that day.

Taking issue with traditionalists, Parker cites the nineteenth-Century philosopher Andrew Lang ("He uses statistics as a drunken man uses lamp posts—for support rather than illumination"), and even when he lays into the Oakland Tribune's Dave Newhouse for a hang-wringing column lamenting the comportment of the face-paint-and-dog-collar set at Network Associates Coliseum, it is plain that behind Parker's Darth Vader face-shield, his tongue is firmly in cheek.

"Newhouse claims that the percentage of out-of-control fans is 'under twenty per cent,'" writes Parker. "That estimation is far too high—20 per cent of 60,000 is, uh, 12,000. I would put the number of maniacally, moronic psychopaths that attend Raiders games at no more than 10,000—plus the two thousand that sneak into the game."

Now that they're about to discover that he can read and write I'm not sure what future reception awaits Craig Parker from his comrades in the Black Hole. I find myself reminded, in any case, of an old Scottish soccer coach who in bygone years developed such a rapport with the fans that, I was told, he became known the length and breadth of Glasgow as 'Dr. Doolittle.'

I couldn't resist asking why.

"Because he can talk to the animals."

George Kimball has been a sports columnist for the *Boston Herald* for the past twenty-three years; he has covered the NFL for three decades. He also writes the "America At Large" column for *The Irish Times* in Dublin.

CHAPTER ONE

Verities

There I was on Labor Day weekend, 2002, attending a second birth-day party for our friends' son. Helping with the camera work, enjoy-ing the September weather and mingling with complete strangers. Overall, it was about as exciting as watching a pro bowlers tourna-ment on television.

But then a serious-looking Black gentleman, noticing the polo shirt with Raider insignia, struck up a conversation about the team's 2002 chances. After a short while of polite speculation, he asked me what I thought of Al Davis. I gave an answer and sensing his anx-iousness, returned the question to him. He began to describe how Art Shell was not given a fair chance by Mr. Davis, and his verbal delivery picked up speed as the vituperation found expression. Suddenly, the man's voice trailed off and he searched for words to capture his pent-up feelings.

Matter-of-factly and looking me directly in the eye, he dead-panned: "I think Al Davis should be assassinated."

Opinion. Everybody's got one.

This is especially true when it comes to discussion about the prin-cipal owner and the general partner of the Oakland Raiders. In terms of cult of personality, Al Davis ranks up there with Joseph Stalin, Adolph Hitler, Fidel Castro, and Richard Simmons.

Ask people what they think of Al Davis and they'll talk of his ducktail pompadour or his penchant for leather dress. They'll talk of how he stole the team away to Los Angeles, his personnel deci-sions, his bathing habits, or that he's ready for the old folk's home. When it comes to expressing a sentiment on this individual born on the Fourth of July, 1929, everyone feels compelled to offer an assessment.

But does anyone really know Al Davis?

The truth is: 98% of people with an opinion on Al Davis have never even met the man.

I met Al Davis once. No, it wasn't at the mall or a porno theatre; it was at his short-lived Southern California playground, the Raiders' offices in El Segundo. The "Los Angeles" Raiders 1989 season was over, and the Pride and Poise boys had pulled that win-two, lose-two excrement that made Raider fans spit nails and curse their own fate. Mike Shanahan was fired in the October Second Massacre after opening the season 1–3 against AFC West opponents.

Art Shell was brought in and had the Silver and Black positioned for a playoff run at 8–6. The Raiders promptly lost their last two road games to finish at a kiss-of-death 8–8 (7–1 at home and 1–7 on the road).

Several Raider Nation friends of mine were sorely disappointed at this turn of events. We felt it was imperative that Coach Shell meet us in person so he could gauge the sincerity of our temperament and the depth of our convictions.

So, on December 28, we embarked on the Mecca pilgrimage from El Toro to El Segundo, stopping every eight steps for El Drinko. We made pretty good time too: 55 miles in 2½ hours. Plenty of scenic vistas along the beautiful I-405 corridor. Gassed and ready to make history, we pulled into the parking lot at 332 Center Street. For those who never visited the Raiders training facility in the City of Angels, be advised: it was a dump. Converted from an old junior high school, the complex more closely resembled a cross between a flophouse motel and a detention center than home to the "Team of the Decades."

El Segundo means "The Second" but, viewing this hovel, a more appropriate term was "El Segundo al último": The Second to Last. Our first impression: if Al Davis wanted to work in a ghetto, why did he leave Oakland? The place was so depressing that Marcus Allen chose to relocate to Kansas City rather than spend another day in these confines. The closest this place came to Versailles fountains was when the kids across the street busted open the fire hydrant to cool their heated skins.

It actually felt better to relax in the parking lot than to go inside—which, after we were told Art Shell was not taking visitors that day—is what we were doing when a black Cadillac pulled into the parking lot.

As fortuitous winds blow, we were standing in the stall next to the sign that said 'Al Davis'; perhaps we were drawn to it. It certainly appeared that we were waiting for him when the American-made luxury automobile pulled to within six feet of us. There we were, three scruffy rednecks from the Pacific Northwest—one a 300-pounder—when out of the car and into our midst stepped the Machiavelli of football, Al Davis.

After a few tentative seconds, we stepped forward, introduced ourselves and shook hands with Mr. Davis. What struck me first was how quiet he was; when he spoke, it was with such a stillness of volume that you almost found yourself leaning forward to hear him. The diminutive manner made him appear smaller than he actually was; his fashion of restraint belied the 6 feet-1 inch frame.

He asked us where we were from and we told him "Washington State." To this Mr. Davis commented, "Well, that would explain the clothes." When we volunteered that we were actually from the Grays Harbor area of Washington, he said, "Yeah, I've heard of that place"—an understatement, since he knew full well that John Madden played football there while attending Grays Harbor College.

Then Al Davis did a strange and most unexpected thing: he apologized to us for the Raiders not making the playoffs. He said: "We let down the city of Los Angeles, we let down Raider fans across the nation, and we let ourselves down." Now, I am originally from Douglas fir country; I have known loggers who could throw a choker around a downed tree the way Raider fans throw an arm around their blow-up doll. And those loggers never apologized for anything.

This is because the curse of loggers—like most sports team owners—is that they know they are right. Yet this Brooklyn native was willing to apologize in a parking lot to complete strangers with hardly $40 between them about something over which he had only marginal control. Maybe he just wanted to make sure he got to the front door in one piece.. Maybe he was just playing us. Or maybe, in his eyes, we weren't strangers.

My 300-pound buddy was wearing one of those gaudy Raider letterman's jackets you see every so often. It had the years of AFC playoffs on the left sleeve, the AFC Championship years on the right. On the front body of the coat were large footballs commemorating the three Super Bowl wins, and on the back were the names of Hall of Fame Raiders (no, Eric Dickerson and Ronnie Lott were not on the coat).

We offered to Mr. Davis that he would be elected to the Pro Football Hall of Fame. No, said Al, he didn't see that happening. On cue, my Raider–nut buddy turned around to show the back of his jacket and said, "You're already in." There at the bottom of the illustrious list of Raider immortals, was the name 'Al Davis.' Surprisingly, this just seemed to make the Raider owner more distant. Perhaps humanity and love do not apply to the public Al Davis.

That was when I asked him if he could loan me fifty dollars, and Mr. Davis walked away in silent disdain.

It's a given: Al Davis has made his share of mistakes. He released Fred Biletnikoff in 1979, even though Freddie had another couple of productive seasons in him. He did the same thing to Matt Millen in 1989; Millen thanked him by garnering two more Super Bowl rings with NFC teams, while Davis time and again came up empty.

Davis' miscues in the annual college draft are legendary, with the years 1985–86 and 1990–91 particularly brutal. His ultimatum to Greg Biekert in 2002—when he offered to cut the middle linebacker's salary from $2.5 million to $1 million per year—was a disloyal slap and a public relations disaster.

Finally, his decision to move the Raiders from Oakland to Los Angeles was the worst mistake of his professional career—worse even than the first-round selections of Todd Marinovich and Patrick Bates. But the ethics of Al Davis have always been in question. This is a guy who, when he worked for The Citadel, allegedly recruited a farm boy in 1956 on the condition that the young man's major could be agrarian studies—even though The Citadel did not offer such a curriculum at the school.[1]

But let us not bury Al Davis; let us praise him. Warren Wells was an Oakland Raiders wide receiver from 1967–1970, a favorite of Daryle Lamonica. Davis worked on several occasions to secure the release of Wells from prison, probably anticipating that many other Raiders were not far behind. Davis brought back Fred Biletnikoff as a coach, and Freddie tutored the likes of Marcus Allen, Tim Brown, Mervyn Fernandez and Jerry Rice.

Al Davis gave '00' a singular honor: each game Jim Otto sits in front of Davis in the luxury box, and to this day Otto will not hear a single bad word about Al Davis. Yes, he unceremoniously unloaded Ken Stabler, Jack Tatum and Dave Casper; but Al Davis also picked up Kenny King, Bob Chandler, Raymond Chester, and Jim Plunkett— all critical players down the stretch in Oakland's 1980–1981 Super Bowl run.

Al Davis stayed by his wife Carol's bedside, addressing her quietly when she was comatose in 1979. "Al would talk to her, squeeze her hand, speak of things only the two of them knew about."[2] Most recently, Davis incurred a $50,000 fine for refusing to attend a 2003 public Super Bowl event, deflecting any chance at distraction and keeping the spotlight where it belonged: on the Raiders team. Too bad he couldn't deflect the furious Tampa Bay pass rush.

Once, after a game, Davis saw a reporter in the locker room who looked awful. Davis grabbed the man by the arm, quickly ushered the scribe to the team orthopedist and said, "Take care of him." The doctor had the sportswriter on the training table right there in the post-game locker room, checking him out. A day later the ink journalist was in the hospital for arterial blockage tests. All this on four words from Mr. Davis.

And, finally, Al Davis created the Raiders and later brought them back to Oakland. Granted, he should not have moved them in the first place, but we all make mistakes—Al Davis just makes them on a larger scale. And who can blame him for making tens of millions of dollars in the process?

In our lives, as we grow older, all Raiders fans seek the same thing: another Lombardi trophy. But, secondarily, we seek that most elusive goal: redemption. Redemption from our past, redemption from our loved ones, redemption from ourselves. Al Davis has been at the head of a football organization that has provided Raider fans with three Super Bowl titles. Granted, the last championship was 1983–84, when the original "Terminator" was still to be released and Ted Watts started thirteen games at cornerback opposite Lester Hayes. As any lifelong Raider knows, it is very difficult to win the Lombardi trophy; currently, there are fifteen football organizations (47% of existing NFL teams) that have never earned a single one.

Al Davis is not a saint, just a man whose efforts have allowed us to drink from the chalice of victory, smell the sweet air of triumph and witness the miracle of a championship season. For those of us who forgive Al Davis his many transgressions and accept his position at head of the table, ours is the greater reward. For those of you who are unforgiving of the man, I still love you as Raiders.

But I know what you are.

You're just like an opinion.

Everybody's got one.

REFERENCES
1. *Slick;* Mark Ribowsky; New York; Macmillan Publishing Company; 1991; pg. 74.
2. ibid., pg. 276.

THE SUPER BOWL IS STUPID

The hype is incredible, indescribable. The glitz and pomp and parties are insufferable. The interviews, interrogations, and innuendo are interminable. And the gaseous retching of announcers—who think that every single, solitary moment of a television broadcast must be filled with sound—is infuriating. It should be a law: during every TV broadcast, radio station identification, newspaper headline, Times Square marquee, Disneyland commercial, Wheaties box cover, playing card picture, White House visit, magazine article, commemorative coin, and funeral epitaph dealing with the world championship of football, there must be a five-word warning displayed as prominently as the Surgeon General's admonition on tobacco.

The Super Bowl is stupid.

The Super Bowl was the brainchild of the late Lamar Hunt, owner of the Kansas City Chiefs. I don't want to cast aspersions on the deceased, but Lamar Hunt was a dweeb-faced hayseed. It is written (somewhere), and I quote: Whosoever believeth in a hayseed is an ill-begotten, inbred, Onan-loving, spasmodic, sycophantic, prostituting, pill-popping poor excuse of a human being. Endquote.

Raider fans sincerely and resolutely detested Lamar Hunt. But more than just Mr. Dweeb-Face, it is the Kansas City Chiefs we really hated. We hated Buck Buchanan, Len Dawson, Elvis Grbac and the waterboy. And the fans. Oh God, the red-clad fans with their stupid tomahawk-chop. If there is an anti-Oakland franchise, it is Kansas City—bless its heart. Raider faithful are a gentle people; we do not believe in capital punishment. But in this case, we're willing to make an exception.

We detest the Kansas City Chiefs because they take from Al Davis what is rightfully his by Manifest Destiny—namely, the AFC Championship. And that is a title worth fighting for.

Super Bowl Champion, on the other hand, is hardly a crown worth wearing. From a fan's perspective, viewing the game is a bit like listening to new age music: exotic and alluring at first, but in the end no more exciting than having sex with yourself. The Super Bowl once was a good idea, but that is no longer the case.

How has this spectacle lost its luster? Let me count the ways. First, few Super Bowls are close. Let's use twelve points as the criterion; any Super Bowl won by twelve points or more is a blowout. For those of you who can count to 37 in roman numerals, how many Super Bowls would you surmise were blowouts? If you guessed two-thirds, you would be correct. 24 out of 37 Super Bowls have been won by twelve or more points. (By this measurement, all five Raider games have been blowouts.) And in fourteen of the 24 blowouts, there was at least a twelve-point lead at the half.[1]

Second, the television coverage is boring. The pre-game show, all forty-two hours of it, was particularly painful to watch:

- A couple of magicians placed their prediction of the game's outcome in a pickle jar outside Times Square, which was then suspended in the air and guarded by U.S. Marines (don't they have terrorists to fight?).
- The on-air developing story of Barret Robbins' benching initially received all of one minute of analysis. Why was there so little time devoted to this lineman's unprecedented tale? Because the story's details were still unfolding and therefore could not be scripted. It takes an incisive mind to filter through all the background noise to get to the root of such a saga. Pressed to wrap up for advertisement breaks, the announcers' minds were as sharp as cantaloupes, spewing hurried and confused sentences like "What happens on a snap late in the fourth quarter will he be tired we'll be back."[2]
- Talk, talk, talk on the USS Preble. Three has-been quarterbacks sitting in director's chairs spouting rhetoric and inanities about the game of football with all the excitement of a glider circling a vacant lot. Junior Seau looked completely ill-at-ease in their midst; perhaps he could see his future after two more seasons of Marty ball. You would be unsettled too, if you had to sit through discerning gems like "The bottom line is you're going to go strength against strength, you're going to do what got you there."[3] Such insights certainly got the viewers there, putting their minds to sleep and sending them running for the acetaminophen.

Name another televised sporting event where, the next day around the water cooler, people talk about … the commercials. Is that football? Incredibly, in a recent survey 40% said they watched the game just to see the Super Bowl commercials (no doubt these viewers lived in the Cincinnati, Detroit, and San Francisco areas).[4] That translates into 52 million television spectators only watching only to see thirty seconds of a man with three arms, a castaway Gilligan or Ozzy Osbourne serenaded by the Osmonds. At $2.1 million per thirty-second ad, the 65 commercials brought in a cool $136 million. Certainly, there were several good thirty-second productions. Unfortunately, there were also several that did not work: Levi Buffalos (missed-tackle art); Subway and Quiznos (tedious and boring); and the pump fake by Rich Gannon in the second quarter—(totally unbelievable).

The ticket prices are outrageous. Who goes to Super Bowls anymore? ABC cameras showed the vanilla crowd at the game's start; it looked mainly like corporate executives, reporters, and prostitutes (is there a difference?). Face value, the tickets went for $400-$500 apiece. Who can afford that kind of action? The answer is: we all can, if we want to mortgage the farm on the backside of Christmas. Meanwhile, we drive cars with 150,000 miles on the odometer and keep putting water in the radiator rather than replace the leaky water pump.

In 1983, Super Bowl XVII was held in the Rose Bowl, capacity 103,667. We rented a Lincoln Town car and drove down from Washington State to see the game. Just before kickoff, the scalpers were sweating bullets as two East coast teams (Miami-Washington) vied after a strike-shortened season. I scalped a ticket that, as luck would have it, placed me in the midst of Redskin fans at about the thirty-yard line. When they saw me show up in the aisle with my cheap black and white No. 12 jersey, they actually glared at me before letting me sit with them. It was a good Super Bowl; Washington took the lead with ten minutes to go when John Riggins lumbered 43 yards for a touchdown on a fourth-and-one left tackle plunge. At the game's end, Redskin fans cried for joy. The price of the ticket: $35.

Now, there has been inflation over twenty years. But a $400 ticket is just another example: the Super Bowl is stupid.

If this sounds like sour grapes, that's because it is. As a Raiders fan, I don't necessarily care to wait nineteen years to have my team return to the Super Bowl and have their helmets handed to them. Tampa Bay was clearly the better team on Jan. 26, 2003: faster, stronger, more focused and better prepared. In the game of their lives, the Buccaneers stood up and stepped forward—while Oakland lay down like a Hobo spider sprayed with insect killer.

But the Oakland organization needn't worry; Raider fans wrote the book on loyalty. If we can forgive Barret Robbins his impromptu tourist visit to the historical enclave of Tijuana, we can forgive a team that won the AFC Championship before taking the final week off. Besides, Raider fans learned a good deal from this year's rendition of the Silver and Black.

What We Learned

- That veterans could inspire young players to a higher level of effort;
- That takeaways are good, but points-off-takeaways are better;
- That Lewis and Clark with a bad case of diarrhea had a more prolific running attack than the Raiders did 200 years later;
- That players can't give up on themselves, even when others are having their doubts;
- That one big play can turn a season around;
- That run-run-pass could beneficially be flipped upside-down to pass-pass-run;
- That complete strangers can be brought together and formed into a cohesive whole;
- That "keep your foot on the gas" applies to more than just automobiles;
- That a football game played in the elements can be a lot of fun, especially if viewed from the warmth of one's home;
- That winning decisively is better than winning ugly.

And we learned one other thing from the 2002 Oakland Raiders. The Super Bowl is stupid.

REFERENCES

1. *Total Football II: The Official Encyclopedia of the National Football League;* Bob Carroll, Michael Gershman, David Neft, John Thorn; New York: Harper Collins Publishers; 1997; pg. 113–177.
2. Chris Berman; ABC Sports; Pre-Super Bowl Warmup; January 26, 2003.
3. Bob Griese; ABC Sports; Pre-Super Bowl Warmup; January 26, 2003.
4. "The Wackiness Is Back"; Dan George; CNN Sports Illustrated; January 27, 2003. http://sportsillustrated.cnn.com/football/2003/playoffs/news/2003/0 1/26/commercial_appeal/; May 7, 2003.

FROM THE PARKING LOT TO
THE PLAYING FIELD

They come. From far and near, by land and by sea, by BART and by bus, by RV, SUV and HOV, by hook and by crook—they come. They come early and they come often, whole caravans of the Raider faithful. Queuing up in long lines that move with relative ease because the forefathers had wisdom to place the destination near a freeway. They bring life's necessities with them: sunglasses, lotion, coolers, ponchos, food, and drinks. They bring their knowledge, voices, and wallets. They bring their attitude and history. Each has a story; each an opinion. Yet these many individuals all arrive at the House of Thrills for the same reason: because live football is its own reward.

In like fashion, the tailgate party before the game is its own attraction. There, in the parking lot, crowded together in a middle-American tribute to free time, friendships are forged, lies exchanged, and a commitment to a certain large extended family takes on a new meaning. If it takes a village to raise a child, it damn sure takes a tailgate to support a football franchise. And the Raiders are the best at this functionality. All colors and creeds are welcome, and the price of admission is small: just wear the proper family colors—silver and black.

When you go to a Raider tailgate party and you're wearing silver and black, then you're wearing fun. It's as simple as that. This is what separates Raider tailgates from other tailgates nationwide. It doesn't matter about your nationality, race, size (big or small, skinny or fat, big-footed or elephant-headed), gender, sexual preference, professional position, income level, or education: if you are wearing the right stuff, you become part of the Raider family and are instantly invited to the biggest block party on the planet. And the party, like our memory, is long.

There are actually three separate and distinct tailgate parties. The first tailgate starts the night before the game. There are four gates that lead in to the Coliseum parking lot (one is strictly for RVs) and vehicles start lining up on the streets the night before. Twenty, fifty, then hundreds of vehicles of all descriptions are driven up and parked along an arterial as trucks and vans drive by with people shouting out, "Go Raiders!" Portable bonfire pits are unloaded, assembled and soon are providing light and heat against the darkness. Tables and chairs quickly appear, DJ music systems spring up, dancing begins— sometimes even between different sexes. Card games are started, Yahtzee is thrown, cribbage is pegged, time ceases to be a hindrance, and the night becomes more like a pep rally than the back of a movie theater. On and on, alive-alive, the hours melt away, until the rollicking gives way to respite and the far-between hardcore pockets of discussion greet the first moments of dawn.

The second tailgate starts when the gates officially open to the Coliseum parking lot at 8 A.M. For the next four hours, convoys and motorcades parade in procession, an orderly chaos toward the best experience you can have as a Raider fan. Take the time to walk through the tailgate areas. Listen to a garage band play "War Pigs" and "Voodoo Child" but change the lyrics to weave football themes. Look around you: it's like a gigantic wedding reception. Inhale the fragrant aroma as the smell of charcoal briquettes, marinated meat, seafood, chicken, deep-fried turkey, racks of ribs, hot dogs, and ham-

burger fat fill the air—as do thrown footballs, few of which are actually caught. Look to your left, there's putt-putt golf; look to your
right, there's miniature ping-pong. There are people having arms
decorated, eyes patched, fingers and toenails painted. One and all
are dressed in silver, black, or white. Everybody has some type of
Raiders paraphernalia: flags, decals, magnets, banners, helmets, dolls,
costumes, canopies, pennants, or propped-out vehicles. Everyone is
laughing, talking, kidding, joking, singing, kissing, posing, predicting, playing happily or sleeping soundly. Everyone has their Raider
game-face on—real or made up. And everyone gets along incredibly
well, a testament to the human spirit and a statement on the commitment of the best professional football fans in the world. Raider
fans are so committed that they practice abstinence lest any surprise
births occur during football season. And why shouldn't they be just
like they are? Raider fans instinctively understand that they are all just
pieces of mud that are on this earth for a short instant, so they might
as well have a good time while they're here. For me, the pregame
tailgate sparks a strange sensation. It felt feels like coming home.

The third tailgate starts after the game. Returning to their vehicles—hoarse and happy, or soused and sad—the Raider fans have
given their all and, hopefully, the players have too. It's time to replay the game: celebrate the great plays, rue the mistakes, and con-
demn the officials. This week's designated drivers sip coffee; everyone
else snacks on the leftover beer, margaritas, and Maalox. The post-
game call-in show is playing softly in the background, but few pay
close attention. Who cares what some stay-at-home know-it-all
thinks. You had to have been there—here in the parking lot, out in
the Coliseum—to have an opinion that matters.

The conversations finally die down. No more stories to tell, no
more injustices to right. All but the most stalwart tailgaters are done
in. It's time to pack up. Time to return the borrowed spatula and
tongs; time to put the kids to bed in the upper bunk. Time to take off
the eye patch and put away the cutlass. Slowly, compelled by tomorrow and the open road now available, the dedicated many get into
their conveyances and crawl toward Hegenberger Boulevard. Their

Raider weekend here is done, but they will be back for the next game, to do it all over again. Raider fans ate, drank and laughed together, cheered their team together, and won or lost together. The bonds of camaraderie that tailgate fans create for each other go far beyond what is experienced in the workweek world. Because of Raider love, every Sunday is a family reunion.

From the parking lot to the playing field: it's not that great a distance. In fact, it's not certain which is the more real game.

RAIDER MYSTIQUE

One hears the words 'Raider Mystique' bantered about throughout the football season and, as with all expressions of French origin—like "a la mode" or "noblesse oblige"—we're not really sure what the term means. We have a general sense that it connotes a sense of mystery, because that's what the word "mystique" sounds like, but we can't be sure, knowing the French reputation for duplicity.

Our search for the meaning of Raider Mystique begins with the Raider players themselves, for they are the most educated and knowledgeable among us.

First, Napoleon Harris, who graduated from Northwestern:

The Raiders have always had a mystique. When you play against the Raiders, you have to bring your game. The Raiders are a team of tradition. I think we're going to continue to grow.[1]

Next, Frank Middleton, who graduated from the school of hard knocks:

We all love blood. We love the smell of blood. Just watch us. When the Raiders get on top of people, the bloodhounds come out. The defense gets riled, the offense gets hyper. And the fans go crazy, man. We're all vampires when we come out on Sunday. That's what the

Raider Mystique is—everybody's blood hungry, fans, players, everybody. We all love going for the throat."[2]

The questions around this subject abound. Just what is Raider
Mystique? Is it an obsessive alliance between fan and team which
transfers into seeing all things through silver-and-black glasses? Could
be, for the visually challenged fan. Is it an immature and unholy
irreverence that transcends the mundane shackles of life's struggles?
Might be, for the mentally challenged fan. Is it a quiet place of reflection where we retreat to consider the glory of championships and
the price that must be paid for success? Certainly, for the thoughtful
fan. Or, simply put, is it a single Silver and Black football helmet nes-
tled among three glistening Lombardi trophies? Yeah, baby!

Is Raider Mystique real? Absolutely. In fact, the only person that
I have ever heard say it does not exist was a sports reporter—and
that right there should prove sports writers don't know squat. Is
Raider Mystique nevertheless a state of mind? Definitely. For wherever there is despair, there is hope—and wherever there is a sports
bar, there are Raider Haters. These are people who have been repeatedly driven to despair by the Silver and Black juggernaut, and fear the
franchise with all the fervor of Republicans toward Bill Clinton. A
San Diego linebacker said:

> It's kind of funny everybody's rival is the Oakland Raiders. I don't
> know why that is, but I think just from the mystique from the his-
> tory of the team. It just seems like everybody wants to get up against
> the Raiders. Everybody is always trying to get them.[3]

Now why do these Raider Haters persecute us so, when we're
just a bunch of loveable funsters? Why doesn't anybody celebrate
the Buccaneers' win in the Super Bowl, preferring instead to gloat
about the Raiders' loss? Why, when the Raiders win, do people at
work the next day simply growl and mumble—but when the Raiders
lose, they go out of their way to stop by and diss us? That's Raider
Mystique.

Can Raider Mystique be inherited? Ask two Silver and Black devotees how they came to be Raider fans, and you will get similar answers. One might give an answer as simple as Julia Roberts trying to explain to her mother why she married Lyle Lovett: "I have no idea." And the other fan will might say: "Oh yeah? 1976? That's when I became a Raiders fan—because that's the year I was born." They don't ever remember making a conscious decision to become a Raider fan but, judging from the myriad of photographs taken— with Raider hats, shorts, shirts and leather chaps—they were always on the Silver and Black side of life. It is almost as if the father took his child aside at an early age and said, "Look, I don't have anything to leave you. I wasted my fortune on RVs, SUVs, DVDs, and STDs. So I am going to bequeath you this advice: don't trust whitey, always respect your mother, and love the Silver and Black as if they were your own." So, you see, it's not just the dysfunction that is genera- tional among Raider families; there's also Raider Mystique.

Can Raider Mystique be shared? When young Raider fans grow up and go through their rebellious stage—drinking, drugs, quitting school—when communication is low and animosity among family members is ever-present, there always exists a subject that is shel- tered from the storm of judgment. It's a safe place, an enclave, a demilitarized zone where either side can retreat and indicate they wish to speak in civilized tones and communicate in peace together. That's Raider Mystique.

Can Raider Mystique be symbolized? Black looks mean. Charlie Garner was asked to compare the San Francisco 49ers with the Oakland Raiders and he initially gave the stock answer about win- ning traditions with different attitudes. Then he was pressed to pick a favorite. "Me? I like wearing black," Garner said with a wicked smile. "Black is more sinister. Black is better."[4]

Indeed, black is better. It was the genius of Al Davis to choose this color scheme. Some say he chose it because he is color-blind, but logic points to his East Coast boyhood love of war, football, and the Black Knights of West Point—"the way the black made them look so much bigger than the other teams."[5] The black uniforms fit perfectly with the helmeted pirate, tell-tale eye-patch and crossed swords behind the head. Who else has a poem written for their franchise that says: "He'll knock you 'round and upside down/And laugh when he's conquered and won,"[6] implying that a Raider takes what rightfully belongs to others? It's all part of the Raider Mystique.

And, while other franchises have changed their uniform colors and logos like they were soda pop cans, the Raiders have always kept the same distinctive colors and block-letter design. Isn't it great, one writer asked, that the Raiders will never have a "throwback" day where they wear their old uniforms?[7] Every day is a throwback. Tradition to Raider fans is important: a tradition of family, loyalty and winning. That's Raider Mystique.

On the football field, winning is a direct result of aggression and intimidation. Said Jim Otto: "We hit harder than anybody, sometimes after the whistle. Well, you can't put a stopwatch on aggression. And if teams didn't like the way we hit them, we'd hit them even harder the next play."[8] The Raiders, over several decades, became one of the top football franchises by the usual standard of winning percentages.

The pirate is symbolically a renegade. Al Davis made a cult following out of last-chance head cases and long-shot reclamation prospects. Coaches shied away from micromanaging and players were left to be free-spirited, so long as they performed their assignments come game-time. In Clifford Branch's view, "If you wanted to be a hippie or a Hell's Angel, that was fine as long as you played Raiders football."[9] Ted Hendricks said that there were only two rules: "Number one: show up on Sunday ready to play. Number two, stay out of jail. Oh ... and number two's not all that important."[10] In return for respect and freedom given them by their coaches, play they did—and won. That's Raider Mystique.

And then there were the unheralded prospects, those players drafted after the third round who fashioned such fine efforts and produced years of Raider productivity: Clarence Davis, (round 4, 1971–78); Clifford Branch (round 4, 1972–85); Dave Dalby (round 4, 1972–85); Skip Thomas (round 7, 1972–78); Mickey Marvin (round 4, 1977–87); Lester Hayes (round 5, 1977–86); Rod Martin (round 12, 1977–88); Reggie Kinlaw (round 12, 1979–84).[11] All of these players started in at least one Super Bowl win. How could the Raiders spot these vital players after everyone else missed them? That's Raider Mystique.

In the 1970s, Raider Mystique was born, as it was personified by a unique blend of characters, athletes and rivalries. It was a team mystiqued. The return to Oakland in 1995 brought a transfer of power: away from the players and to the fans. Today, it is the fans that hold the mystical power, as they seek to outdo each other for most outrageous getup worn to a football game. Be it a skull face, gorilla head, vampire, voodoo queen, Zulu warrior, two-headed Raider, sombrero man, or spiked shoulder pads, everything and anything is fair game as spectators seek to match football players' weird superstitions with their own unusual sense of style. In true Mardi Gras fashion, the fans' message is: we are the keepers of the spiritual secrets in the House of Thrills. That's Raider Mystique.

But the players have recently started their own movement to re-establish Raider Mystique. First, there are the reclamation projects such as Tyrone Wheatley, Rich Gannon, and Jerry Rice—players who find a home after travel or rejection among other franchises. Then there are the Raiders who are "too old." Gannon, Rice, Bill Romanowski, Rod Woodson, Tim Brown, and Trace Armstrong are out to prove that professional football can be led by a gang of six— with a little help from their (young) friends—even though their combined maturity nearly equals the age of the United States (225). Together as a team, the Raiders seek to remake their own image into a twenty-first century model: "We don't just want to have this image of nastiness," Gannon said. "We want to have a character and personality that reflects that but is unique to us. It's important to be very tough and physical but at the same time be disciplined. That's the big thing. You've got to play smart in this league and be disciplined. If you do that, you have a chance."[12]

And always, the naysayers keep predicting doom on the House of Al: They're too old; they'll wear down in the second half; Tim

Brown has lost a step; Rich Gannon doesn't have a strong arm; Jerry Rice is forty; Bill Romanowski can't cover; Rod Woodson isn't the player he once was; Trace Armstrong cannot come back from the Achilles tear. And when these players helped their team to win the AFC Championship, that line of reasoning was jettisoned and a new argument was hatched: the Raiders are $50 million over the salary cap; they're going to cut the entire team; they can't afford to sign any free agents; they can't re-sign their existing players; they won't be able to restructure themselves out of this one. And yet the Raiders keep winning. That's Raider Mystique.

So it goes. On and on, through charge and vindication, victory and defeat, good against bad, us against them. Supreme in our confidence, deranged in our commitment and molded by loyalty, Raider fans revel in the assessment that we are the last true believers.

Raider Mystique. Is it real? It's more than real.

It's a way of life.

REFERENCES

1. "Crockett Wheeled Off Field with Neck Injury"; Jerry McDonald; *Oakland Tribune*; September 9, 2002.
2. "Frank Talk from O-line"; Nancy Gay; *San Francisco Chronicle*; January 22, 2003.
3. "Raiders Nemesis Sports New Stripes"; David Bush; *San Francisco Chronicle*; December 7, 2002.
4. "Raiders Just Living in the Present Tense"; Nancy Gay; *San Francisco Chronicle*; November 3, 2002.
5. *Slick*; Mark Ribowsky; New York: Macmillan Publishing Company; 1991; pg. 119.
6. Poem written by Steve Sabol; www.silverandblackattack.com; April 30, 2003.
7. "Off-Season Plan to Stop Leaking: Call a Plummer"; Jerry McDonald; *Oakland Tribune*; December 1, 2002.
8. *The Pain of Glory*; Jim Otto with Dave Newhouse; Champaign, IL: Sports Publishing, Inc.; 1999; pg. 118.

9. *Raiders Forever;* John Lombardo; Lincolnwood, IL: Contemporary Books; 2001; pg. 184.

10. *You're Okay, It's Just a Bruise;* Rob Huizenga, M.D.; New York: St. Martin's Press; 1994; pg. 45.

11. *The Team of the Decades 2002;* Oakland Raiders Media Guide.

12. "NFL 2002 Raiders Preview"; Nancy Gay; *San Francisco Chronicle;* September 3, 2002.

RULE CHANGES

There he was, tall and beautiful, lazing in the California sun on the grass near the practice field. You know, he explained, the NFL would look nothing like it does today if not for the Raiders. You'd still have five-yard chucks, Holy Rollers, hook moves, and stickum. Yep, if it weren't for the Raiders, pro football would look a lot different.

Then Ted Hendricks got on his horse and rode out onto the playing field, beholden to nothing except the rulebook.

So let's revisit the NFL Digest to see in what areas the Raiders were influential in this rulebook realm of subjects, predicates and handcuffs:

1976: A defensive player is prohibited from "running or diving into, or throwing his body against or on a ball carrier who falls or slips to the ground untouched and makes no attempt to advance, before or after the ball is dead."[1]

This rule doubtless found its roots in the Oakland Raiders' game at Kansas City, November 1, 1970. Leading 17–14 against the Silver and Black, on third down QB Len Dawson ran a bootleg for a first down with 1:08 left in the game. The play supposedly ended when Dawson tripped over a teammate's leg but, as Dawson lay prone on his stomach—not attempting to rise—out of nowhere came defensive end Ben Davidson. Running full blast, Davidson plowed his helmet into Dawson's exposed back like a cruise missile seeking vengeance on an Iraqi palace bunker.

At first, Davidson held to the position he was simply hustling on the play: "If he had fallen, he still had to be tackled."[2] Only in later years would Gentle Ben admit the obvious. "We needed a touchdown to win and field goal to tie, so when Lenny rolled out, he tripped over a leg, and I figured if I could hurt him, we'd be back in first place next week, so I speared him and did a somersault over him."[3]

1978: Within a five-yard zone from the line of scrimmage, a defensive player may chuck an eligible receiver. Beyond this five-yard limitation, the defender may not contact a receiver who tries to evade him.

The five-yard chuck rule was the NFL's raised white flag to the "bump and run," a defensive tactic employed by cornerbacks against world-class track stars masquerading as wide receivers. And the prototype of bump-and-run tactics? The Oakland Raiders. Coach Al Davis first witnessed the combative nature of cornerback tactics in 1963 with Oakland's Fred Williamson. "He would get up on top of receivers and knock the crap out of them, then run with them," said Davis. "So we began to teach the bump-and-run. It was predicated on the fact that we could always keep the free safety free and give the cornerback the security to play tight man-to-man based on a basketball concept." Kent McCloughan became the Raiders' first bump-and-run cornerback, playing for Oakland from 1965–1970.

In 1967, the Raiders would trade Rex Mirich to the Denver Broncos for a guy named Willie Brown, and Brown would revolutionize the bump-and-run. Said Al Davis, "God, he was great. The best who ever played that. One reason was he was fearless."

"I wanted to stop all passes, everything," Brown said. "I wanted to start as close as possible without being offsides and deny everything—the out, the in, the long pass. Everything. I would hit him at the line, then mirror his every move, always staying as close as possible."

Added assistant coach Charlie Sumner, "I don't recall anybody playing up on a receiver that close until we did it consistently with McCloughan and Brown."[4]

1978: If a pass is touched by one eligible offensive player before being caught by a second offensive player, it is a legal pass completion.

This was the December 23, 1972, "Immaculate Reception" in a playoff game with the Pittsburgh Steelers. At the time, the rules stated that if an offensive player touched the ball, another offensive player was ineligible to catch the deflected pass unless a defensive player touched it in between. Nearly every Raiders' book ever written pays homage to this play, but the words of Jim Otto summarize it best: "It remains the most incredible, implausible finish of a football game that didn't involve a marching band running onto the field. It also was the birth of television instant replay."[5] And it's the play that gave John Madden an ulcer. We Silver and Black fans call it the "Immaculate Deception," for obvious reasons—no Raider defender ever touched the ball!

1979: If a player fumbles on any down inside the two-minute warning in either half, only the fumbling player can recover and/or advance the ball.

Ah, the infamous "Holy Roller" play. Down 20–14 to San Diego with ten seconds to go, Oakland threatens to score from the Chargers' fourteen-yard line. On fourth down, QB Ken Stabler is sacked and fumbles the ball forward; running back Pete Banaszak can't quite get a handle on the ball and winds up shooing it forward toward the goal line where tight end Dave Casper reaches down and kicks the ball into the end zone, falling on it for a the winning touchdown. Saints preserve us, how did that happen?

In the post-game locker room, 'W' in hand, Stabler freely admitted that he fumbled the ball forward on purpose. In fact, all three players came clean about the miracle play.

When asked if his fumble was intentional, Stabler replied, "I had to. We had no timeouts left. I tried to fumble." Pete Banaszak owned up to his part: "You bet I batted it toward the goal line. If I'd picked it up, I'd never have scored. It was the logical thing to do." And the third of the Cheating Three Musketeers, Dave Casper, said "At first I tried to pick it up, but I kept missing it. So I just tried to kick it in the end zone. When I saw that fat line go by, I knew I could fall on it."[6]

What the bizarre finish to this game overshadowed was made apparent during the subsequent fourteen games: the Raiders weren't any good that year. They were swept by both Denver and Seattle, finished the season 9–7 and out of the playoffs for the first time in seven years.

But to anyone who witnessed that play in any way, shape or form, the memory brings a big, fat smile to their face and a single thought: that was one great cheater play.

1980: It is illegal for a player to strike, swing, or club an opponent in the head, neck, or face even if the initial contact is below the head.

In 1963, during which every AFL team except one scored an average of three touchdowns per game, Raider defensive-back coach Charlie Sumner helped teach cornerback Fred Williamson to use his forearms as weapons to pound a ball-carrier across the head. Soon Williamson's nickname was "The Hammer." Said John Rauch, coach of the Raiders from 1966–1968, "It was, when you're gonna make a tackle, make the guy know it, and one way to ensure you're getting your arm around him is that you come with the hammer."[7]

But the defensive back's shot-to-the-head truly found expression when a speedster named George Atkinson taught an underling named Jack Tatum how to use the "Hook." In Tatum's words, "The purpose of the Hook was to strip the receiver of the ball, his helmet, his head, and his courage." No. 32 went on to explain: "Using a straight forearm and swinging it into a player is illegal, but I would keep my arm in tight against my body. I would attempt to strip the ball from the offensive man while at the same time trying to catch his head in between my biceps and forearm. Believe me, it was legal, and what's more, the Hook was always the best intimidator in the business. I've probably used the Hook at one time or another on every receiver and running back in the NFL."[8]

1981: It is illegal for players to use any form of adhesive substance while participating in a game.

It was Fred Biletnikoff who first popularized the use of stickum. Fingers, hands, wrists, and forearms: the man was one giant appendage of flypaper. The sticky paste was so pervasive, each time Biletnikoff caught a pass, the football had to be removed from the playing field—where it was cleaned off with a special solvent.[9] "But I never used it in practice," Biletnikoff said. "It was more like a psychological thing for me. It was something that made me feel comfortable on Sunday."[10]

After Biletnikoff introduced rookie cornerback Lester Hayes to stickum in 1977, Hayes used it extensively—especially during the 1980 season when he pulled in a total of nineteen interceptions, counting playoffs. But John Madden argued that Lester did not use stickum to snare interceptions; he used it to stick on wide receivers. The bump rule said that if your hands slid off a receiver, you could not bump him a second time. The stickum allowed Hayes to adhere to his prey like "a big Band-Aid."[11] After the substance was outlawed, Hayes still found ways to get it on his hands, surreptitiously using the spray solution, which facilitated the adherence of medical tape to the skin.[12]

1983: A player may not use a helmet (that is no longer worn by anyone) as a weapon to strike, swing at, or throw at an opponent.

Yes, Article 13, illegal use of a helmet as a weapon. How could that be anything but a Raider rule?

It was the second round playoff game with the New York Jets on January 15, 1983, in the Los Angeles Mausoleum, I mean, Coliseum. And the protagonist on this day was the Raider who once told Tom Flores: "I never knew a man I didn't want to fight."[13]

Lyle Alzado was either loved or despised, depending on which side of the ball you lined up on. Near the end of a tight third quarter, Alzado—incensed that he was being held every play—ripped off the helmet of Jets tackle Chris Ward and then threw it at him. He missed him, but it's the thought that counts.[14] "He got mad because

I tried to drive him over the pile," Ward said. "He grabbed me by the facemask, the chinstrap came up and off went the helmet."[15] Alzado was vicious in battle but magnanimous in defeat. "They tried to intimidate us as much as we tried to intimidate them," Lyle said. "And for that, I salute them"[16] But first, please allow me to rip off your helmet and attack you with it.

1999: Twelve (12) new footballs, sealed in a special box and shipped by the manufacturer, will be opened in the officials' locker room two hours prior to the starting time of the game. These balls are to be specially marked with the letter "k" and used exclusively for the kicking game.

This was the NFL's answer to Ray Guy, prolific Raider punter from 1973–1986. Taken in the first round when a punter was usually picked up at the bus stop, Guy would boot the pigskin 1,049 times for 44, 493 yards, an amazing 42.4-yard career average.[17] Said John Madden: "I was never much on hang-time until we got Ray, but then we started clocking how long his punt hung in the air. Sometimes he kept it up there as long as six seconds."[18] Like right-wing conservatives searching for the explanation of Led Zeppelin's attraction to their children (the band must belong to the devil), the NFL's sleuths searched for answers to Ray Guy's incredible punting ability. Their answer? Al Davis was putting helium in the footballs Ray Guy was using. Hence, the hermetically-sealed "k" ball approach, used exclusively to keep cheater Al in line.

2001: If a defensive player intercepts a pass **or catches or recovers a fumble** . . . and his original momentum carries him into the end zone where the play is declared dead in his team's possession, the ball belongs to the defensive team at the spot where that ball was intercepted, caught or recovered.

For an explanation of this Raider rule change, travel back with me in time to a mythical land with big trees and fans with bigger mouths . . . Seattle.

The date was December 16, 2000, a game attended by tens of

thousands of Raider fans, including myself. A cold, wet, miserable day at Husky Stadium for the 11–3 Raiders, who were trying to clinch the AFC West crown for the first time in ten years against the hapless 5–9 Seahawks. Although leading 24–19 with 2:40 left in the game, the Raider D was playing a subpar fourth quarter. Lots of individual tackles, shuffling to the ball carrier—they looked like they just wanted to dry off, warm up, and go home. Judging from their performance, you would have thought they wanted to play in the sunny climate of Denver on December 31 rather than obtain a free pass through a first-round bye. Somebody had to make a play. And somebody did. Unfortunately, he was wearing a Seahawk uniform.

Seattle's Rickey Watters took a handoff at his own nineteen-yard line and weaved his way to the left sideline where he was coming right at us in the end zone corner, lumbering for an apparent 81-yard touchdown. As he got to the Raider 35-yard line, we were all holding our breath, because we could see what Rickey Baby could not—that No. 24 Charles Woodson was closing on him from behind much like the way I get rejected in a bar: fast and furious.

THUMP! Woodson knocked the football to the carpet at the 28-yard line, where it continued on its journey toward the end zone like some determined Conestoga wagon headed alone along the Oregon Trail. At the two-yard line, right in front of us, Marquez Pope fell on the loose football and slid into the end zone, cuddling his prize as if it were a magic lamp that would grant him a blanket and a space heater on the flight home. With a 24–19 Raider lead and about two minutes left, the game was over.

But wait: there was bewilderment among the referees on the field. That confusion quickly turned into disbelieving anger among Raider fans when referee Bernie Kukar started doing a walk-like-an-Egyptian dance, signifying a safety. If a pass interception that carries into the end zone is ruled a touchback, how was this any different? Kukar had a litany of rule-out explanations—including the bridge was up, the dog ate his homework, and his nephew bet $2,000 on Seattle to win. In the end, Kukar said: "Therefore it is a safety. That's the only thing we can do with it."

There were about 25,000 Raider fans in attendance at that game—won by Seattle, 27–24—who can tell Bernie Kukar, to this day, what he can do with it.[19]

The Raiders football organization has won over 380 games during its 43-year history. Every year, opposing owners go home and spit nails in frustration at the Raiders' winning ways. And every year, these same owners meet during the off-season to discuss rule changes. "If you can't beat 'em, join 'em" is how the saying goes, but somehow I don't see NFL owners hand-clasping with Al Davis to cross America with love and harmony. So they came up with a new saying.

If you can't beat 'em.

Change the rules.

REFERENCES

1. "Rules of the Name"; Jim Campbell; *Professional Football Researcher's Association*; The Coffin Corner; Vol. 21, No. 2 (1999).

2. *Hey, Wait a Minute (I Wrote a Book)*; John Madden with Dave Anderson; New York: Ballantine Books; 1984; pg. 238.

3. *Raiders Forever*; John Lombardo; Lincolnwood, IL; Contemporary Books; 2001; pg. 158.

4. *Super*; Edited by Murray Olderman; Oakland, CA: The Oakland Raiders and Murray Olderman; 1981; pg. 17–19.

5. *The Pain of Glory*; Jim Otto and Dave Newhouse; Champaign, IL: Sports Publishing Inc.; 1999; pg. 163.

6. "Raiders Bend Rules to Win"; Bruce Jenkins; *San Francisco Chronicle*; September 11, 1978.

7. *Slick*; Mark Ribowsky; New York; Macmillan Publishing Company; 1991: pg. 141.

8. *They Call Me Assassin*; Jack Tatum with Bill Kushner; New York: Everest House; 1979; pg. 16, 45.

9. Madden, op. cit., pg. 149.

10. Lombardo, op. cit., pg. 205.

11. Madden, op. cit., pg. 171.

12. *You're Okay, It's Just a Bruise;* Rob Huizenga, M.D.; New York: St. Martin's Press; 1994; pg. 31.

13. *Just Win, Baby;* Glenn Dickey; New York: Harcourt, Brace, Jovanovich; 1991; pg. 207.

14. *Cruisin' with the Tooz;* John Matuszak with Steve Delsohn; New York: Charter Books; 1987; pg. 193.

15. "A Coal Miner Kept Getting in the Way of the Raiders"; Gordon Edes; *Los Angeles Times;* January 16, 1983.

16. "Raider Season Ends, 17–14"; Alan Greenberg; *Los Angeles Times;* January 16, 1983.

17. *Total Football II; The Official Encyclopedia of the National Football League;* Bob Carroll, Michael Gershman, David Neft, John Thorn; New York: Harper Collins Publishers; 1997; pg. 855.

18. Madden, op. cit., pg. 162.

19. "Playoff Picture Muddied"; Bill Soliday; *Oakland Tribune;* December 17, 2000.

STATISTICS

He uses statistics as a drunken man uses lamp posts—
for support rather than illumination.

—ANDREW LANG (1844–1912)[1]

You are cruising the Internet, reading the newspaper, listening to the radio or watching the television. Whether you hear, see, dream, or imagine it, the numbers come at you like a phalanx of night fighters in a Star Wars movie:

- In 2002, the Oakland Raiders controlled the time-of-possession clock in eight of sixteen regular season games. In that stretch, they were 8–0;
- On offense, Oakland finished ninth in the AFC in rushing and first in passing (first in the NFL overall). On defense, the Raiders were third in the AFC against the rush and twelfth in

pass coverage (eleventh in the NFL);
- The Raiders scored on their first possession of the second half in ten of sixteen regular season games (five touchdowns, five field goals). During those ten games, they were 7–3;
- Oakland averaged 28.1 points per game and gave up 19.0 points. Its 9.1 positive point differential per game was second-best in the NFL, behind Tampa Bay (9.3).

What on earth do all these numbers mean?

Statistics are to football what money is to politics and sex is to marriage: an integral part, a lubricant to understanding and some-times—when used as the sole focus of interest—a one-way trip to hell.

Used properly, statistics are no more than an indicator used to promote the point that one is trying to make. Unfortunately, too often writers and announcers use statistics as the end point, result-ing in confusion and consternation on the part of the football fan.

Several examples illustrate this point:

Pointless: In the third quarter of the 2002 Raiders-Jets Divisional Playoff, QB Chad Pennington was picked off by the Raiders' Tory James. A graphic dutifully came on proclaiming that was the quar-terback's first interception in 240 attempts.

What does that statistic tell the fan? That he seldom made a bad pass? Any witness to his performance that day would scoff at such a statement. That Pennington was overdue to throw an interception? Was it just bad luck? Perhaps Green Man would not throw another interception until 240 more pass attempts were made? Judging from the Silver and Black pressure being unleashed at the time on the Chad, my guess was that it would be about ten more passes before Mr. INT again visited the Jets' column—which was exactly correct, in retrospect (it is amazing how knowledgeable football fans are in hindsight).

The 240-attempt statistic was pointless; it did no more than show-case some tight-lipped troll's penchant to master the inane. The fan's understanding of the game was not advanced one hashmark yard marker.

Insightful: Make no mistake, when it comes to football statistics, the line between insightful and pointless is as thin as our wallet the day before payday. For example:

- Rich Gannon was No. 1 in the NFL in pass attempts, pass completions, passing yardage, and pass yards per game; he was second in completion percentage, fourth in yards per pass attempt, and tied for fourth in touchdown passes (26). His overall quarterback ranking: 97.3 (second in the NFL);
- Charlie Garner gained 962 yards rushing and 941 yards receiving, basically earning sixty yards a game in each category. In games where Garner's rushing/receiving total topped 100 yards, Oakland was 9–2; in games Charlie failed to reach 100 total yards, the Raiders were 2–3;
- Although Tim Brown's 81 receptions in 2002 were the sixteenth-best in the NFL, the 11.5 yards per catch and two touchdown grabs were the lowest of Brown's career in these categories. Over fifteen seasons and 1,018 receptions, Tim Brown lost only three fumbles;
- In five games against AFC teams, Zack Crockett ran 21 times for 31 yards—and seven touchdowns. In the seven touchdown runs, Crockett gained eight yards.

While interesting, these numbers ironically showcase the axiom that statistics are for losers. Why? Because the figures do nothing to advance the fan's understanding of the game. If a football team wins 6 out of 16 games but the quarterback throws just ten interceptions, who cares? Only losers do.

Prescient: Politicians and gamblers have long used statistics to predict the likelihood of a successful outcome. Football is no different. On January 5, 1986, early in the first quarter of the Raiders-

Patriots AFC Divisional Playoff, the black-jersey 1980 franchise draft choice threw an out-pattern pass to wide receiver Dokie Williams, who was guarded by the Patriots' Ronnie Lippett. Hedging on the knowledge that statistically the Raiders shied away from slant routes toward the middle of the field, Lippett played the outside, waited for Williams to cut his way, and made the interception.[2]

Statistics can also be used to predict the likelihood of an unsuccessful outcome. Following that play, across the bottom of the television screen appeared this graphic: That was Marc Wilson's first pass in a playoff game.

My reaction to this insight was ominous and physically debilitating—somewhat like receiving your stockbroker's latest annual statement. Because, as Raider fans the world over know: in the playoffs, a team only goes as far as its quarterback's arm.

Sure enough: by the game's end, the Raiders had committed six turnovers (three interceptions, three fumbles) and New England prevailed 27–20. That was a real punch-in-the-stomach statistic that cannot be forgotten. The value lay in its prescience.

Misleading: On the back cover of the 2002 Oakland Raiders media guide is this table: "Top Professional Football Records (1963–2001); #1. Raiders, Winning Percentage—.628."

This is a correct statistic. Or is it? Didn't the Oakland Raiders begin play in 1960? Perhaps they were a different franchise from 1960–1962. Possibly they were the Senors, Snores, or Snorkelers during those three years.

My hunch is that the missing three Raider years, like Nixon's 18½ minute gap, were excised due to the damage they could inflict on the Raiders' claim as the winningest franchise in pro football. From 1963–2001, the Raiders were 361 wins–214 losses–11 ties, a .628 winning percentage. If one includes the 1960–1962 years (during which they went 9–33), the numbers become 370–247–11, a .600 winning percentage. This would drop the Raiders into third position of top all-time records—an unacceptable rung if the hype of winningest franchise is to be continued.[3] Benjamin Disraeli must have been talking football when he said, "There are three kinds of lies: lies, damn lies, and statistics."[4]

Along a six-game stretch, during which the Raiders went 5–1, the following players made unsung contributions:

Doug Jolley: 24 catches for 348 yards, 14.5 yards-per-catch average;
Sebastian Janikowski: 15 field goals made in 17 attempts (88%);
Rod Coleman: 7.5 sacks for 54 yards.

These are impressive statistics, but they are also quarantined from the impact the plays made on the field. Statistics cannot substitute for the nuances of timing, individual athleticism, and team momentum. What makes statistics so alluring is that they seek to quantify and give order to what is essentially a complicated game. On any one play, there are 30+ factors interacting to produce success or failure.

Safely ensconced on our couch, we football fans can achieve perfection with numbers, something unattainable for the players on the field. Sitting on bar stools and swilling down beer, we play with numbers because we lack the courage or ability to run with the big dogs. Unable or unwilling to be in the NFL, we instead give what we can to the team we love.

We give our money, our Sundays, our voices, and our loyalty to the Silver and Black.

And, in return, we become Football's Blackest Hole.

So go forth and learn the lessons of pigskin jargon. Believe (if you will) in one God, reflect (if you must) on one world—but know in your heart that the only important football statistic is the final score when the clock shows 0:00.

Listen to the naiveté of the announcers who says "If Charlie Garner gains 150 total yards"—dropping their pencil lightly on the writing tablet for emphasis—"the Raiders win the game." Laugh because you know they neglected to mention at least eleven other factors that affect the result.

Be not afraid of the tongue-wagging know-it-alls. Appreciate David Stockman's point when he said, "None of us really understands what is going on with all these numbers."[5] Accept that, when there is a circle of Raider fans talking football, nobody is really listening; they're only waiting for their turn to talk. Jump into this den of liars with eyes open and lungs filled. Enjoy the give-and-take of rushing first downs and defensive turnover ratios. Memorize quick bursts of statistics and deliver them with verve and confidence.

Just don't be hanging on a lamp post when you do so.

REFERENCES
1. www.brainyquote.com
2. "Raider Offense Couldn't Overcome its Mistakes"; Bob Oates; *Los Angeles Times;* January 6, 1986.
3. The official Raider position is that 1963 was the year Al Davis became head coach.
4. www.brainyquote.com
5. "The Education of David Stockman"; William Greider; *The Atlantic Monthly;* December 1981.

I REMEMBER

In a world of strange occurrences—a lady successfully sues McDonald's and wins because her spilled cup of coffee was served too hot, a kid steals an airplane and flies it into a Florida high-rise, this book gets published—it is a bit weird how we always think of football players as young. It seems natural enough but it isn't. These athletes play their seven seasons, give or take a few, and then go away somewhere—on with their lives, I guess. But in the fan's mind, they remain eternally youthful. Still able to gather in the catch, go low for the tackle, make that first-down marker. In a sense, these remembrances are like a painting: immortal and immutable.

So it always comes as a shock to hear that our Raider legends are human after all. Like when I recently read a headline that defensive back Mike Davis had lost hearing from all the head-banging hits he inflicted over the years.[1] This realization gave me pause. Although Davis bestrode the Raiders' secondary twenty years ago (1978–85), in my mind he was still a lithe leopard who struck fear into receivers' hearts and once made the catch of a lifetime.

When reading the news, I responded as a Raider fan should: I reflected.

How much more severe was our response when we heard that a Raider player had died. How can someone consistently be expected to win a matchup against an opponent yet lose in the ultimate battle with the Angel of Death? The Raiders were larger than life, or so it seemed—frozen in our mind's' eye in a colossal display of athletic prowess that somehow served to remind us that once, if only for a moment, life made sense.

Now they were gone, not just from the playing field but from this earth, and our response as Raider fans can only be that small part of ourselves we have left to give.

We remember.

John Matuszak: Died June 17, 1989, Age 38.

The Tooz. The duality of man stuffed into a massive construction of contradictions. At 6 feet-8 inches, 290 pounds, he was (by his own admission) bigger, badder, and stronger than most small cities. Inserted into a 3-4 defense where the linemen needed to control the line of scrimmage, Matuszak was instrumental in the defensive effort resulting in two Super Bowl wins. But there was always the other bookend: Tooz's poor performance at the 1977 AFC Championship loss to Denver was a result of drinking and popping Quaaludes the night before. Denver ran the football right at him the last three minutes of the game, and a lethargic Matuszak was unable to come up with the needed big play.[2] "All through my career, I seemed to place obstacles in my path," wrote Tooz.[3] He finally met an obstacle he could not overcome. In the end, a lifetime of alcohol and drugs led to an accidental overdose of Darvocet—an incomplete end to a completely original Raider.[4]

Stacey Toran: Died August 5, 1989, Age 27.

The youngest of six Raiders to die prematurely, Toran is ironically better remembered for the tragic way he died off the field than the strong safety position he played on the field. Drafted in the sixth round out of Notre Dame in 1984, Toran was a respected hitter in the Jack Tatum style of play. A young man who was quiet off the field, Toran let vicious hits do his talking on it. As his sixth professional season approached, he stood on the verge of a breakthrough season. August 5, 1989, he tried two death-defying stunts—driving while blind (alcohol level: .32%) and not wearing a seat belt. The result was a classic alcohol-related driving fatality: he slammed his BMW into a tree one block from home and was ejected. "We knew, his teammates knew—we all knew—he was All-Pro," eulogized Raider assistant coach Willie Brown.[5] That didn't make him immortal or All-World. Sadly, in the end, he was simply all gone.

Lyle Alzado: Died May 14, 1992, Age 43.

Reflect on the two sides of this man who said, "I should have played my whole career as a Raider." The hard man who would rip the helmet off an opposing player and throw it at him versus the soft man who earned a degree in special education and spent untold public service hours to benefit sick and disabled children. The tough, aggressive take-no-prisoners pirate juxtaposed against the all-too-human man of courage who cried as the seconds ticked down on Super Bowl XVIII. The handsome, perfectly chiseled physique of an athlete on steroids contrasted with the gaunt, hollowed look of a dying man with T-cell brain lymphoma. "You can never give up. Giving up is the worst thing you can do," Alzado said.[6] See the two sides of a Raider fan remembering Lyle Alzado: happiness tinged with regret.

Bob Chandler: Died January 27, 1995, Age 45.

I met Bob Chandler. It was before the home-and-away opener against the San Francisco 49ers, the first game of the Los Angeles Raiders franchise, September 12, 1982. We were milling around

the lobby of the Oakland Airport Hilton. I looked over and there
he was, checking in. I went running up to Chandler like I was a
Beatles groupie—I might have shrieked. Chandler only stood 6 feet-
1 inch, 180 pounds, with a slender, almost fragile body build. But
he was a tenacious pass receiver and instrumental in the 1980 drive
to New Orleans, and that is why I was honored to meet him. I kept
buzzing around all sides of him like I had ADD, ADHD and ALG
(Annoying Little Gnat) disease as he tried to fill out the registra-
tion card. I kept asking him questions but, before he could answer,
I would go in a different direction, telling him that I was at the
1981 opener in Denver when he was nearly killed by a vicious hit
that lacerated his spleen. I asked him where his car was and he
pointed proudly behind him. There, seen through the front window,
was the most beautiful metallic blue Porsche—waiting like a beloved
sister at a train station.

Chandler could not know, although he may have suspected, that
he would play in only two more games and never again catch a pass
in a professional uniform. He retired from football, became a radio
commentator and, at the next (and last) Los Angeles Raiders opener
against the 49ers some dozen years later, complained of a persistent
cough. Although he didn't smoke, Chandler had lung cancer—the
bad kind. He passed away less than five months later.[7]

Eric Turner: Died May 28, 2000, Age 31.

It is the oldest saying in sports: wait 'til next year. We cling to
life, buoyed by some absurd notion that tomorrow is guaranteed.
Oh, sure, we have the rhetoric down about hug your kids, love your
wife, and leave all your money to Sun Myung Moon. Even if one
lives to reach eight decades, see how long it takes you to count to
eighty. Not long. But I still believe I am immortal; I cannot imagine
that, one day, I will never again see a Douglas fir tree. Eric Turner's
death changed that for me in some small way. His untimely passing
from abdominal cancer seems at times more like a mystical warning to me than the testament to Turner's courage it really was. That
is because, as Steve Wisniewski said, "You always think of athletes

as being invincible because they are young and strong."[8] One day Turner was in the NFL sealing a victory with an interception at the Raider goal line; seven months later he was gone. When he was signed in 1997, Turner said: "They've got great defensive players here, great tradition, and I just wanted to be a part of that.... There were other teams, but there was no other team I was interested in."[9] That is how I prefer to remember Eric Turner. I cannot imagine that I will ever again see another one like him.

Dave Dalby: Died August 30, 2002, Age 51.

What goes through one's mind moments before they die? For most people, they keep on trying to live. But for Dave Dalby, he just wanted the pain to stop. He wasn't the first alcoholic to do himself in, but Dave Dalby was first in other ways. He was asked to fill the shoes of a legend—Jim Otto, who retired after fifteen seasons and 210 consecutive starts. Dalby not only met this challenge, he created a new standard, playing fourteen seasons, 205 consecutive games and starting in three Super Bowl wins.[10] Dalby liked to quote a small study that purported to show that NFL linemen only lived to age 52. "It's no use, doc," he would say to the team doctor, "we're all going to die by fifty, so I might as well have fun."[11] When he died, Dave Dalby was not having fun—but he was 51 years old.

The average career span in a Raider uniform is three years.[12] There may come a time when, for whatever fortuitous reason, you have the opportunity to meet a Raider but are embarrassed to bother him. It is good manners to respect this privacy, but don't forget that you may never see a Raider again. To this day, in 1987 I wish I had taken only a short bus-ride to where John Matuszak was signing his book, *Cruisin' With the Tooz.*

The players in Silver and Black may seem larger than life, but they're not. I know this because I met Bob Chandler.

I remember.

REFERENCES

1. "Mike Davis No Longer Hears Cheering"; Lance Pugmire; *Oakland Tribune;* January 26, 2003.

2. "Part 8: The End of the Party"; Pat Toomay; *ESPN Page 2;* http://espn.go.com/page2/s/toomay/021021.html; April 25, 2003.

3. *Cruisin' with the Tooz;* John Matuszak with Steve Delsohn; New York: Charter Books; 1987; pg. 122.

4. "Matuszak Death Is Accidental"; Mark Heisler; *Los Angeles Times;* June 28, 1989.

5. "Police Seek to Reconstruct Last Hours of Toran's Life"; Julie Cart and John Kendall; *Los Angeles Times;* August 12, 1989.

6. "The Cannon is Quiet"; Mary Ann Hudson; *Los Angeles Times;* January 26, 1992

7. "Bob Chandler Didn't Get Much of a Chance to Say Good-By"; C.W. Nevius; *San Francisco Chronicle;* September 1, 1995.

8. "Turner's Death Sinking In"; Bill Soliday; *Oakland Tribune;* May 30, 2000.

9. "In Memory of Oakland Raider Eric Turner"; http://www.raider-shack.com/den.html; April 25, 2003.

10. *The Pain of Glory;* Jim Otto with Dave Newhouse; Champaign, IL: Sports Publishing, Inc.; 1999; pg. 176.

11. *You're Okay, It's Just a Bruise;* Rob Huizenga, M.D.; New York: St. Martin's Press; 1994; pg. 159.

12. *The Team of the Decades 2002;* Oakland Raiders Media Guide.

CHAPTER TWO

Livin' in the Past

LIVIN' IN THE PAST

Oh, we won't give in
Let's go living in the past.

—JETHRO TULL, 1972[1]

There we were, a tight-knit group of suffering Raider fans, ticked off that the Raiders had lost another game along the endless ant trail of losses between 1994–1999. We were just sitting there, too mad to move. Talking with other fans who had come to this sports bar to watch their favorite teams play on the dozen or more television sets high up against the walls.

Invariably, amid the clink of glasses and clank of plates being picked up from the tables by busy waitresses, the regular thrust-and-riposte got up and going between Raider and Seahawk supporters.

"How many Super Bowls do you have? We have three."

"So what. You guys never had anyone as good as Largent."

"Speaking of over-rated Seahawks, how's the Boz? Has he recovered from his accident?"

"What accident?"

"Being run over by Bo Jackson!"

"Hardee har har har. Your Dad is stupid and your father's ugly; I knew them both."

Sensing the give-and-take with Seattle fans was about to get out of hand, we returned to talking among ourselves. Our conversation invariably wove itself back to the glory years, back to the time when the only thing longer than a Raider's rap sheet was his hair. And the time when the beards most Raiders sported made them look like willing protégés of Charles Manson. About this time, a gentleman— a Dallas Cowboy fan with an easy movement that matched his Texas drawl—flicked his cigarette cinders into the cheap, plastic ashtray, leaned back on his bar stool and said: "That's what I love about y'all Raiders. Yore livin' in the past."

I never knew if the Cowboy fan was mocking us or paying us a compliment. I'd like to believe it was a little of both. Because that is what Raider fans do: we root like the dickens for our beloved Raiders, then we spit and curse at the injustice of a loss as if it were the first instance we have ever experienced such a cataclysm.

Our conversation drifted—casually but purposefully, like a desultory river that inevitably reaches the open sea—into a discussion of the AFC Championship years. The good old days. Our favorite plays, favorite players, greatest games, best coach, All-Pro waterboy (Run Run Jones always wins this one), rip-off calls, special moments, tailgate stories. Our vocal delivery became rich, vibrant, and animated as we spun tales of conquering multitudes of Silver and Black. Perhaps we were using these memories to mythologize our past and remind ourselves that, once, we too were young. Perhaps we just like being a Raider fan. For us, it's more than just a job—it's a way of life.

And we have gratitude. We are grateful for VCRs. That way, come the designated January day if our heroes are not involved—as they have not been for the past eighteen years—we can simply plug in a tape of a time when this world made sense, the good guys won, and truth ruled supreme. So, if you ever come home and you walk in the back door carrying groceries but your mate doesn't get up off the couch to help, doesn't turn to greet you, and just sits and stares at a clouded screen, understand what that means. Ask the question—"What're you doing?"—in full awareness of what the answer must be.

"Just livin' in the past."

REFERENCES

1. "Living in the Past"; Jethro Tull; EMI; 1972.

1976 AFC Championship
Pittsburgh vs. Oakland
December 26, 1976
Oakland, California

AT LAST

Picture yourself in a snapshot's moment of peace in a lush, green field. The sun is shining, the warmth inviting, and the shadows serenely reminding you that all of life's ambitions are temporary. Verdant, individual blades of grass dance about you on the gentle breeze, as if they had found nirvana in their own simplicity. The aroma of your favorite food and beverage wafts in the air, and you hear a much-loved song in the background. A football rests on the grass, its symmetrical tips pointing left and right, and the grassy laminae reach toward its stitched laces in haphazard fashion. A solitary bumblebee flies lazily around the ball, its robust and hairy appearance accentuated by the jet-black body with broad yellow bands. It circles at close range, hovering with indifferent aplomb.

Suddenly, this idyllic, peaceful scene is invaded by eleven giant men descending on either side of the football—over four thousand pounds of motivated anger, technique and power. As the front lines get down in their three-point stances, the bumblebee—having never read Charles Darwin—alights onto the grass near the pigskin. Just before the play begins, No. 50 Dave Dalby sees the bumblebee in the grass. He looks up at his snorting opponent and, without taking his gaze away, brings his right fist down hard into the grass—pulverizing the bee's thorax like Godzilla crushing Bambi with a massive strike from above. Dalby did not do this out of hatred for nature. He simply didn't like the bumblebee's colors.

And suddenly, you realize: this is it. Now is the time.

At last.

Let it be known: the Oakland Raiders defeated the Pittsburgh Steelers 24–7 on the day after Christmas, 1976. In doing so, they repaired the errors of six former AFC Championship appearances and applied a healing balm to the souls of 500,000 Raider fans nationwide. They delivered to their head coach his first AFC Championship after 83 regular season wins in eight seasons. They did it with a team effort as varied as the myriad scoundrels portrayed in *All the President's Men*. And the reason for their success was that the Raider teammates were all on the same page: like Howard Beale in *Network*, they were mad as hell and they weren't going to take it anymore.

Said Mike Rae, who replaced Ken Stabler after he was shaken up in the third quarter: "I've never seen a bunch of guys want something more." George Atkinson agreed: "We wanted this one more than we wanted the games in the past."[1] Ken Stabler's assessment was straightforward and to the point: "We hate them; they hate us. Beating them that bad in the playoffs was sweet indeed."[2]

The TV announcers tried their best to limit the sweetness of this decisive victory. In the first half alone, they referred to the absence from the championship game of Pittsburgh's running back duo, Franco Harris and Rocky Bleier, no less than eighteen times. Had these announcers worked for the Nazis in World War II, they would have argued that the Holocaust was a minor misunderstanding and that the 1938 terror of Kristallnacht was just a kegger that got out of hand. As Al Davis said, "Last year in the championship game, we were missing Willie Brown and Tony Cline, and Fred Biletnikoff and Marv Hubbard were hurt. We didn't complain."[3] Raider fans don't complain because we understand that professional football is a vicious game played with aggression and determination—and that injuries are part of this greatest sport in the world. "If those had been our backs hurt," said defensive end Otis Sistrunk, "they would have played on crutches."[4] Whining about injuries is as demeaning as an appointed vice-president pardoning his criminal superior and then running for the country's highest office himself. My hunch is that sports people, so accustomed to using Oakland as a doormat when it came to AFC Championship games, could not reconcile themselves to a Raiders team in the ascendant—and so became willing apologists for the old Pete Rozelle order.

Out with the old, in with the new. "All week long, the coach has said that he didn't want us to beat the Steelers. He wanted us to whup them," said wide receiver Clifford Branch.[5] And that is precisely what Oakland did, dominating Pittsburgh through a balance of offensive and defensive prowess which left the Steelers demoralized and disbelieving. A key play early on showed the Raider purpose. Mark van Eeghen ran for ten yards over the middle and fumbled when hit by Pittsburgh's Jack Ham. The inimitable Curt Gowdy made the call: "Recovered by Pittsburgh." Pause. "Oh, they give it to Oakland." Pause. "WHAT?" he exclaimed in apoplectic surprise. Dave Casper had jumped in at the end of the fumble recovery and wrestled the football away from Jack Lambert. I would guess that, had he been playing middle linebacker instead of that slouch Lambert, Franco Harris would have made the fumble recovery for Pittsburgh.

Meanwhile, what Oakland was making was headway via the run against the vaunted Steel Curtain. After Hubie Ginn partially blocked a punt, giving the Raiders the football on the Pittsburgh 38, Oakland capitalized with a step in its gait: run on first down for three yards; left-side run for five yards; and on third-and-two, van Eeghen followed as Dave Dalby blocked Lambert and rumbled for a first down. Earl Mann's 39-yard field goal made it 3–0 at the end of the first quarter.

In that first quarter, guess how many first downs the Pittsburgh Steelers gained? Try zero. Let's focus for a moment on the highly rated Pittsburgh offense that scored 342 points during the regular season: Run for one yard, pass nearly intercepted, pass incomplete, punt. Next series: overthrown pass due to nervous feet against the defensive rush, run for three yards, incomplete pass (hard and high), punt. After another bad pass on first down, quarterback Terry Bradshaw was 0 for 6; on the next series, Bradshaw finally completed a pass—to the Silver and Black.

On second-and-eleven, the beleaguered Steelers QB again threw too hard and out in front of Frenchy Fuqua; the tipped ball was picked off by Willie Hall, who promptly got up and raced down the right sideline to the one-yard line. After two goal-line Steeler stops, on third down Clarence Davis followed Pete Banaszak's lead block in to the end zone for a 10–0 Raider lead.

After a Pittsburgh score cut the lead to 10–7, Oakland ran the ball and the clock in a way that left the Steelers' defense befuddled. Mark van Eeghen left, five yards. Clarence Davis left, five yards. On third-and-five, Davis again left for sixteen yards into Pittsburgh territory. Banaszak left for five yards to the 28-yard line; on third-and-five, Davis up the middle for eight yards, did I tell you Rocky Bleier's hurt? Banaszak on a sweep left for ten yards, and a pass interference call on Fred Biletnikoff puts the football first-and-goal on the Pittsburgh four-yard line. "We brought in our three-tight-end offense that we used in short-yardage situations. Two of the ends were on the line and Warren Bankston set in the slot," wrote Ken Stabler. "On our first-down play we faked a handoff to van Eeghen and Bankston faked a block, slipping into the end zone all alone." With the play-action fake freezing the opposition, Stabler threw to a wide open Bankston to make the score 17–7 with 19 seconds left in the first half.

In the second half, Oakland scored again, using a 28-yard pass thrown up against the blitz which Branch adjusted to nicely; a fourth-and-one completion to Bankston (the same play used as on the touch-down catch) to keep the drive alive and, finally, the five-yard pass to Banaszak, his first of the year. Said Stabler: "I didn't see linebacker Jack Ham coming on a blitz from the blind side and he put a double-duty lick on me, bruising my ribs and knocking the cap off a tooth."[6] But it was hard to knock the sweet sound coming from the raptur-ous vocal chords of the Silver and Black faithful, as nearly 54,000 Raider fans gave their boys a standing ovation.

After that, with the score 24–7, it was all over except for the glee and the crowd noise. "That crowd," said Stabler "really stirred us up. I'd hear them coming off the field and yes, I heard them when I got hurt." Behind superb blocking, the Raiders simply had too much run in them: 51 rushes for 157 yards. "Kenny asked us to give a little extra and we did," explained guard Gene Upshaw. "We blocked. We controlled the line of scrimmage."[7] In contrast,

Pittsburgh had little or no offense and was unable to control the time clock against a formidable Raider D. "When you have three downs and out, then your defense is going to be on the field a lot," explained Pittsburgh coach Chuck Knoll. "And even our defense is going to have trouble."[8]

The only trouble for Raider players was in getting to sleep that night. For Raider fans, the trouble came in waking up for work the next day. Awash in suds and euphoria, cleansed by the baptism of victory of all those previous dreadful losses, both players and fans stayed awake through the wee hours, replaying and reliving the drama and triumph over and over again—until exhaustion overwhelmed their mortal bodies and they slumped in their easy chairs and hard beds. Unable to go on, they bravely succumbed to sleep, the poor man's opera. But, just before the consciousness ebbed and their breathing became rhythmic, each of them shared one final thought.

At last.

REFERENCES

1. "Raiders Long Wait Over"; Betty Cuniberti; *San Francisco Chronicle*; December 27, 1976.

2. "Getting' Nowhere Fast"; Robert Jones; *Sports Illustrated*; Vol. 47, #12; September 19, 1977; pg. 98.

3. "Steelers Bemoan the Missing Stars"; Art Spander; *San Francisco Chronicle*; December 27, 1976.

4. "Raiders: Ecstasy and Tears"; Betty Cuniberti; *San Francisco Chronicle*; December 27, 1976.

5. "Raiders Long Wait Over"; Betty Cuniberti; *San Francisco Chronicle*; December 27, 1976.

6. *Snake*; Ken Stabler and Berry Stainback; Garden City, NY: Doubleday & Company, Inc.; 1986; pg. 131.

7. "Dull Enough to Be Super"; Art Rosenbaum; *San Francisco Chronicle*; December 27, 1976.

8. Spander, op. cit.

Super Bowl XI
Oakland vs. Minnesota
January 9, 1977
Pasadena, California

YEAR OF THE SNAKE

The Chinese New Year dates back to 2,600 B.C., which coinciden-
tally was the last year the Oakland Raiders defeated the Pittsburgh
Steelers in a playoff game. Until this year, 1977. The legend of the
Chinese Lunar Calendar is that Buddha invited all animals on earth
to come visit him before he departed from this planet. Only twelve
animals showed up. Buddha rewarded them by naming a new year
after each one. It is not obvious to most Americans of non-Chinese
descent why these twelve species were singled out for this honor.
At least one is loathsome—the rat. Another is fearsome—the
dragon. Others are merely common domestic animals—the horse,
the rooster, and the dog.

But, in 1977 there occurred a Chinese Lunar year that would
touch Raider fans with its wisdom and insight. For that year, the
Chinese tradition celebrated an animal which was charming, bright
enough to check off at the line, and capable of finding the open
receiver against the blitz.

The Year of the Snake.

Ken Stabler was the quarterback of the Oakland Raiders and, as
he admitted, he knew he "would never be a Terry Bradshaw or a Joe
Namath. Only God gives out those kind of passing arms. But I dra-
matically improved what I had and I felt confident I knew how to
win with it."[1] During an interview, Stabler was more candid: "In the
NFL, there are 25 guys who can throw better than I can. But I can
make guys win."[2]

And his teammates loved him for it. According to offensive guard
Gene Upshaw, "You can be losing your block, and the Snake will
still make you look good. He's mobile. He doesn't cling to a pattern.
He moves here, there—he's a snake, man."[3] Stabler was like a master

of martial arts, sinking while deceptively twisting away, presenting the mirage of a target while actually removing the mark and gaining leverage for his next movement. With slippery elusiveness, Stabler could bedevil onrushing linemen, slither away, buy some time, then sting with a pass completion.

George Blanda, no slouch himself, said:

> Stabler is a great passer. He has accuracy, great timing, great touch. He can throw the ball through a linebacker or over a linebacker. He has a good touch on the long pass or he can drive it in there. But his greatest knack is being able to read defenses. He knows where to go with a pass.[4]

And now they were here, in the Rose Bowl at Pasadena, ready to play the Minnesota Vikings in Super Bowl XI. Under the watchful eyes of 103,000 spectators and a world-wide viewing audience of 130 million, the question was: would Stabler, the No. 1 passer in the NFL , know where to go with the pass? Would the Raiders run? Would the Raiders run to set up the pass?

It did not take long before the answer came: the Raiders would run. They would run left. And they would run wild.

This strategy was because their offensive line, led by the dynamic duo of Art Shell and Gene Upshaw, far outweighed their Viking opponents'. By Stabler's estimation, the Raiders' line averaged just under 270 pounds against the Purple People Eaters' 242 average girth.[5] Goodness, how this offense ran the ball. By my estimation, they ran left twenty-four times, right seven times, and up the middle nine times. That means sixty percent of the time, Oakland ran left. And, when they weren't running left, center Dave Dalby was firing out like a supercharged rocket—on one play moving linebacker Jeff Siemon back into another time zone. By game's end, Oakland's two leading rushers—Clarence Davis and Mark van Eeghen—had 220 yards between them. And, while the big men ruled the trenches, the big plays ruled the game.

The game didn't start off smoothly: the Raiders stalled after marching in crisp fashion from their own 34-yard line to the Viking 11, and Errol Mann banged his 29-yard field goal attempt off the left upright (George Blanda, where art thou?). Later in the first quarter, Ray Guy had his first punt blocked, and Minnesota stood poised at the 3-yard line. But Phil Villapiano came across the pit on a Brent McClanahan dive play that McClanahan will rue forever. Breaking across the line of scrimmage, he gave a look like "You got something for me?" then stuck his helmet right into the football, knocking it loose. Willie Hall recovered and the Raiders then went on a ninety-yard drive that culminated in a field goal and a 3–0 lead. Key plays were a 34-yard Clarence Davis run (off the left side) on third-and-six from the Oakland six-yard line, and Stabler's eight-yard toss to Dave Casper, who then turned up field and ran sixteen yards after the catch.

The next time they got the ball, Oakland made their ball-control offense pay dividends. Starting at their own 36, the Raiders capitalized on Casper's third reception, a four-yard pass with a run adding fifteen more. Then Carl Garrett juked, hesitated and spun for a four-teen-yard run, presaging by twenty-five years another CG who would make such a move his trademark. On third-and-three from the six, Kenny Stabler took his eight-yard drop and hit Fred Biletnikoff with the second of four first-rate catches he would make on the day. In what looked like a ballet timing-pattern, Biletnikoff came back out of the end zone for a beautiful leaping grab in front of the right pylon. On the ninth play of the 64-yard drive, Stabler heaved to Casper while retreating after a play-action, to make the score 10–0 in the second quarter. As he trotted off the field, Stabler told Madden, "There's more where that came from."[6]

And indeed there was. Neal Colzie returned a 38-yard Minnesota punt for 23 yards to the Viking 35. Two runs moved the Raiders to the 27, where, on third-and-two, Dalby took down two defenders with one block—resulting in an eight-yard gain to the nineteen-yard line. Then Biletnikoff made his what-a-grab catch, looking a low pass by Stabler over the middle into his hands as he was hit by two defenders and downed at the one. "Ken is the best quarterback who's ever played football," Biletnikoff explained later.[7] A one-yard plunge by Pete Banaszak, followed by a missed extra point, made the score 16–0 at halftime.

But the game wasn't all offense, as the second half provided witness. Skip Thomas playing tough on the pass all day, harassed receivers and batted away potential gainers. The Patchwork Boys— John Matuszak, Dave Rowe, and Otis Sistrunk—ruled the front line as their domain nearly the entire game. With eleven different teams on their resumes among them, these three stoppers had more miles on them than Greyhound tires—but in Oakland they found a home. And, on third-and-one in the third quarter—with Minnesota trying to get something going—these guys found the ball carrier. Matuszak submarined low while eight Raiders stacked the line; no gain for the Vikings, forcing a punt.

After Oakland scored another field goal to go up 19–0 (the key play here was Clarence Davis running left for 17 yards, sprung mainly due to a bruising lead block by Mark van Eeghen that could be heard in Compton), the defense again rose up. Dave Rowe made a five-yard push against his blocker—churning his legs as if crushing purple grapes—while John Matuszak was bearing down on Fran Tarkenton like a pirate pillaging a tavern, and the pass was batted down by Rowe. Then, Sistrunk whacked Tarkenton's passing arm down from behind. After a roughing-the-kicker penalty kept the ball with Minnesota, Matuszak made a two-yard stop, and he and Phil Villapiano started head-slapping each other.

Later, with the score 19–7, Minnesota's rookie Sammy White caught a first-down pass over the middle, but Skip Thomas ("Doctor Death") took his helmet off with a sweet hook move. Sistrunk and Matuszak then converged on a passing Tarkenton like he was holding their bag of Super Bowl money; the completion lost two yards. After Sistrunk and Rowe smothered a draw play, White again lost his helmet—and nearly his head—while gathering in another first-down pass. On the catch, Skip Thomas attacked from behind while Jack Tatum rushed in full bore and unloaded the lumber with his left shoulder into White's head. Sammy crumpled to the ground while

Tatum stood over him. In Tatum's words: "That type of devastating hit has a tendency to discourage other receivers and running backs from trying anything over the middle."[8] Two plays later, on third-and-four, Ted Hendricks blitzed and Fran Tarkenton dodged, then threw a dying quail into the thick of the Raider D that was intercepted by Willie Hall and returned near midfield. "No way," insisted Dandy Don Meredith. "No way should you ever throw that ball." Maybe the Minnesota offense just wanted to get off that field. "Thank God we came out alive," sighed Minnesota's Brent McClanahan.[9]

Then, with ten minutes left in the fourth quarter and the football at the Raiders' 49-yard line, Stabler and Biletnikoff hooked up one last time for the game breaker. Stabler took his typical nine-yard drop and let fly with a spiral over the middle that Freddy took in, wide open on the run, at the 32-yard line. He didn't stop until downed at the three. Pete Banaszak immediately took the ball in over the right side to make the score 26–7. In celebration, he heaved the pigskin into the Rose Bowl stands. It was nearly anticlimactic when cornerback Willie Brown raced 75 yards with an interception to add Oakland's final points; it was anything but anti when the entire Raider team ran out to congratulate him in the end zone.

And then, the game was over, a 32–14 Raider victory. John Madden was carried off the field by his teammates before the caravan toppled head over tea kettle from the weight. Fred Biletnikoff cried and thanked his comrades. And Ken Stabler, after an extended round of well-wishes and interviews, just wanted to slip away. To be by himself and savor the moment in private. See what it's like to awaken as a world champion.

When daylight dawns and she's still with you
And the crowds and scalpers are gone
And you've locked her in your mind and soul and psyche
This is where she belongs
When the Sunday strains become life's remains
And the calls and invites are few

Just know that what you did this one day
In part defines you.[10]

The Year of the Snake.

REFERENCES

1. *Snake;* Ken Stabler and Berry Stainback; Garden City, NY: Doubleday & Company, Inc.; 1986; pg. 83.
2. "The Super Bowl—Special Advertising Insert"; *Sports Illustrated;* Vol. 60, #2, January 16, 1984.
3. Stabler, op. cit., pg. 93.
4. ibid., pg. 106.
5. ibid., pg. 133.
6. "Raiders Win the Biggest One"; Glenn Dickey; *San Francisco Chronicle;* January 10, 1977.
7. "Biletnikoff: We're Brawlers"; Betty Cuniberti; *San Francisco Chronicle;* January 10, 1977.
8. *They Call Me Assassin;* Jack Tatum with Bill Kushner; New York: Everest House; 1979; pg. 172.
9. "A Viking Analysis"; *San Francisco Chronicle;* January 10, 1977.
10. Sung to the melody of "Year of the Cat" by Al Stewart and Peter Wood; *Year of the Cat;* EMI; 1976.

1980 AFC Playoff
Oakland vs. Cleveland
January 4, 1981
Cleveland, Ohio

HE CAUGHT THE BRICK

In the most extreme conditions of nature, you may find the resilience of Raider purpose.

Such was the case on January 4, 1981, as the Oakland Raiders met the Cleveland Browns in a second round playoff game in Cleveland's Memorial Stadium before 80,000 loud and hardy. As the two teams prepared to do battle with each other, they both confronted a second, more sinister enemy: a brutal temperature of one degree at kickoff with a wind chill of minus 30. These climatic conditions made the contest the second-coldest professional football game ever, the most frigid being the infamous "Ice Bowl" on December 31, 1967, between the Green Bay Packers and Dallas Cowboys—minus thirteen degrees, wind chill minus 48. Third place went to the German Eighteenth Army versus the beleaguered citizens of Leningrad on January 12, 1943.

Despite these High Arctic conditions, the rules of football still applied: the field was 360 feet long and 160 feet wide; each end zone totaled thirty feet and the hashmarks were 70 feet, 9 inches from each sideline. The only problem? The field was under a two-inch blanket of frozen water. "On the first play of the game, I looked down and I was standing on a sheet of ice," said tackle Art Shell. "All I could do was spin my wheels. I was in neutral."[1]

That assessment pretty much described both teams as they trod the tangled tundra of mud and ice in the first half. In the first twenty-five minutes, both offenses could concisely be summed up in four syllables: one, two, three, punt. Nobody could run and, with the pigskin weighing seven pounds in the Neptune-like air, that meant the game's successful outcome rested on performing one unnaturally difficult act in facile fashion.

Catch the brick.

It was not as easy for receivers as one would think, because—on this terrain—the rules were changed. Under normal conditions (as pointed out by TV commentator John Brodie), getting open was the challenge—catching the football was second nature. In this environment, players could get open. It was pulling in the pass that presented the problem,—and then they still had to worry about the defensive hit. Cleveland's Dave Logan couldn't cradle one ball properly and it slipped to the ground. Oakland's Kenny King caught a first-down pass but dropped it when pummeled by defenders. The Browns' Reggie Rucker was unable to haul in an over-the-shoulder post-pattern airmail. The Raiders' Raymond Chester couldn't secure the rock when battered after a seeming catch. Cleveland's Calvin Hill ran an out-pattern and the rifle pass went through his hands faster than *The Empire Strikes Back* shot to No. 1. It was trouble all around.

After Cleveland took a 6–0 lead in the second quarter on a 42-yard pass interception (Ted Hendricks blocked the extra point), Oakland began to blow the warm breath of offense into their cupped, frostbitten fingers. It started when Bob Chandler made an incredible sideline grab where he stretched out farther to make the first-down catch than we stretch our weekly paycheck. Said quarterback Jim Plunkett: "Bob planted 2 feet just inside the sideline, caught the ball and then fell over like an axed tree. We call this our 'Timber!' pattern."[2] Kenny King then caught a swing pass for five yards and Mark van Eeghen caught another toss over the middle for a first down—which was incorrectly spotted one yard short of the first-down marker, prompting third down. On a broken play, Plunkett couldn't make a clean handoff and alertly dove over the pile for it. Now, the Raider offensive line began to control its destiny: King ran a draw for seven yards; van Eeghen gained two and then five up the middle. In a huge play, Plunkett fired a strike to Chester, taking the football down to the two-yard line. It looked like a skating rink out there, and van Eeghen uncharacteristically slipped and fumbled on first down. The ball bounced off a Raider leg, however, and the carrier quickly covered it. On third-and-two, van Eeghen bulled over the right side of the line behind Mickey Marvin and Henry Lawrence, and the Raiders were on the board. Holder Bob Chandler took the extra-point snap and placed it down on the ground as gently as parents turn their infant daughter over on her belly before sprinkling powder on her bottom. Chris Bahr nailed it through and, suddenly, Oakland led 7–6 at halftime.

The third quarter completely belonged to Cleveland. The Raiders were lucky they came out of it only down 12–7. On three consecutive drives, the Browns drove down to the Raiders' thirteen-yard line, nineteen-yard line, and thirteen again—yet only came away with six points. On one field goal attempt, the holder fumbled the snap (see, they didn't have Bob Chandler). Oakland did not gain a first down the entire quarter. Probably it was the cold, open-field wind whipping at hands too frozen to feel.

Once the teams switched sides to begin the fourth quarter, the Raiders showed that although they might be captives of the elements, they were masters of the game at hand. Starting at the Oakland 26-yard line and facing third-and-four, Jim Plunkett—who heaved the frozen brick all day with amazing power and predictable inaccuracy—put together three completions over the middle which moved the Raider ball as fast as the Federal Reserve was raising interest rates. First was the scramble and shovel-pass to van Eeghen to the Raider 39-yard line. Next, Clifford Branch made a leaping, leaning grab from a standstill, coming down on the Browns' 42. Third, Raymond Chester went up high while falling backward, bringing the brick down with him at the Cleveland 15. Then, on third-and-three amid the mud-stained chunks of wearied humanity, Plunkett hit Kenny King in the breadbasket crossing at the seven-yard line; King turned up field and plowed to the two. Three plays later, van Eeghen followed the left-side blocks of Art Shell and Gene Upshaw into the icy tundra for six points. The point-after-touchdown made the score 14–12, Oakland, with 9:22 remaining on the clock.

Now Jack Frost began to sap the last reserves of players' commitment and metabolism. Bodies weighed heavy on the hashmarked moonscape, and debilitated muscles responded weakly in the tormenting cold. Plunkett and Cleveland quarterback Brian Sipe had surprisingly similar statistics: Plunkett was 14 for 34, 149 yards, 0 touchdowns, 2 interceptions; Sipe was 11 for 34, 131 yards, 0 touchdowns, 2 interceptions. After the teams traded punts, Sipe took off running for yardage and, when he was hit by Mike Davis, the football flew as high into the air as the prime rate (21%). When it came down, Oakland's Odis McKinney recovered at the Cleveland 24-yard line.

With 4:18 left, amid the brutal solstice climate, the battle was joined. Oakland was fighting a slippery, icy mixture of mud, snow, and blood. Cleveland was fighting the clock with frozen, frostbitten fingers desperate to find feeling and grip everything, anything. The Raiders needed ten yards to secure a first down; the Browns held them to nine yards, 30 inches and took over on downs with 2:22 left in the game and the ball on their own fifteen-yard line. The crowd was as loud as if 125,00 Cuban refugees—newly arrived on the Mariel boatlift—had just learned Fidel Castro was dead. They could sense what was about to happen. Twenty-four of Cleveland's previous thirty-two games had been decided in the last two minutes.[3] The Kardiac Kids were about to embark.

On second down, Sipe hit Ozzie Newsome with a 29-yard gain, significant because Odis McKinney fell down while covering the play but still saved the touchdown by making an ankle tackle at the Browns' 44-yard line. Cleveland was unable to move but received a first down after a penalty on Oakland for an illegal chuck. Greg Pruitt then caught a 23-yard sideline pass to the Raiders' 28, and a draw play picked up fourteen more to the Oakland fourteen-yard line. After a one-yard gain, 46 seconds remained in the game. Referring to the Browns' veteran place-kicker, Ted Hendricks said, "I was really concerned. Cockroft missed every field goal on that side of the field, but he made two in the third quarter and he was getting his confidence back. I had a real bad feeling about him trying another one."[4]

After a timeout to talk things over, Cleveland trotted back onto the field. "We figured the Browns would run the ball up the middle then kick it," safety Mike Davis said. "What they did, though, was baffling."[5] As the Browns came to the line of scrimmage, Davis was surprised to recognize by the formation: "They're going to pass!"[6]

At the snap, Ozzie Newsome—who had caught four passes for 51 yards—was lined up on the right He headed for the end zone and tried to cut left into the middle of the field. Davis covered Newsome, and Burgess Owens came over to help out, forcing Newsome to go deeper into the end zone than he would have liked. This depth put Davis in the inside position between Sipe and Newsome. Sipe let fly with a spiral toward Ozzie that quickly turned into a waffler in the face of the 16-mile-an-hour wind blowing in from Lake Erie. Davis broke with Newsome and was with him step for step. When the pass arrived, Davis was in position to knock it away. But then Mike Davis did something extraordinary, something so unbelievable that the eyes saw it but the mind was unable to register its reality. With pain peeling away precious layers of ability, eyes stinging from the severe blast of wintry lake air, and body parts numb with exhaustion and cold, Mike Davis forever placed himself in the annals of Raider lore.

He caught the brick.

Final score: Oakland 14, Cleveland 12.

REFERENCES

1. "Browns Gone With the Wind"; C.W. Nevius; *San Francisco Chronicle*; January 5, 1981.
2. *The Jim Plunkett Story*; Jim Plunkett and Dave Newhouse; New York: Arbor House; 1981; pg. 235.
3. "Raiders Freeze Out Cleveland"; C.W. Nevius; *San Francisco Chronicle*; January 5, 1981.
4. ibid.
5. *Super*; Edited by Murray Olderman; Oakland, CA: The Oakland Raiders and Murray Olderman; 1981; pg. 122.
6. "Eerie End by Lake Erie"; Bruce Newman; *Sports Illustrated*; Vol. 54, #2; January 12, 1981; pg. 13.

1980 AFC Championship
Oakland vs. San Diego
January 11, 1981

San Diego, California

THE SIX-MINUTE EGG

It was a conversation not picked up by the television microphones.

Down by a touchdown late in the game, San Diego's stalwart defensive line was waiting and ready. After nearly 54 minutes of all-out battle, their mission now was simple: get the Oakland offense off the field as quickly as possible and put the football into the capable hands of the Air Coryell General, Chargers quarterback Dan Fouts.

"All right, Louie," said Chargers' defensive end Fred Dean. "It's time to crack a few eggs and make an omelet. Then we'll eat it in New Orleans." Louie Kelcher nodded but stared straight ahead. With a billowing blue-gray dusk settling over Jack Murphy Stadium, beads of perspiration rolled down his face and massive neck. Through his facemask, Kelcher could see the Oakland offense trotting up to the line of scrimmage, hear the roar of the home crowd, and he knew what he had to do.

What Kelcher did not know was that the Oakland Raiders would deliver exactly as promised. For the next 360 seconds of violent battering and blocking, in the game of their lives, what San Diego's future held could be cupped in the palm of a small child's hand.

A six-minute egg.

At the beginning of this wild AFC Championship game, though, San Diego's future looked more like a six-second egg. That's about how long it took Oakland to put the game's first touchdown on the scoreboard—thanks to one tight end named Raymond Chester. With five yards to go on the game's third play from scrimmage, Raider quarterback Jim Plunkett threw too hard for Kenny King and the football caromed off his outstretched fingertips and continued downfield. Chester, who was crossing right to left farther on, reached up

61

and tipped the errant ball with his left hand, stabilized it to eye level, grabbed it, and took off running to the end zone—all within a blink of a patched eye. Jim Plunkett called it the Immaculate Deflection.[1] That quickly, Oakland went on top, 7–0.

After San Diego tied the game on a 48-yard scoring strike from Dan Fouts to Charlie Joiner (a scoring drive that took 1:21), Plunkett came right back and, rolling right, found Clifford Branch for a 47-yard gain. A thirty-yard pass interference call on a Charger defender against a Raider newcomer named Todd Christensen put the ball inside the San Diego ten-yard line and, two plays later, Plunkett scrambled in. Oakland led 14–7 with 3:45 left in the first quarter.

After holding the Chargers to a three-and-out punt, Oakland started at the opponent's 49-yard line and scored quicker than Al Davis puts on leather. Bob Chandler took in a pass for fourteen yards, Chester grabbed a catch for eleven more, then Plunkett threw a 21-yard beauty to lead a crossing Kenny King into the promised land and a 21–7 lead. The four-play drive took 1:33.

Following an Oakland interception of a Dan Fouts pass, brought on by a blitzing Ted Hendricks, Oakland failed to move and punted. On San Diego's second play, John Matuszak stripped the football from the ball carrier and Hendricks recovered it on the Charger 29-yard line. A penalty pushed Oakland back to third-and-20, where Plunkett hit Clifford Branch on a crossing pattern at the 32; Branch then ran with a speed and quickness that made defenders grab at the air, the same air viewers were forgetting to breathe as they watched this modern-day Mercury scamper to the San Diego fifteen-yard line. Mark van Eeghen scored untouched four plays later and Oakland led 28–7 with over six minutes to play in the first half.

But San Diego would claw its way back, scoring a touchdown before the half ended and adding a field goal on its first possession of the third quarter to make the score 28–17. They then added another touchdown and, as quickly as you can say *Coal Miner's Daughter,* it was Oakland 28, San Diego 24. Hendricks found Plunkett on the sideline. "You've got to keep scoring," he pleaded. "We can't stop them."[2] At that point, with nine minutes gone in the second half, the Raiders had yet to notch a first down. "I think we could have been in real trouble then," Bob Chandler said. "A less experienced team might have panicked."[3] It was time for the Raiders to get as mad as Robert De Niro in *Raging Bull*. They did, putting together a nice drive and increased their lead to 31–24 as the fourth quarter began. After trading field goals in the first part of the final period, Oakland put together the drive that can only be termed egg-cellent.

Their two previous possessions had resulted in field goals and each consumed over five minutes of play, so the Raiders knew that they could move the ball on the Chargers. Oakland took possession of the football with 6:43 left on the clock and the pigskin resting on its own 25-yard line. Basically, each rushing play takes about 35 seconds. On first down, behind Dave Dalby's fire-out block, van Eeghen gained five. Next, over the left side, with Kenny King providing a tough lead block after Shell and Upshaw took care of their opponents, van Eeghen picked up ten yards—first down at the Oakland 40 with 5:29 remaining. At the snap of the ball, with the clock showing 4:59, van Eeghen followed Mickey Marvin and Henry Lawrence over the right side for four yards. King plunged for two yards. On third-and-four at the 46, with 4:10 remaining and behind good protection, Plunkett dumped off a quick toss to Arthur Whittington for another first down. More than once during the drive, Dalby was heard to say, "A few more first downs, and we're in the Super Bowl."[4] Behind Dalby and Marvin, Derrick Jensen moved forward for three yards; then van Eeghen added two on the next play, bringing up third-and-five with 2:55 left in the game. But a San Diego player jumped offside on third-and-five, and van Eeghen easily got the first down behind Dalby, Marvin, Lawrence, and Chester. At the 2:00 warning, the football was placed on the San Diego 35-yard line and Oakland had a new set of downs fresher than Wilbur Mills chasing Fanny Fox. And, after San Diego burned two of its timeouts on a pair of short runs, Plunkett's scramble up the middle on third-and-four ended the Chargers' hopes for a post-game party faster than the Jimmy Carter reign ended. All that was left was for Charger coach Don Coryell to give his infamously grimacing, acerbic, bile-inducing scowl.

In the final six minutes of the game, San Diego's powerful offense gained no yardage, got no first downs, never reached Oakland's territory, and put no points on the board—all because they could not get on the field. Said Charger Kellen Winslow, "I was looking for something, anything—a fumble, a penalty, an interception—anything to get us the ball. But it never happened. They were perfect."[5] Mark van Eeghen provided this one insight into why the Raiders didn't turn the ball over: "I can count the fumbles on the fingers of two hands and the fumbles I lost on one hand."[6] As the exuberant Raider players walked to the tunnel that would take them to New Orleans, Gene Upshaw held the game ball aloft with his right hand. There, with the scoreboard behind it showing 0:00, the elliptical form of the pigskin took on a new shape. It suddenly looked like a giant goose egg.

The six-minute egg.

REFERENCES
1. *The Jim Plunkett Story;* Jim Plunkett and Dave Newhouse; New York: Arbor House; 1981; pg. 241.
2. ibid., pg. 243.
3. "Superstitious Raiders Were on Edge Until the End"; C.W. Nevius; *San Francisco Chronicle;* January 12, 1981.
4. "Plunkett Stars in AFC Win"; C.W. Nevius; *San Francisco Chronicle;* January 12, 1981.
5. *Super;* Edited by Murray Olderman; Oakland, CA: The Oakland Raiders and Murray Olderman; 1981; pg. 125.
6. "Back to the Basics"; Paul Zimmerman; *Sports Illustrated;* Vol. 54, #3; January 19, 1981; pg. 19.

Super Bowl XV
Oakland vs. Philadelphia
January 25, 1981
New Orleans, Louisiana

CELEBRATION

Celebrate good times, come on!
It's a celebration.

—KOOL & THE GANG, 1980[1]

Isn't it amazing how a song can take us to a specific moment or place? There are certain tunes that, for whatever reason, transport us in time and space to a realm in our mind that is reserved for just that song. Whether it is a picnic at the beach, the first time we heard The Beatles, a youthful dance, finding ourselves, or losing our virginity (which for some is the same moment)—music has the power to carry us back to a specific occasion.

And that's how it is with the Kool & the Gang song, "Celebration." In my mind, "Celebration" will always take me back to the event that took place on January 25, 1981, in the New Orleans Superdome.

Super Bowl XV. Oakland 27, Philadelphia 10.

For on that day, the Oakland Raiders made history as they climbed to the top of the mountain known as the National Football League. No team before them had ever won the Super Bowl by going through the wild card bracket, meaning the Raiders had to win four playoff games—in all of which they were the underdogs. Of course, they were never underdogs to Raider fans, and one month to the day after Christmas, they showed why they were, as Al Davis said, "magnificent."

The game started favorably for Oakland. Philadelphia picked up its initial first down by two running plays. Then, from the 35-yard line, Eagle quarterback Ron Jaworski (the "Polish Rifle") ran the play-action and retreated seven yards, set, looked left and fired his first pass in a Super Bowl game. Intercepted! Linebacker Rod Martin, the fourth year pro out of Southern Cal who had watched hours of Eagles' film, spotted where the play would go and made a good read on a terrible throw. The Eagles' tight end, John Spagnola, was open to a touch pass over the heads of Martin and Bob Nelson, but Jaworski tried to muscle it in—and paid the price. "Spagnola hooked right behind me, and I just dropped back and played the ball," said Martin, who added, "It was kind of wobbly—more like a duck than an Eagle."[2] Oakland suddenly had the ball at the Philadelphia 29-yard line. Four plays later, we saw a snapshot of what was to come when quarterback Jim Plunkett took the snap and a ten-yard drop, stood there nearly five seconds, and hit Clifford Branch with a completion to the five-yard line. From there, on third-and-two, Plunkett dropped to pass, thought to scramble, and instead threw a two-yard touchdown to Clifford, who had masterfully caused the Eagle defender to turn his back on him. Branch slid the other way. Oakland 7, Philadelphia 0.

Meanwhile, the Eagles' offense was having fits with themselves as well as the Raider D. Philadelphia's main goal was to run wide, and one play early on showed that—on this day—such a game plan had about as much chance of success as Ted Kennedy outrunning his past in a bid to become president. A quick left pitch to Wilbert Montgomery became problematic for the Eagles because Rod Martin was already in the backfield waiting for him, forcing Wilbert to turn upfield. Ted Hendricks was running from the left side along the line untouched and, with Matt Millen, crunched Montgomery for a one-yard loss. The game's second big break came when Jaworski rifled a forty-yard touchdown pass, but the play was called back because Harold Carmichael, in motion before the snap, had turned upfield too soon.

After the punt, Oakland started at its own fourteen-yard line with 1:06 left in the first quarter. After two plays netted six yards, the Raiders faced a third-and-four—but were about to get so much more. Plunkett dropped back to the twelve to pass but no one was open as the pocket collapsed around him. He scrambled left in his own inimitable style and, seeing running back Kenny King "standing all alone jumping up and down waving his hands," let fly an intention toward King.[3] "I was running a simple six-yard pattern," said King, "when I saw Plunkett scramble. I took off up the field."[4] King was running up the left sideline, facing in and looking over his right shoulder. As the football came toward him, King rotated to his right, backed up a few steps, snared the pass over his right shoulder at the Oakland 38-yard line and took off dashing down the left sideline. Bob Chandler—who was primary receiver—was executing a pass pattern from right to left and so was right next to King as he sprinted for the end zone sixty yards away. Stride for stride the two sped for paydirt, with Chandler throwing the insurance block at the Eagles' 15 that guaranteed the 80-yard touchdown.

It was an amazing play in several regards. First, everybody worked to make the play: Mickey Marvin blocked his defender to the ground; Plunkett made his escape and threw a pass which gave the choreography a chance; King made an excellent catch and kept his balance; and Chandler used his adrenaline to stay with King and throw the finishing block. It was sweeter still because Al Davis had craftily engineered the acquisition of three major players involved in this broken play. Davis picked up Plunkett off of waivers in 1978 (in 1979, Plunkett threw fifteen passes; in 1980, he threw 320 passes, and the Raiders won 12 of 14 games he had started before this one) He traded Jack Tatum to Houston for King in 1980 (King had nine yards of offense in 1979, 906 yards in 1980). And he traded Phil Villapiano to Buffalo for Chandler that same year (in 1980, Chandler had 49 receptions for 786 yards, a 16.0 average, with ten TDs).[5] When all efforts were linked together, it was the longest touchdown pass in Super Bowl history. That pass stands as my favorite Raider play of all time. At the end of the first quarter, the score now stood Oakland 14, Philadelphia 0.

The Eagles got on the board with their next possession, making good on a field goal attempt to close to 14–3. Although the Raider defense was playing tough—John Matuszak running at Jaworski like a 300-pound train wreck, Dave Pear applying pressure, Bob Nelson

on a relentless and violent blitz—Philadelphia was a worthy opponent and stood poised to tack three more points on the scoreboard.
But Ted Hendricks got his hands on a low 28-yard field goal
attempt—his 20th career block of PATs or field goals, an NFL
record—and the score remained 14–3 when the first half ended.

As the third quarter began, Oakland took the kickoff at its 23-
yard line and began tearing off chunks of yardage like hungry men
tear off pieces of French bread to dip in their bowls of onion soup.
On second down, a swing pass went for thirteen yards, with King
carrying the football out in front of him like he was holding a bou-
quet of flowers. On first down at the Raider 35, Plunkett showed
why he was a first-rate quarterback—and that he listened to his
receivers. Plunkett wrote that Chandler, miffed that Branch had
already caught four passes, came back to the huddle earlier and
groused "Dammit, look at my side!" Off play-action, Plunkett took
a ten-yard drop, and stood there a good five seconds before hitting
him in stride running right to left with a pass perfectly dropped in
between Eagle defenders for a 32-yard gain. Added Plunkett, referring to receivers: "They all want the ball."[6]

Two plays later, Plunkett again threw deep, toward Branch—but
he made a mistake. "I missed the defense," Plunkett said. "I was
expecting a zone. If I'd read it earlier as man coverage, I would have
thrown it differently—deeper and farther."[7] As we have seen him do
time and again, Branch adjusted his body while the ball was in flight
to place himself in proper position to take the ball away from rookie
Roynell Young. Moving right to left along the goal line, Branch was
shadowing Young like two pegs in a close cribbage game; as the
underthrow arrived, Branch put on an afterburner burst, leaped like
a gazelle, shielded Young from the ball and took what was his, simply
because he is a Raider—and because Clifford belongs in the Hall of
Fame. With just over eight minutes left in the third quarter, the score
was now Oakland 21, Philadelphia 3.

Philadelphia came back with a drive to the Raiders' 35. On third-
and-three, Jaworski faked play-action, quickly dropped back six
yards, and threw left and high. Rod Martin, who was silhouetting the

receiver, stepped in front and put his hands up like a shopper reaching for a 2-for-1-sale item on the top shelf of a supermarket. Martin's second interception of the day was in his big paws, and the linebacker drafted in the last round of 1977 went to the sidelines and let his fingers do the talking, raising two digits toward his sisters and mother in attendance. Before the day was over, that sign became three, as Martin set a Super Bowl record with three interceptions.

Just in case there were any doubt, the Raiders set the record straight concerning who was the best team in football. They did it with a stay-at-home pass blocking scheme that allowed only one sack.[8] They did it with a running game that amassed 117 yards on 34 carries. They did it with a quarterback throwing 13 completions in 21 attempts for 261 yards and three TDs. And they did it with a smothering defense that dominated the line of scrimmage, shut down the Eagles' running game, and harassed Jaworski all day.

In the end, one is left with singular memories of this great victory: how crowded it must have been for Philadelphia's offense with Dave Browning and Reggie Kinlaw already in their backfield; Dave Pear and Dave Browning, two University of Washington grads, lined up side-by-side on a running play; Lester Hayes trailing on a pass into the end zone but closing and batting the football away at the last second; an Oakland offense that averaged 6.2 yards on first down throughout much of the game and averaged 11.7 first-down yards in the third quarter; Plunkett throwing with precision and scrambling in confusion; and all the cast-away Raiders who finally got a Super Bowl ring.

Al Davis summed it up nicely in the post-game awards ceremony: "You know, when you look back at the years of glory of the Oakland Raiders . . . but this was our finest hour, this was the finest hour in the history of the Oakland Raiders. To Tom Flores, the coaches, and the great athletes: you were magnificent out there today, you really were."[9]

Raider Al was uncharacteristically exuberant in victory. Gone was the need to hold something in reserve. Absent was the nagging feeling of self-doubt that accompanies victory by the undeserving or humble. At the very moment of triumph, the win is nothing—because it's only a game, after all. But even if there are more important things in life, it does not make the memory of this victory less precious. To Raider Al, and to all Raider fans, it is the victory, glory and accomplishment of the Silver and Black that matters. And the moment.

It's 1981. The hostages are free. Ted Koppel is out of a job. There's only one thing left to do.

Celebrate. Come on.

REFERENCES

1. "Celebration"; Kool & the Gang; 1980; Funk Essentials.
2. "He Had the Winning Hands"; Steve Wulf; *Sports Illustrated*; Vol. 54, #5; February 2, 1981; pg. 23.
3. "Raiders Dominate Eagles to Win Super Bowl"; C.W. Nevius; *San Francisco Chronicle*; January 26, 1981.
4. *Great Moments in Raider History*; Editor in Chief, Al LoCasale; Playa del Rey, CA: CWC Sports, Inc.; 1998; pg. 119.
5. *Black Knight*; Ira Simmons; Rocklin, CA: Prima Publishing; 1990; pg. 152.
6. *The Jim Plunkett Story*; Jim Plunkett and Dave Newhouse; New York: Arbor House; 1981; pg. 253.
7. Nevius, op. cit.
8. "Raiders Out-Think Eagles"; C.W. Nevius; *San Francisco Chronicle*; January 26, 1981.
9. Post-Game Super Bowl Show; NBC Sports; January 25, 1981.

1983 AFC Championship
Seattle vs. Los Angeles
January 8, 1984

Los Angeles, California

THE FAIR LADY

Chuck Knox, the coach of the Seattle Seahawks, likes to espouse classic sayings to his players in the hopes of motivating them to greater effort. One such aphorism of which Coach Knox is fond goes "Remember, a faint heart never won the fair lady." This line, I am told, is from J.R.R. Tolkein's classic, *The Lord of the Rings.*[1] Now I can't read this seminal work, mainly because it is three books totaling 65,000 pages and I can only read twelve pages before I have to take a nap. What I can do is watch football all day long, and I am here to tell you: it may be true that the faint heart never won the fair lady but, this last Sunday, the fighting heart won the AFC Championship.

The Oakland ... er, Los Angeles Raiders defeated the Seattle Seahawks 30–14 before 89,000 fans in Memorial Coliseum. It was a game not nearly as close as the final score indicates. But going into the game, it was potentially as troublesome as any game the Raiders played this year. Or any two games. For the Raiders lost both of their games to Seattle this year; why I don't know. Perhaps the Silver and Black have trouble getting psyched up against the Silver and Royal Blue. Or maybe the Kingdome is their real nemesis with its ear-splitting decibel level and rock hard Astroturf (somebody ought to blow the place up). Or maybe it was the lack of coaching (Lyle Alzado said the losses were because "they had a better game plan than we did"[2]). For whatever reason, the Raiders incurred 50% of their regular-season losses (and 100% of their AFC defeats) to a team that has a non-existent fowl as a mascot. So the Raiders had to dig deep to pull out this victory, and—from the very beginning—they came out fighting.

The Raiders knew what they had to do to win this football game: they had to stop the leading ground gainer in the American Football

Conference, rookie Curt Warner. During the year, Warner ran for 1,449 yards Against the Raiders, he gained 176 of those yards and scored two touchdowns. If they were going to stop this 5'-11" bundle of finesse and power, the Raiders would have to beat him down. And that is exactly what they did, holding Warner to a meager 26 yards in eleven rushes. "We didn't just tackle him, we punished him," concluded linebacker Matt Millen.[3] The tackling team of Alzado-Reggie Kinlaw-Howie Long-Ted Hendricks-Bob Nelson-Millen-Rod Martin was up to the task of tackling Warner and harassing Seahawk's quarterback Dave Krieg. But, just in case they weren't, the Raiders had added a couple additions to the team: intensity and intimidation. "When we stepped in that tunnel," said backup nose tackle Dave Stalls, "I realized I had never seen a team like this. This team was utterly possessed."

It was just plain scary to see how psyched those Raiders were at the start of this game. I swear, more fights broke out on the field in the first quarter than hand-to-hand combat in the entire Granada invasion. Millen described the tactic in these terms: "I call it playing the three P's . . . pointing, pushing, and punching."[4] Seattle's running back Dan Doornink agreed: "About every time there was contact, they'd be pushing or hitting somebody in the face, something like that."[5] The Seahawks unfortunately brought it upon themselves. "We've got pride," said Long, "and we didn't like what they were saying about us. They said Jacob Green deserved to be All Pro and that I didn't, that I'm all talk. They said the guy who plays opposite Lyle would dominate him for the third time this season." Added safety Mike Davis: "Hey, they were mouthing off all week. We read it in the newspapers, their fans sent telegrams to us. There's no question they were playing a game of psychology with us, but they forgot all the Raiders flunked psychology."[6] At least *that* psychology.

The first turnover came early, and the penalties came even earlier. After a phantom pass interference call on cornerback Lester Hayes ("My shadow must have bumped him"[7]) put the ball on the Raider 32-yard line to start the game, Krieg was sacked hard by blitzing Rod Martin. "Dave Krieg has had an excellent season," said free safety Vann McElroy, "but I think Rod got to him early and his confidence was shaken. When you're a quarterback and you get hit like that, your timing goes."[8] After a roughing the kicker penalty gave Seattle a first down, Krieg took a two-step drop and threw to the right side to Steve Largent, but he wasn't even close. Lester Hayes stepped in front, intercepted, and returned the football 44 yards to Seattle's 27-yard line. Said Krieg: "They blitzed and he guessed we'd throw a quick out, which is what we did."[9] A twenty-yard field goal followed, making the score 3–0—which is where it stood at the end of the first quarter.

Seattle played the Raiders tough, stopping them in the second quarter on third-and-one and again on fourth-and-one. But the Raider D was even more unforgiving, allowing the Seahawks just one first down in their next three series following the interception. Then the Raiders got the offensive engines going.

From their own 38, on second down quarterback Jim Plunkett took advantage behind a wall of protection to wave Clifford Branch to the middle of the field—where he hit him for a twelve-yard gain to midfield. Running back Marcus Allen then blasted sixteen yards over the left side behind the blocks of Charlie Hannah and Bruce Davis. Plunkett then threw right to wide receiver Malcolm Barnwell at the 22-yard line, who ran to the 15 before being dragged down. Two plays later, a pass to tight end Todd Christensen moved the football near the five-yard line. On third-and-one, Allen took the handoff and immediately began climbing invisible steps as he went vertical. Remember how ET went airborne on the bike? That's how it looked. A second later, Allen was flying like a cruise missile, seven feet in the air, moving horizontally over the stunned defenders and parallel with the ground below. When he came down, the Raiders had a first-and-goal. Two plays later, Frank Hawkins bulled over the right side and it was 10–0 with 4:17 to go in the second quarter.

On its next possession, the Raiders' defense gave Seattle no yardage and no quarter. First, Krieg was sacked for the third time, Martin getting to him again. (By the time he was pulled in the third quarter, Krieg had a "hat trick": 3 completions, 3 sacks, 3 interceptions.)[10]

Then a Warner draw netted no gain—by this time, Curt had 18 yards in ten carries. On third down, a swing pass to Doornink went nowhere when Long brought the running back down with one hand holding his jersey—prompting me to remember the line of Ted Hendricks: "When I grab 'em they're grabbed."[11] Seattle was forced to punt for the fourth time in the first half.

The Raiders wasted no time putting more points on the scoreboard. On second down, Plunkett took a 6-yard drop and uncoiled an arrow that found Barnwell at the Seattle twenty-yard line, and Malcolm continued on to the Seahawk 7. The Seattle defender mistakenly thought Barnwell was running an out-pattern, but he simply ran around him and upfield. Two plays later, Hawkins scored his second rushing touchdown and the Raiders led 20–0 at halftime. A third-quarter score made it 27–0, and it was all over except for the statistics. As Allen said: "Our goal was the Super Bowl and the Seahawks were the obstacle in our path."[12] With this dominating and convincing win, the Raiders removed the last impediment to the Super Bowl as easily as a bulldozer takes out a tree stump, winning the AFC Championship for the third time in eight years.

And what of the fair lady, the one alluded to earlier? She flew on ahead to Tampa, Florida for the January 22 game. There she waits, nubile and curvaceous, with her right arm outstretched and her palm turned upward. In the cup of her hand is a ring.

And its colors are Silver and Black.

REFERENCES
  1. http://middlearth.pitas.com/part2.html
  2. "Raider Tag-Team Tactics Take Toll on Hawks"; Steve Kelley; *Seattle Times*; January 9, 1984.
  3. "Dissecting Raiders' Game Plan"; Scott Ostler; *Los Angeles Times*; January 9, 1984.
  4. "Raiders Use Their Three P's to Break Hawks"; Blaine Newnham; *Seattle Times*; January 9, 1984.
  5. "Raiders' Nastiness Envelops Seahawks"; Art Thiel; *Seattle Post-Intelligencer*; January 9, 1984.

6. Newnham, op. cit.

7. "They Had a Corner on the Championship"; Ralph Wiley; *Sports Illustrated;* Vol. 60, #2, January 16, 1984; pg. 18.

8. Newnham, *op. cit.*

9. "Zorn for Krieg? Krieg Says It Was a Good Move"; Mark Heisler; *Los Angeles Times;* January 9, 1984.

10. "The Seahawks Were Made-to-Order Foe"; Bob Oates; *Los Angeles Times;* January 9, 1984.

11. *Cruisin' with the Tooz;* John Matuszak with Steve Delsohn; New York: Charter Books; 1987; pg. 192.

12. "Marcus Gave a Heisman Performance"; Georg N. Meyers; *Seattle Times;* January 9, 1984.

Super Bowl XVIII
Washington vs. Los Angeles
January 22, 1984
Tampa, Florida

BACK IN BLACK

In the past two seasons, counting playoffs, they totaled 23 wins and 6 losses. Their defense looks like a *Who's Who* of pain and mayhem, this season allowing a third-down conversion percentage of only 32.3% . They won their two previous playoff games by a combined score of 68–24. They were led by an owner who thinks he alone is The Establishment. They have been in the Super Bowl three times previously, winning two. On January 22, 1984, they were back again, in Tampa, Florida.

And this time, they were back in black.

Appearing for the first time in their home field black jerseys, the Los Angeles, nee Oakland, Raiders demolished the Washington Redskins 38–9 in Super Bowl XVIII. Firing on all cylinders like a perfected juggernaut, the Raiders dispensed with the defending champions by beating them at their own game. "Basically, after all the motion, they're just a team with one formation and they dare you to try and stop them," Howie Long observed. "It's just power football and no one had been able to stop it."[1] Added Mike Haynes: "No matter what formation they ended up in, in the end it just came down to man-to-man, very basic stuff—you take that guy, I take this one. My kind of football. . . ."[2] That's Raider kind of football: line up and let the smash-mouth begin.

What was most interesting about this kind of football was that, in the first half, the game revolved around a single syllable: punt.

After an opening-series punt by the Raiders, Washington took over at its own 20. The Redskins gained a first down on three John Riggins' runs. Then quarterback Joe Theismann attempted three straight passes: all against cornerback Haynes, all incompletions. One pressure, one hurry, and one quick-out, and the 'Skins offense performed its own quick out—off the field. In came their punting unit and, at the snap, in came the Raiders' Derrick Jensen—with a vengeance and a goal in mind. Blasting up the middle, Jensen not only blocked the punt with his arm but also had the wherewithal to stay with the caroming football and fall on it in the end zone for the game's first score. Said special-teams coach Steve Ortmayer: "We thought the wind was blowing so hard that it would be tough for a punter to get a good snap, catch it smoothly and get off a good punt."[3] Jensen added, "It's the first time in six years we've used that play early. Usually we're more conservative."[4] Hardly conservative, Raider fans were suddenly as smooth and happy as Ronald Reagan surrounded by "Star Wars."

The happiness continued as the Raider defense held Washington to a three-and-out series. It was at this time that the word "punt" reared its second head in Hydra-like fashion—or should I say "hand." After only a 27-yard punt, the football took an odd bounce and hit Ted Watts on the right wrist as he blocked a Redskin; Washington recovered and took over on the Raider 42. But the Redskins could tack only fifteen more yards to their lucky break, and the score remained 7–0 Oakland when the 'Skins' 44-yard field goal attempt sailed wide left.

Both sides did little with their next possessions, so kicked. As the Raiders' Greg Pruitt ran back the punt return to the 38-yard line, he was knocked off his feet while a Redskin tried to strip the football from his grasp. Was it a fumble? Would the breaks continue to go against the Raiders? Every Raider knows that the ground cannot cause a fumble, unless the ball is dislodged before the player hits the ground. It was a close call, but I would agree with the referee that Pruitt was down before the ball came loose. Chalk one up for truth and justice.

After a seventeen-yard sweep to the left side by Marcus Allen, the Silver and Black drive stalled and in trotted punter Ray Guy. Little did he know that he was about to make one of the most memorable individual plays in Super Bowl history.

It was the third play of the second quarter. Standing back to punt on his own 44-yard line, Guy reacted immediately as the snap sailed two feet over his head. Jumping straight up from a standing-still position, Guy looked like he had been launched from a trampoline. Arching his back and curling his legs under him to get greater extension, the man widely considered the "best athlete on the team" shot his right arm into the air like a student who knows the answer in sixth-grade algebra class. Then, incredibly—at the height of his extension—Guy caught the ball with his right hand, brought it under control and down to earth in one fell swoop, and executed perfectly the two-step dance of the punter against a charging Redskin rush. The football traveled out of the end zone, preventing certain disaster. At 34 years old, Guy was the oldest punter in the NFL—and also the best. What he did on that play has never been done in a Super Bowl game—before or since. It is immortal.

On first down at the Redskin's own twenty-yard line, Riggins ran a sweep for one yard. This 240-pound bulldozer of a fullback, who set a Super Bowl record in Pasadena a year earlier by rushing for 166 yards, now had twenty yards in nine attempts against the Raiders. By this time, the Silver and Black defense was showing that the vaunted Redskin offense was a worse forgery than Hitler's fake diaries. For every Washington action, there was an equal Raider reaction: Riggins plows into the middle; Reggie Kinlaw meets him at the line of scrimmage for no gain. Theismann tries a controlled scramble to the right, but Howie Long is waiting there for Joe like a wolf waiting for a lamb. Theismann takes off left but is run down by middle linebacker Matt Millen for a six-yard loss. Theismann runs the controlled scramble and throws the football 45 yards downfield, but cornerback Lester Hayes is on receiver Charlie Brown like bark on a tree. In frustration, Brown whined for an interference call, but there was only minor contact and the pass was long anyway. Said Hayes: "The Silver and Black fears no mere mortal. Even Smurfs. We are Jedi."[5]

After the inevitable Redskin punt, the Raiders took over at their own 34 and—on first down—quarterback Jim Plunkett showed the Redskins how the long pass was supposed to be executed. Off play-action, Plunkett dropped back eight yards and unloaded a 51-yard pass that only had eyes for Clifford Branch. Running down the middle of the field and past defenders at Mach One, looking back over his right shoulder, Branch took rightful possession of the heave at the 15-yard line as casually as we take a tray from a buffet line. Two plays later, Plunkett made a twelve-yard touchdown pass to Branch look like a yawner (Clifford's third career touchdown reception tied a Super Bowl record) and the Raiders led 14–0 with 9:14 left in the second quarter.

The Redskins finally got on the scoreboard with a field goal to close to 14–3 with 3:00 remaining before intermission. Then came another memorable moment. The Raiders had run an eight-play series and then punted, giving the football to Washington on their own 12-yard line with twelve seconds remaining. You'd think the 'Skins would have sat on the ball and headed into halftime down by only eleven points, but you would be as incorrect as Interior Secretary James Watt describing a certain commission that year as "a black, a woman, two Jews, and a cripple."[6] Linebacker coach Charlie Sumner remembered that, when the Raiders had met the Redskins back in October, the 'Skins ran a screen play left to Joe Washington that went for 67 yards. Playing a hunch, Sumner pulled Millen, substituted the quicker and faster Jack Squirek, and told him to shadow Mr. Washington. Sure enough, Theismann faked the downfield look and tossed a lazy spiral over a drifting Lyle Alzado and toward a flanking Washington. Said Theismann: "I never saw the linebacker. I was concentrating on trying to get it over Alzado."[7] Suddenly, as if in slow motion, into the picture came a charging No. 58, snatching the football out of mid-air and waltzing the five yards into the end zone as easy as you please. Squirek raised the football above his head in a salute to jubilation while his teammates poured onto the field. "I must have had 2,000 pounds jump on top of me," Squirek said. "I never got a chance to spike."[8] At least he got a chance to make a play, and the interception was another Raider immortal moment.

It was a total first-half team effort (three scores: one from offense, one from defense, and one from special teams).

The half time score was now 21–3, and the Raiders would protect this lead for the rest of the game in the best way they knew how—
by ground. They would entrust this task to Marcus Allen, and in the
second half he would run. Oh, how he would run. Allen had eleven
carries for 51 yards in the first half, but it was the second half that
Raider fans would remember. Allen picked up an eight-yard gain to
the Redskin 11 early in the third quarter over the right side behind
Mickey Marvin and Henry Lawrence blocks. Then he slid into the
end zone off a Dave Dalby obstruction to up the score to 28–9.

Allen was about to uncork his longest run of the game, but first
a statement needed to be made by the group Long called "The
Slaughterhouse Seven"—the three down linemen and the four linebackers.[9] After a fumble recovery, the Redskins were at the Raider
36-yard line, down 28–9 and trying to make a game of it. A first
down pass netted six yards, but Riggins was held to two yards on
second down and Joe Washington gained only one on third. That
brought up a crucial fourth down and the play went to Riggins over
the left side. Unfortunately for the Redskins, that was the side linebacker Rod Martin played, and he was lined up against tight end
Rickey Walker. Martin, while at USC, had previously played against
Walker, who suited up for arch-rival UCLA. Before this game Martin
promised, "He didn't block me in college, and he won't block me in
the Super Bowl."[10] Martin made good on his vow, standing Walker
up and sliding in to meet a charging Riggins, bringing him down
with those massive hands short of the first down. Making light of
his and Kinlaw's draft position in 1977 and 1979, Martin said:
"Reggie and me, just two 12th-round draft choices trying to get
by."[11] On this day, they did more than got by; they got it done.

But it would take Allen to put the exclamation point to an all-
around stellar day for the Raiders. Taking the handoff on the next
play, Allen originally went left, but his way was blocked. So he
reversed direction back to the right and then, as suddenly as Bilbo
Baggins found the secret entrance into the mountain, he cut up the
middle of the field. "I was just picking myself up off the ground,"
Marvin said. "Then I looked around and a rocket went through."[12]

The "rocket" was Marcus Allen, who later said:

> They kind of over-pursued and I just cut it back. Actually, it was
> kind of my fault it ended up that way. I should have been inside but
> I was outside so I had to try to make something out of nothing.[13]

By the time he was done running a record 74 yards to the opposite end zone, it was the Washington Redskins on the outside, looking in at the new World Champions as they danced and skipped on the sidelines. Allen finished the game with 191 rushing yards, also a Super Bowl record.

All that was left was for us to watch the tears flow from defensive end Lyle Alzado, and he didn't disappoint us. The great warrior who embodied the gentle heart and vicious spirit of Raider Mystique broke down and cried at the game's end. "This was my first time I've been champion," said Alzado. "This is my first and possibly my last championship."[14] We love you for that moment, Lyle.

This Silver-and-Black effort showed us how the game of professional football should be played. Perhaps another Raider team will find itself in a similar position.

Back in the Super Bowl.

Back in black.

REFERENCES

1. "Millen's Impression of Sugar Ray Leonard Fires Up the Raiders"; Rick Reilly and Rich Roberts; *Los Angeles Times;* January 23, 1984.

2. "A Runaway for the Raiders"; Paul Zimmerman; *Sports Illustrated;* Vol. 60, #4; January 30, 1984; pg. 24.

3. Reilly and Roberts, op. cit.

4. "To Win Super Bowl, the Raiders Put In Calls for Jensen, Squirek"; Scott Ostler; *Los Angeles Times;* January 23, 1984.

5. "Hayes and Haynes Handcuff Smurfs"; Mark Heisler; *Los Angeles Times;* January 23, 1984.

6. *The Columbia Chronicles of American Life;* Lois Gordon and Alan

Gordon; New York: Columbia University Press; 1987; pg. 699.

7. "Raiders Send Hogs to Slaughter, 38–9"; Alan Greenberg; *Los Angeles Times;* January 23, 1984.

8. "He Made His First Score a Big One"; Jack McCallum; *Sports Illustrated;* Vol. 60, #4; January 30, 1984; pg. 20.

9. Reilly and Roberts, op. cit.

10. Quoted by John Madden, NBC Sports, January 22, 1984.

11. Zimmerman, op. cit.

12. Zimmerman, op. cit.

13. Greenberg, op. cit.

14. Reilly and Roberts, op. cit.

CHAPTER THREE

Preseason

PRESEASON

The urine in referee Walt Coleman's Depends drawers was barely dry before Al Davis began making plans for the 2002 Oakland Raiders football season.

First, in February Mr. Davis traded the head coach for $8 million and four draft picks.[1] The same month, he signed free agent linebacker Bill Romanowski. At his news conference, Romanowski said that he couldn't wait to hit somebody, adding "And the fans are, in my mind, amazing. These guys, if you're not a true professional and can't handle what these people can dish out, they'll scare the daylights out of you."[2] In March, defensive tackle John Parrella put black ink on a Raider contract with silver lining. Said Parrella: "I can't wait for the first home game because the Raiders have the best fans in the world. I was so jacked up when I signed with the Raiders, I wish we had a game on Sunday so I could go out and hit someone."[3]

Then Bill Callahan, who spent the previous four seasons as offensive coordinator for Oakland, was named the thirteenth head coach in the franchise's history. Before Callahan could enthuse at his press conference that he couldn't wait to hit somebody, Al Davis took the microphone and said that Callahan had "been a great part of the motor that drives this organization on the football field."[4] Offensive guard Frank Middleton was signed off waivers that same month, and defensive back Terrance Shaw was also added later.

In fateful April, Al Davis and the Raiders stunned the football world by masterfully trading up several times to draft Phillip Buchanon and linebacker Napoleon Harris in the first round.[5] In retrospect, the Buchanon draft was not surprising, since Davis always believed one built a football team around cornerbacks.[6] The Raiders also took Langston Walker and Doug Jolley in the second round. And, on the last day of April, the Raiders announced that defensive back Rod Woodson would play for Oakland. That brought the number of new defensive players in Silver and Black to six. No doubt, this was a conscious effort to improve the Raiders' defensive standing in the NFL above last year's marginal 18th position.

In July, Al Davis opened his wallet and signed quarterback Rich Gannon to a six-year $54 million contract—the largest in team history—although the first two years reportedly only paid Gannon $250 a season.[7] In August, the Raiders added a large piece of real estate to their front line, signing Sam Adams.[8] To make room under the salary cap, Davis offered to cut middle linebacker Greg Biekert's salary by 60%. Biekert—who had started in 124 out of 128 games since 1994—played his final series of downs and asked for his release.[9]

Finally, Labor Day passed, and it was time for the Oakland Raiders to open the 2002 season at home against a nemesis of 25 years—the Seattle Seahawks.

REFERENCES

1. "Al Strikes Again as Bucs Fork Over Farm for Gruden; Art Spander; *Oakland Tribune;* February 19, 2002.

2. "New Raider Romo Ready to Rumble"; Carl Steward; *Oakland Tribune;* February 28, 2002.

3. "Raiders Sign Parrella"; Raider Newsroom; Official Web Site of the Oakland Raiders; March 7, 2002.

4. "Callahan Press Conference"; Raider Newsroom; Official Web Site of the Oakland Raiders; March 14, 2002.

5. "Busy Raiders Get Defensive"; Bill Soliday; *Oakland Tribune;* April 21, 2002.

6. *Hey, Wait a Minute;* John Madden with Dave Anderson; New York: Ballantine Books; 1984; pg. 90.

7. "Gannon Deal Reveals Kinder, Gentler Davis"; Monte Poole; *Oakland Tribune;* July 17, 2002.

8. "Adams Bolsters Defensive Line"; David Bush; *San Francisco Chronicle;* August 20, 2002.

9. "Biekert Situation Divides Raiders"; Nancy Gay; *San Francisco Chronicle;* August 29, 2002.

50 WAYS TO LEAVE YOUR LOVER

We are mavericks, misunderstood, often motley and sometimes mistaken. Treated with all the respect of the usual suspects, we are loyal, contentious and prideful. Immature beneath our years, we are nevertheless feared beyond our borders. Within our Walter Mitty world, we yearn for the autumn wind, sing the past-glory praises, and grind our teeth at missed opportunities. We are the Raider Family.

And in our family, for twenty-five years we have wanted to beat the Seattle Seahawks like a red-headed stepchild. Part of this animosity is institutional. After all, Seattle was our direct rival within the American Football Conference (AFC) West. That reality guaranteed two meetings (one home, one away) each year between the vaunted Silver and Black and upstart Seahawks. But something happened to turn this institutional animosity into a heated, personal rivalry.

What happened was that Seattle kept beating the Raiders. This single reality made the Seahawk-Raider competition personal. The Oakland/Los Angeles/Irwindale/Anchorage Raiders have always prided themselves on winning. And winning, by definition, means totaling more victories than losses (significantly more if you hope to reach that holy grail of postseason possibilities, the playoffs). Yet Seattle's 25-year record against the Raiders is 23–27, basically a .500 draw dating back to a time when the space shuttle was still a vision and Billy Carter relieved himself on White House shrubbery. The Seahawks swept the regular season series no less than six years and split the home-and-away contests another ten. Personal? You'd better believe it. It wasn't just the effeminate SeaFerry/Seapigeon/Seasquab/Seaturkey team colors or ridiculous nickname that we mocked with glee. Name one other team that could sweep the Raiders during the regular season. Okay, Kansas City and Denver, but we hate those guys too.

The losses were particularly galling given their disastrous effect on Raider playoff hopes. From 1979–2001, the Seahawks bounced the Raiders from—or dealt a mortal blow to—the promised land of Silver and Black playoffs on six different occasions. SIX DIFFERENT

TIMES! In the limited-opportunity parlance of second-season football, this is the moral equivalent of asking Moses to walk his merry band of miscreants around the desert-block another twenty years. Consider these happy Seahawk highlights/tormented Raider nightmares:

12/16/1979: Seattle 29, Oakland 24
Jim Zorn completed 23 of 35 passes for 314 yards and two TDs in the last game of regular season; Sam McCallum had eight receptions for 173 yards and one TD (career best); the Raiders drank from the happy-hour chalice of Guyana Jim Jones and were knocked out of playoff picture (except for Kenny Stabler, who was traded to Iran).

12/22/1984: Seattle 13, Los Angeles Raiders 7
Dan Doornink rushed for 123 yards (career best) to eliminate the defending Super Bowl champions in an AFC Wild Card playoff game; the Raiders did not get inside the Seattle 40-yard line until 5:05 left in the fourth quarter. Raider offensive uniforms were fumigated when their emanating stench was mistakenly identified as matching Union Carbide's deadly Bhopal gas.

12/8/1986: Seattle 37, Los Angeles Raiders 0
The 7–6 Seahawks hand the 8–5 Raiders their worst defeat since 1962; Raider QBs sacked eleven times; Raider management shrewdly picked up the Chernobyl No. 4 reactor at a garage sale to fuel their well-oiled machine, promptly lost the following two games, and fell out of playoff picture.

12/18/1988: Seattle 43, Los Angeles Raiders 37
The 8–7 Seahawks won their first division title in 13 years as they jarred the 7–8 Raiders with 490 yards in total offense; Dave Krieg passed for 410 yards and four TDs; eliminated from a second season, the Raiders looked like playoff contenders about as much as Michael Dukakis embodied the commander-in-chief while riding around in a tank.

12/17/1989: Seattle 23, Los Angeles Raiders 17

In final game of season, the 7–7 Seahawks outplayed the 8–6 Raiders as Krieg completed 25 of 34 passes for 270 yards and two TDs; John L. Williams had twelve catches for 129 yards and one TD; after Raiders lost the following final game of the season, they were eradicated from making the playoffs like a willow ptarmigan lounging in Prince William Sound as the Exxon Valdez visited Bligh Reef.

12/17/1995: Seattle 44, Oakland 10

The 7–7 Seahawks thumped the 8–6 Raiders; Chris Warren rushed for 105 yards and three TDs and Seattle gained 175 yards on kick-offs and punts in this laugher; the Raiders lost their following final game of the season and fell out of playoff picture; O.J. Simpson was acquitted and signed onto Oakland's special teams roster for his slashing style of play.

After each of these losses, when chancing upon Raider fans, women invariably locked their doors and gleeful children grew quiet and hid in the shadows. But the situation for Seattle fans is more complex. Now that they don't have Dick Nixon . . . I mean Raiders . . . to kick around anymore, who are Seahawks fans going to hate? Are they going to hate San Francisco with its indicted management and phony "re-inventing football" mantra? How are they going to detest St. Louis? They don't even know what state the Rams are in (Ohio) or which side St. Louis supported in the Civil War (America had a Civil War?). And the only people who even know about the existence of the Phoenix Cardinals are NFC East teams, which have feasted for two games per year on the carcasses of the Buddy Ryan Express. Cast into the Paul Tagliabue Diaspora of NFL reorganization, Seattle fans may one day pine for the "good old days" when the Seahawks could put a whoopin' on those Raiders.

A word needs to be said about "Raider Hater" Seahawk fans. Many of them too often reminded me of hyenas: brave and bold in a victory pack but sullen and timid if they fell behind by even a single point. Perhaps this fair-weather outlook is a natural outgrowth of suffering twelve losing seasons in twenty-five years. But God, could they make noise. The deafening decibels generated by Kingdome crowds could sound like the Rolling Stones and Blue Oyster Cult playing directly into a Raider's left ear as Billy Graham proselytized into the right one while brandishing a Husqvarna chain saw. Any Raider who sat through the 33–3 shellacking (1985) or 37–0 embarrassment (1986) can feel my pain. Northwest Raider fans would sit in the stands and patiently wait for those perfectly hushed Kingtomb moments where 60,000 fans were as quiet as when a manager asks for volunteers at a staff meeting. Like watching in 1987 as Bo Jackson ran eighty yards down the left sideline for a touchdown, chased in plodding futility by Seattle's worst draft choice ever—Brian Bosworth. Seahawk (and Northwest Raider) fans loved to turn out to root for their respective teams: three of the four highest-attended games in Seahawk history were against Oakland (all Seattle wins).[s] After one of those games (2000), as they filed from Husky Stadium with their sixth and final win of the year, one fan said "This was our Super Bowl." As a fan of the team which flat-out derailed the Seahawks in their only AFC Championship appearance, 30–14 in 1984, allow me to say: "The pleasure was all ours."

It is a pleasure I hope to build upon in the 2002 season, with an asterisk of course. Football is a fascinating confluence of forces: physical stature combined with athletic ability channeled through technical expertise and fueled by human passion—all taking place among the mass histrionics of 65,000 fan-atics. For Raider fans, the spectator role amounts to reasoned chess-game analysis translated into spontaneously-screamed incoherent sounds in conjunction with orchestrated two-syllable words (De-Fense!). Seattle opens the regular season in Oakland against the Raiders on September 8. My wife and I will be down at the game, incoherently cheering every deserving Raider play in general and screaming in frustration at the mistakes in particular.

Seattle now resides in the NFC West, so the institutional territorial imperative between the Raider and Seahawk fans no longer exists. Now, for the first time in twenty-five years, Raider fans can root for

Seahawk victories in earnest, without fear of playoff reprisal. Wouldn't it be something if, ensconced in their own stadium and buoyed by an amazing convergence of newfound support, brewskies and cooperation among Seahawk and Raider fans, Seattle began to defeat the 49ers and Rams and win far above its humdrum 54.6% career home-winning percentage? Wouldn't it be double-something if the Seahawks made the playoffs for only the second time in fourteen years, and moved beyond the first round for the first time since defeating the Raiders in 1984?

Good luck, Seattle, in the 2002 football season. Shorn of duty, mindful of history and accepting a chance to be better, this Raider fan will be rooting for you.

Starting September 9.

REFERENCES

1. *2002 Seattle Seahawks Media Guide.*

CHAPTER FOUR

2002: First Quarter

Seattle at Oakland
September 8, 2002

As dawn broke Sunday morning, U.S. citizens across this land could see the time fast approaching which would commemorate the darkest day in their young nation's history. For Americans in general, their deepest worry was that Arab terrorists could get into the vulnerable country with subversive intent.

For Raider nation fans in particular, their shallow concern was that the Seahawk's Shaun Alexander could enter the Oakland secondary in upright gallop.

It was back on November 11, 2001 that Seattle's Alexander shredded Oakland's defense like a clam in a Cuisinart, gaining a ridiculous 266 yards on 35 carries in a 34–27 Raider loss. The rushing yardage gained in a single game was the fourth-highest of all time, behind Corey Dillon (278 yards, 2000), Walter Payton (275 yards, 1977) and O.J. Simpson (273 yards, 1976). Coming into that 2001 game, the Silver and Black were 6–1; after the debacle, Oakland would stagger to the finish line at 4–4. Following the defeat, only once would the Raiders win a game by more than ten points. Defensive end Tony Bryant said, "After that game, a lot of teams got to see things that even we didn't know were there. After that, it was kind of a long season for us."[1] No doubt about it: the Seattle game crushed Oakland's veneer of invincibility.

Today, Alexander would face a Raider defense that, after a mediocre year (22nd out of 31 teams in rushing defense), had gone through a restructuring more severe than the American intelligence agencies which had failed so spectacularly before 9/11. Nine new starters would wear the defensive black jerseys. Gone were the likes of Elijah Alexander, Eric Allen, Greg Biekert, Johnnie Harris, Grady Jackson, Marquez Pope, Darrell Russell, Josh Taves, and William Thomas. Raider fans would have to familiarize themselves with the names and numbers of fourteen new defensive personnel. That's a tall order for fans who can barely spell BART.

The Seattle game plan would be simple. "I am sure they are going to come down here and establish the run early and try to control the clock and the tempo of the game," new Oakland coach Bill Callahan said.[2] Bryant was more succinct: "Alexander made a highlight film out of us last year."[3]

Let's hope the highlight film this year shows that a Seahawk in hand, especially eight Raider hands, is better than a Seahawk in open field.

ONE IF BY LAND

Walking on the outskirts of downtown this last Sunday evening, I noticed something peculiar. Off in the distance, there was a light shining in the belfry of the Tribune Tower. Only too aware of today's dangerous world—and dimly recalling the revered poem line, "One if by land, two if by sea"—I took a second look. Were the Russians coming? Was the Iraqi navy sailing up the San Francisco Bay in North Korean junks? There amid the flowing moonbeams, I keenly followed the rhythmic motion of the tower light. When it reached 31 sways and stopped, I snorted and went on my way. Some fool was just letting us know: all was well with Raider Nation.

Let the record show: the Oakland Raiders opened the 2002 football season with a convincing 31–17 win over the Seattle Seahawks. But it wasn't really that close. Had they been able to move the ball by sea, the Raider offense would have wracked up nautical miles. QB Rich Gannon (19 for 28, 214 yards, 2 touchdowns) needed a sextant more than a time clock to manage the open field before him.

Vaguely reminiscent of Buffalo during its offensive heyday, the Raiders drove the pigskin at will. They even ran the no-huddle in their opening drive, culminating with an eight-yard TD toss to Tim Brown, the 101st of his career. One moment Oakland would be at their own 30, the next (don't look away) they were threatening from the Seahawk 20. Their four touchdown drives of the first half entailed possessions of 4:13, 0:44, 2:37 and 4:41. "The way it works is if we complete 65 percent of our passes and don't turn it over, we win the game," Gannon predicted.[4] During an effort where the offense controlled 58% of the 60-minute clock, the Raiders chewed up yardage like Tom Likus dominates two-way conversation: brutally and with attitude.

Although it was a team victory in which no position played poorly (although tight end and special teams raised a few eyebrows), the most valuable player would have to be identified by completing the following: "Charlie *(blank)*." Most Raider fans would answer "Manson," but that would be wrong. As are Tuna, Joiner, McCarthy, Chaplin and Brown. I can assure you: if you asked the Seattle Seahawks to complete the name, to a man there would be only one answer.

Charlie Garner.

Charlie Garner was nothing less than sensational on a day when a major question on fans' minds was "Can Oakland return to the run?" Garner's all-purpose yardage (15 rushes, 127 yards; 5 catches, 64 yards) transfixed the Raider faithful and sent historians running for their reference books to see when the century rushing mark was last achieved. This regular-season 100-yard game was the first by a Raider since Tyrone Wheatley carried for 146 yards over twenty months ago.[5]

In order to better understand Garner's critical contribution to the Raider victory, consider this: he played a part in 42% of the Raider's initial 65-yard TD drive; he touched the ball in 87% of their next 38-yard TD drive; he contributed 38% of the third 69-yard TD drive, and he helped account for 79% of the yardage in the Raiders' 67-yard drive which resulted in a goal-line fumble. Said Gannon, "He is as dangerous in the passing game as he is in the running game, and he's probably pound for pound the toughest guy on our football team."[6] To opposing defenses, Charlie Garner is a heathen of slashing bursts and stealthy tread. A North-South wind and a flare-out nightmare. To Raider fans, he is so money.

And yet the best play did not come from No. 25. It came from No. 32, Zack Crockett. After scoring on their initial possession, the Raiders gave up a ridiculous kickoff return and were soon tied at

7–7. They were then outplayed by the Seahawks for their next two series. Someone had to make a play, and that someone was Zack Crockett. Racing down the field after a Kevin Stemke punt, he delivered a solid torpedo-tackle while suspended in mid-flight. Play of the Game. A crowd which had cheered loudly just moments before when a Seattle player was slow to get up now stood in stunned silence as the fourth-year Raider remained down and motionless on the field. Whispers of "Get up Zack" could be heard from drunken Raider fans more accustomed to screaming epithets. After minutes that seemed eternal, Crockett was removed from the field on a stretcher. From then on, the Raiders were a team transformed. "You try and turn those things into positives, where you play for Zack," observed Tyrone Wheatley.[7] Crockett did return, but it was only to the post-game party, where it is rumored he drank torpedoes.

And the vaunted running game of Seattle? It never broke free, shackled instead by an unforgiving defense with vengeful intent. On thirteen occasions, Seahawk Shaun Alexander took the handoff; time and again, he made less headway (36 yards) against the men in black than George Bush trying to form an international coalition against Iraq. "It seemed like we were swarming from every direction. It was like he had nowhere to go, nowhere to hide," said linebacker Bill Romanowski (5 tackles, 0.5 sack).[8]

Led by the posse of John Parrella, Tony Bryant, and Napoleon Harris, Raider defenders repeatedly tackled with a force as lethal as a fusillade of 2,000-pound smart bombs. Deprived of their his running game, Seattle quarterback Matt Hasselbeck took to the air, completing 23 passes but gaining only 155 yards in the attempt. By halftime, the score was 28–7 and the rout was on. In the end, the Seahawk plan of run-run-pass was about as effective as a United Nations summit to preserve the planet and reduce poverty.

The most entertaining play of the game came from an unlikely source when another Shaun—Shawn Springs—scooped up a Raider fumble near the Seahawk goal line. He found his way to the middle of the field and continued on across the hashmarks until he was racing up the opposite sideline. Gannon saw he was last man and drew a straight line of pursuit that would have made a mechanical engineer proud. "I was chasing up the field, and I just tried to take a good angle," Gannon said.[9] The y-intercept occurred at about the Raider 30. Grabbing Springs by the shoulder pads from behind, Gannon employed leverage as if trying to bring down a small steer. Using his momentum, Gannon windmilled the Seahawk out of bounds, Springs' legs and arms flailing about like a scarecrow in a jet stream. Leaving Springs lying in disheveled bewilderment, Gannon walked across the field at a deliberate pace, accompanied by a deafening Raider ovation.

His message was clear: not in this house, Shawn. For this house is our house. We are Raiders. We shall bear any hangover, protect any child, respect most elders and oppose all hijackers. With an obsession for Sundays and an eye on San Diego, we recite the pledge: ask not what your Raiders can do for you—ask what you can do for your Raiders.

Next Sunday the Silver and Black travel to Pittsburgh to play the AFC Championship that never was. For those who watch or listen, they will see an Oakland effort to remain in the unbeaten ranks with an early bye week the just reward. If you miss the game, just look towards the Tribune Tower Sunday night. With lantern sways, QuasiRaider will tell you the score and the means to its outcome.

One if by land, two if by air.

REFERENCES

1. "Seattle's Alexander Sent Raiders Run 'D' in a Spin"; Bill Soliday; *Oakland Tribune*; September 5, 2002.
2. "Raiders Move from Paper to Field"; Bill Soliday; *Oakland Tribune*; September 8, 2002.
3. "New Defense Makes a Good First Impression"; Carl Steward; *Oakland Tribune*; September 9, 2002.
4. "Consistent Gannon Makes the Difference"; Jerry McDonald; *Oakland Tribune*; September 4, 2002.
5. *The Team of the Decades 2002*; Oakland Raiders Media Guide.

6. "Raiders Running Game Returns"; Jerry McDonald; *Oakland Tribune*; September 9, 2002.
7. "Crockett Wheeled Off Field with Neck Injury"; Jerry McDonald; *Oakland Tribune*; September 9, 2002.
8. "Romp Kicks Off Callahan Era"; Bill Soliday; *Oakland Tribune*; September 9, 2002.
9. "Crockett Wheeled Off Field with Neck Injury"; Jerry McDonald; *Oakland Tribune*; September 9, 2002.

WEEK 2
Oakland at Pittsburgh
September 15, 2002

Like all Americans, Raider fans rejoiced that July 28th as a team of coal-diggers survived a most harrowing ordeal just 55 miles southeast of Pittsburgh. One by one, every fifteen minutes, they were raised from the certitude of death to rejoin family and friends amid the dance of the living. Nine miners buried for 77 hours 240 feet underground—men that had "decided early on they were either going to live or die" as a team—used strength and resolve to carry them through the blackness of despair and into the silver light above ground.[1]

With determination like that, they should've been Raiders. But, alas, they lived near Pittsburgh and were probably Steelers fans.

Raider fans don't like the Pittsburgh Steelers. Without a win to show in nearly twelve years against them, and the Silver and Black history of heartbreaking lost opportunities borne, we would like nothing better than to beat the Steelers fifty times in a row.

And the feeling is mutual. Asked about the significance of the rivalry, Pittsburgh's Jerome Bettis said, "Steelers vs. the Raiders is a game you circle. Everyone in our organization understands that game is a must win." Asked what he hated most about the Raiders, Bettis offered: "That color, that black and silver. We're black and gold. The good guys. The black and silver is the bad guys."[2]

For our part, after the beatitudes of saying dinner grace, Raider fans usually end the prayer with "Never forgive. Never forget. Amen." Vengeance may be the Lord's prerogative, but it is the Raiders' motivation. With two AFC Championship losses (1974 and 1975) as well as the worst play in the history of pro football coming at their hands, Raider fans have a good deal to detest about the Pittsburgh Steelers.

- 12/23/1972: "There was no way they were going to call it on the field," said coach John Madden after the illegal pass not only gave Pittsburgh an undeserved 16–10 playoff win but also brought down a government in Italy. "With all those people there, somebody might have been killed." Madden stated categorically, "Our films show that Tatum never touched the ball."[3]

- 12/29/1974: In the Coliseum featuring an AFC Championship game of finesse against muscle, Oakland rushed 21 times for 29 yards while Pittsburgh gained 224 yards on 50 carries in a 24–13 Raiders loss. Asked if he had ever seen such a dismal running effort, Coach Madden said, "There may have been a game sometime, somewhere, but I can't remember it."[4]
- 01/04/1976: In Pittsburgh's unfriendly Three Rivers Stadium amid nature's hostile six-degree wind chill, Oakland lost its sixth straight AFC Championship appearance, 16–10. As the return flight approached Oakland Airport, a telephoned death threat was made against all Raiders. "Get away from me," Coach Madden warned a reporter. "Where I am may be the most dangerous place in this airport."[5]

For years, Raider parents would not let their children watch "Mister Rogers' Neighborhood," simply because he was from Pittsburgh.

It only makes it worse when we read what some loud-mouthed Steelers scribe wrote:

Don't worry about Bill Callahan outcoaching Bill Cowher tomorrow night. . . . Callahan (is) the football equivalent of a substitute teacher, and we all know how ineffective they are. Callahan won't make any bold moves.[6]

Such jargon sounds like bold talk from a one-eyed fat man. All of America saw Pittsburgh's opening-game laugher against the New England Patriots, a 30–14 loss. Tailback Jerome Bettis gained only 35 yards on 8 carries after rushing for nearly 8,000 yards the previous six seasons—and he lost a fumble for the first time in over 580 attempts. Coming off a season when the Steelers ran for more yards than any other NFL team, quarterback Kordell Stewart was a passing fool; he threw two interceptions in his first three pass attempts and suffered five sacks during the Monday night game.

Still, Coach Bill ("The Face") Cowher was optimistic of the Heinz Field strategy. The Face declared, "We're going to be patient, we're going to be persistent, as long as the game's close, we'll probably be able to run the football."[7] For the Raiders, Coach Bill Callahan sought to defuse talk of the tactic used so effectively against Seattle the week before: "We're not going to use the no-huddle every game. It's something we can use as needed, but we're not inclined to use it all the time, especially on the road in a hostile environment."[8]

And it will be a hostile environment. There is no love lost between these two teams. The Steelers seek to break into the win column and please the hometown crowd in an effort to repeat as division champions. Oakland seeks to raise their record to 2–0 in the quest to win an AFC West for a third straight year.

In doing so, with strength and resolve, the Raiders just might bury one haunting memory.

Raider fans hope such an eventuality comes to pass.

RAIDERS PASS THE TEST

We are strangers—ships passing in the night—yet we do things which bind us together in commonality. We pass on the left, pass judgment, pass out, pass it around, pass legislation, pass on a decision and, of course, we pass gas.

Sunday night, before a nationally televised audience, the Oakland Raiders bound themselves to the unbeaten eight by doing what AFC West Champions do.

They passed the test.

More to the point: they passed.

In a fitting homage to the man who wrote the book on passing, ex-Steeler John Unitas—who passed away earlier this week at age 69—Oakland used aerial acumen and total team effort to topple Pittsburgh 30–17. The final tally was not unique; the Raiders trounced Seattle by almost an identical score a week earlier. What was surprising, after racking up 221 yards rushing in game one, was the means employed toward the end.

To say Oakland threw the football is like saying Al Davis has detractors. Quarterback Rich Gannon's 64 pass attempts (Terry Kirby also threw one) were a team record, and his 43 completions were the highest number for a non-overtime game in NFL history. During the entire game, the Raiders owned the pass. They lofted, they timing-patterned, they shovel-passed. Receivers curled, split, slanted, squared out, turned in, screen-passed, and flared out. They played the game as if the run had been outlawed by the Taliban.

If you diagrammed each potential Raider receiver's dedicated and alternate routes over the 65 passes thrown, the schematic would resemble a Star Wars intercept drawing of incoming Scud missiles. The total time the Oakland ball was in the air surpassed a season-premier episode of "Friends." The most widely-requested mechanical device in the pressroom was a pencil sharpener.

How crazy was it? Their first series—using the no-huddle—Gannon threw 12 times in 13 plays, with only one toss moving the ball more than ten yards. The next series: six straight passes for 35 yards before Charlie Garner, on his way to a 36-yard touchdown, blasted up the middle like Bigfoot, the Monster Truck. Series No. 3: five pass completions resulting in 53 yards before Gannon was intercepted. Incredibly, the Raiders passed 29 times in their first 31 offensive plays; when the first half ended with Oakland leading Pittsburgh 20–10, Gannon had thrown 42 times in 47 snaps.[9] Ever the paragon of hyperbole, Callahan offered, "We thought we could throw it and spread it out a little, just change it up, try to neutralize the blitz...."[10] If that isn't an understatement, then Saddam Hussein is the Iraqi George Washington.

Time and again, Gannon's passes found their mark. Jerry Rice, one month shy of his 40th birthday, made ten catches for 85 yards in the first half alone. "I'm not tired," Rice said. "Whatever I'm doing (in terms of physical conditioning), I'm going to keep doing."[11] Jerry Porter caught his first NFL touchdown since becoming a second-round draft pick of the Raiders in 2000. ("Wow. It's been a long time," Porter said. "I haven't had one since college."[12]) By game's end, Gannon had thrown for 403 yards to nine different receivers, completing more passes than Catholic edicts clarifying their position on Jews and God.[13] The Steelers defense hardly stood a ghost of a chance.

That is because the Silver and Black had a ghost to purge in this game. The Raiders played with a chip on their shoulder, but they were actually seeking to unload a burden from their backs. Time after time after time, as Oakland stumbled through yet another 1990s 8–8 non-playoff season, the song remained the same: the Raiders would play on the road and—be it Tennessee, Denver, Miami or Kansas City—come out smoking against their opponent. They would control the clock, the run, the secondary and the line of scrimmage on both sides of the ball. They would be in command of nearly every facet of the game except one: the scoreboard. Miraculously, Oakland would own only a 3-point lead over the rival. Then, when the home team made a run at them—which the good teams always do—the momentum would swing against the Raiders and defeat would be snatched from victory.

True to form, Pittsburgh made their run at the Raiders, capitalizing on a Joey Porter interception runback for 84 yards that was noteworthy mainly for Charlie Garner running the length of the field to make the tackle and nearly force a fumble. Said Gannon of the pick, "It was really a bad decision ... in my 15-year career it is probably the worst play I've ever had."[14] The resultant five-yard Pittsburgh toss to Hines Ward cut the lead to 20–17 on the last play of the third quarter. And that's when the third-year Raider out of Virginia, Mr. Terry Kirby, did against the Steelers what I like to do with my women: go all the way.

Subbing for the injured Tyrone Wheatley and Randy Jordan, Kirby had already caught 3 passes for 39 yards. On the first play of the fourth quarter, he took the resulting kickoff at his 4-yard line, hurdled a couple of wedge-blocking Raiders at the 20, outran the Steelers' kicker at midfield and found an extra gear of speed to beat the last Steel man down the right side of the field. "People don't know how tough that (beating the kicker) is," Kirby said. "He is just standing there and can see it coming. He only has to slow you down." In doing so, Terry Kirby outran the past. "I have been in this league 10 years, and this is what I have done—wait for my opportunity," said Kirby. "You just have to take advantage of the next chance you get."[15] Suddenly the Steelers' comeback chances looked like the ruins of Yasir Arafat's hot tub in his West Bank headquarters. The score was 27–17, game firmly in Raider hands, ghost soon to be exorcised and Kirby's "next chance" was the flight home to be enjoyed. Play of the Game.

This is the test the Raiders passed; they elevated their game to a higher level. This higher level of performance is now enjoyed by Oakland, Denver, and New England. The challenge is to maintain that level of play, week in and week out. So far they're 100%. And with a head coach hardly playing the part of a substitute teacher ("I felt that you had to keep pushing and be aggressive and continue to attack"[16]), they figure to stay that way.

One of the Raiders' greatest weapons that finds its way to the football is Rod Woodson. In one of the stranger displays of opportunistic takeaways, Woodson recovered three fumbles—two inside the Oakland red zone—the first Raider to ever record such a feat. We all remember the 1981 Super Bowl XV win over Philadelphia when linebacker Rod Martin intercepted three Ron Jaworski passes. But three fumble recoveries? To give you an indication, it had not been done in nearly four years of NFL play. Fifteen years plus into his career, Woodson is still unforgiving when the ball is on the ground.

And two weeks into this season, the Raiders are unbeaten and unbowed in their quest for football supremacy. Today they have achieved their initial goal; tomorrow they rest. "We can go into our bye with our heads up, knowing we might have something special brewing here," cornerback Charles Woodson said. "But we have to take it for what it is—two wins—and we've got a long ways to go."[17] On Sept. 29, Tennessee rolls into town, one of five franchises so stupid they have to be named for a state. Oh yeah, we remember the Titans, a team the Raiders have yet to beat since their return to Oakland.

When the fifth Sunday of this month dawns over Jack London Square, pack up the ice chests, load the barbecue grills, slap on the decals, and unfurl the flags. Sit with generations of Raiders, enjoy good conversation, play the music and radios, eat a lot. Cook up some shish kabobs, hot dogs, hamburgers, and jalapeños.

And don't forget to pass the ketchup.

REFERENCES

1. "Rescued Pa. Miners Recount Ordeal"; Larry Neumeister; *The Philadelphia Inquirer*; July 28, 2002.
2. "Steelers' Bettis Hits as Hard as He Gets Hit"; Dave Newhouse; *Oakland Tribune*; September 12, 2002.
3. "Madden: Pittsburgh TD Illegal"; Darrell Wilson; *San Francisco Chronicle*; December 26, 1972.
4. "Raiders Miss Super Bowl Again"; Glenn Dickey; *San Francisco Chronicle*; December 30, 1974.
5. "On the Air—Grim Threat"; Art Rosenbaum; *San Francisco Chronicle*; January 6, 1975.
6. "Madden: Raiders Won't Copy Patriots' Game Plan"; Mark Madden; *Pittsburgh Post-Gazette*; September 14, 2002.
7. "Raiders Know What Lurks in Pittsburgh"; Jerry McDonald; *Oakland Tribune*; September 15, 2002.
8. "Don't Expect the Raiders to Copy New England's Plan"; Nancy Gay; *San Francisco Chronicle; September* 15, 2002.
9. "Air Callahan Sets Records, but Defense Seals the Deal"; Nancy Gay; *San Francisco Chronicle*; September 16, 2002.
10. "Raiders Air Out Steelers"; Jerry McDonald; *Oakland Tribune;* September 16, 2002.
11. "Gannon Armed and Ready"; Dave Newhouse; *Oakland Tribune;*

September 16, 2002.

12. "Porter Scores an NFL First for Raiders"; Jerry McDonald; *Oakland Tribune;* September 16, 2002.

13. "Catholics, Jews and the Work of Reconciliation"; Daniel J. Wakin; *New York Times;* September 15, 2002.

14. "One Bad Pass Gnaws at Gannon"; Jerry McDonald; *Oakland Tribune;* September 16, 2002.

15. "Kirby's Return Breaks Steelers"; Mitch Pritchard; *Oakland Tribune;* September 16, 2002.

16. "Callahan Still Has Plans for Offense"; Bill Soliday; *Oakland Tribune;* September 17, 2002.

17. "Raiders Air Out Steelers"; Jerry McDonald; *Oakland Tribune;* September 16, 2002.

WEEK 3
Bye Week
September 22, 2002

It is barely pro football season, autumn has not even officially begun, and the Oakland Raiders have finished two games in a 16-game season. They are undefeated and have raced over their opponents by an average of 14 points. That can mean only one thing: it's time for a week off.

Incredibly, just when things were getting going for the refitted Raiders, they have to take down the sails and drop anchor. Historically, in the twelve-year history of the bye week (started in 1990), the Silver and Black have on average had the time off in week seven. Rumor has it that, next year, the Raiders' one-week hiatus will come during the preseason. A bye this early in the season is about as confusing as the current color-coded national terror-alert system. There can be only one explanation: in the NFL's eyes, organizations like the Oakland Raiders (along with their terrorist cheerleaders) constitute an axis of evil.

Oakland also constitutes a threat to opposing teams. Consider these numbers: with eight quarters behind them, the Raiders are No. 1 in total offense (No. 6 rushing, No. 4 passing) and No. 3 in total defense (No. 4 against the run and No. 6 defending the pass).[1] Oakland also leads the NFL in third-down conversions, with 19 successes in 32 deadlines.[2] Thus far in this young season, the ageless Raiders have scored 45 points in the first half, forcing the opposition to come from behind. They have called 57 rushing plays and 100 pass plays, gaining a total of 887 yards in the effort. And now, they get to sit on their butts.

For his part, Raiders' Coach Bill Callahan was fatalistic about the bye week. "I like it at the midpoint so you give your guys a break and kind of collect yourself and regroup for the stretch run. This is a little early. But that's the way it goes." Actually, the Raiders have nothing to complain about. With the exception of 1987—the scab season—the NFL played its 16-game season with nary a breather from 1978–1989. Later, Callahan tried to spin a positive note as he contemplated playing fourteen games without a break. "I think you stay in rhythm," he said. "You allow your team to work on a consistent basis and don't get out of synch . . . especially if you are fortunate enough to be on a run."[3]

Which is how Oakland hopes to hit the ground when they face Tennessee at home September 29.

BLACK AND WHITE

*CB Charles Woodson injured his right shoulder
and was icing it after the game.*

—OAKLAND TRIBUNE, SEPT. 17, 2002.[4]

There is something to be said about the power of the written word. Eyes racing over the computer screen, electrochemical impulses slamming across neural synapses like bullet water slides at hyper speed. None of the audio creativity involved in radio listening, no impulse overload and blather of television. Just black and white, words strung together into vision, thoughts and emotions.

Which is why the reaction was so predictable when I learned that Charles Woodson fractured his shoulder in the 30–17 Pittsburgh triumph and was expected to miss the next 3–6 weeks.

WHAT?

Suddenly there was neither blood pulsing through my veins nor air flowing into my bronchioles. Gone was the extended euphoria as a result of the triumphant black-and-white victory along the shores of the Monongahela River. In its place were despair, surrender—and a reflective acceptance that it could have been worse.

For injuries, a few of which we can pronounce, are part of this sport we follow. Cartilage tears, pinched nerves, plantar fasciitis, strained backs, muscle hematomas, anterior cruciate ligament, sprained thumbs, separated shoulders. Football is an activity where attrition is brother to retreat and injury sounds the bugle. Ask John

Parrella what Oakland needs to return to the Super Bowl and he answers, "We just got to stay injury-free this year, play well together, and see what happens."[5] Jack Tatum said the three biggest factors in a Super Bowl run were spirit, avoiding injuries, and luck. He would know: he embodied the first, inflicted the second, and received a bad dose of the latter when his jarring 1972 hit of Frenchy Fuqua on fourth down resulted in the Immaculate Deception.[6]

The Oakland Raiders played practically the entire 2000 season injury-free and went to the AFC Championship, while the defense knocked the stuffing out of nine opposing quarterbacks during the run. Then came the Saragusa flop that separated Rich Gannon's shoulder and the Silver and Black from its fourth Super Bowl title. In 2001, the Raiders fought the dark cloud of injury from the moment Barret Robbins was carried off the field in the Miami sunshine of the second game.

The average football fan cannot fathom what a professional football player goes through each week to play the game he loves. Bob Chandler's spleen was lacerated in a life-threatening hit on Opening Day 1981; six weeks later he played against Tampa Bay. Jim Otto tore five ligaments in his leg yet started in 210 consecutive league games; he suffered dozens of concussions and as many broken noses, a detached retina, and enough broken ribs to build the entire Raider cheerleading squad; today he walks on titanium knees. John Matuszak called them "hangnail" injuries—physical hurts that pained but were not enough to keep one off the field that Sunday. Then he gave examples: "groin pulls, twisted ankles, dislocated fingers, pulled hamstrings and slightly fractured bones."[7] I can't speak for you, but any one of these injuries would have sent me bawling to my mommy like Edmund Muskie crying in New Hampshire.

Professional athletes appreciate only too well what can happen in a single instant to their incredible athleticism, the chiseled bodies, that granite resolve. "It's something that's in the back of your mind every time you take the field," said sixth-year Raider Randy Jordan. "It's the part of football that nobody wants to think about."[8]

It showed itself to Zack Crockett near the end of the first quarter on Opening Day against Seattle. Hit from behind while pursuing a punt return, Crockett lay face down and motionless as team doctors toiled above and players rubbernecked from a distance. "The way his position was, it didn't look too good," cornerback Charles Woodson said. "He had no feeling below his waist for a few seconds," explained team physician Warren King.[9] Strapped to a board, moved to a cart and driven from the field is not how players visualize their contribution to team effort, but it used to be worse. At one time, Raider management frowned on the use of stretchers, feeling it hurt the morale of the team and made them play less aggressively.[10]

Ironically, while No. 32 was immobile on the field and teammates were shaken on the sidelines, good-looking young ladies frolicked for male pleasure in television beer advertisements. What the average TV football fan doesn't understand is that, when injury timeouts occur and the break is made to commercial, the injured player remains down. He doesn't get up and run off the field.

What makes an athlete play larger than life? Raider fans know the rhetorical phrases and buzzwords: play with pain, pay the price for victory. Probable, questionable, doubtful, out—these are indicator-words that camouflage the human toll and remove us from understanding the game. Charles Woodson played over two quarters last Sunday night with a broken shoulder, made three solo tackles, forced a fumble, and was anteloping back to the pass long before his interception. After the game, he put ice on his shoulder and probably took two Indocin.

Jim Otto toiled fifteen years and persevered through 38 major surgeries, only three of which were football-related.[11] Eric Turner played ten games of the 1999 season and then died of abdominal cancer. Maybe the higher pain threshold focuses them to play better. Perhaps they just want to get back into the fight.

Certainly there is the organizational imperative to consider. Al Davis opens his wallet and millions of dollars fly out into the ether, finding their way to players' pockets like transferring files with Windows '98. Playing is how football athletes earn their livelihoods.

Hand cast, knee brace, neck roll: regardless of the black-and-blue debility, they'd better be padded up and on the field come Sunday. Peter Gent said it best in *North Dallas Forty*:

> Pain is nothing more than the property perceiving the disintegration of its parts. Teach it the difference between pain and injury. If it is felt by the property it is pain. If it is felt by the corporation it is injury.[12]

That is a valid axiom, but it still doesn't explain why an athlete's season can be ended—or a team's fortunes irrevocably altered—in one play. Several season ago, Eric Allen was tackled routinely after making an interception at home against Seattle; the 20–17 victory raised Oakland's record to 7–3 halfway through November. But Allen stayed down after that tackle with what was later diagnosed as a season-ending torn ligament. Wrote one columnist, "The Raiders that day won the game but lost their spirit."[13] The team then went on a 1–5 skid and closed out the season a miserable 8–8.

The Woodson shoulder injury is alarming for its very intimation of mortality. If one discounts the Opening Day game, our best cornerback has been injured since last October, 2001.[14] It is difficult for the spectator fan to fathom how debilitating this game is on the human body.

And it is even harder to justify why, halfway through the season, Woodson will be harping a soliloquy about returning punts again.

Adrift of explanations, faced with complexities and surrounded by spin, today's Raider fan remains loyal and makes the best of the situation. We hold these truths to be self-evident. Oakland is unbeaten. Dave Dalby is dead. Charlie Garner is alive. Charles Woodson is injured.

Keep it simple.

Simple as black and white.

REFERENCES

1. "Callahan Still Has Plans for Offense"; Bill Soliday; *Oakland Tribune*; September 17, 2002.
2. "Gannon is Golden on Third Downs"; Bill Soliday; *Oakland Tribune*; September 18, 2002.
3. ibid., Soliday.
4. "Porter Scores an NFL First for Raiders"; Jerry McDonald; *Oakland Tribune*; September 16, 2002.
5. "Parrella Loves Being in Trenches with Raiders"; Dave Newhouse; *Oakland Tribune*; August 8, 2002.
6. *They Call Me Assassin*; Jack Tatum with Bill Kushner; New York: Everest House Publishers; 1979; pg. 140–149.
7. *Cruisin' with the Tooz*; John Matuszak with Steve Delsohn; New York: Charter Books; 1987; pg. 100.
8. "Crockett Hopes to Play Sunday in Pittsburgh"; Nancy Gay; *San Francisco Chronicle*; September 12, 2002.
9. "Scary Neck Injury Fells Crockett—Tests Negative"; Nancy Gay; *San Francisco Chronicle*; September 9, 2002.
10. *You're Okay, It's Just a Bruise*; Rob Huizenga, M.D.; New York: St. Martin's Press; 1994; pg. 124.
11. *The Pain of Glory*; Jim Otto and Dave Newhouse; Champaign, IL: Sports Publishing Inc.; 1999; pg. 3.
12. *North Dallas Forty*; Peter Gent; New York: Signet Classics; 1974; pg. 157.
13. "There's No Debating Allen's Importance to Raiders' Resurgence"; Monte Poole; *Oakland Tribune*; May 26, 2002.
14. "Raiders' Glass Half Empty"; Bill Soliday; *Oakland Tribune*; November 6, 2002.

Tennessee at Oakland
September 29, 2002

The autumn wind is a pirate
Blustering in from sea
With a rollicking song he sweeps along
Swaggering boisterously
— STEVE SABOL[1]

Strangely enough, the Oakland Raiders returned to the friendly confines of Network Associates Coliseum with something to prove.
Although they stood 2–0 after home-and-away wins against Seattle
and Pittsburgh, the Silver and Black were in third place in the AFC
West—since Denver and San Diego each possessed 3–0 records. With
a bye week chafing their ulcerated skins, Raider fans were more than
ready to see if the undefeated streak could continue.

And who were these guys, anyway? With a rookie (Phillip
Buchanon) replacing a franchise-cornerback, led by a clean-shaven
quarterback whose face would shatter if he ever smiled (Rich
Gannon), and powered by a runner whose last post-game interview
was in the twentieth century (Charlie Garner), they hardly looked
the part of Raider lore. They seemed more likely to tour the United
Way circuit than the late-night barroom scene. Did this team have
what it takes to exemplify the insignia worn on their helmets?

His face is weather beaten
He wears a hooded sash
With his silver hat about his head
And a bristly black moustache

Fortunately, as Pete Banaszak exemplified so well for Oakland,
the game is played on Sundays.[2] After two games, the Raiders have
shown they know how to succeed. On this particular day they face
a thorny nemesis: Tennessee's Eddie George. In three previous games

against Oakland, George has gained 438 yards with three touch-downs in three Titan wins.[3] He brings along an impressive resume combined with a foot injury to face a stingy rush defense that has already smothered two marquee runners (Seattle's Shaun Alexander—39 yards; Pittsburgh's Jerome Bettis—42 yards). "Nobody is going to run the ball on us," proclaimed tackle Sam Adams after opening day. "That just isn't going to play here."[4]

The autumn wind is a Raider
Pillaging just for fun
He'll knock you 'round and upside down
And laugh when he's conquered and won.

It is now officially autumn, a time when blustery currents can whip clouds of dust across Hegenberger Boulevard and make children rub both eyes with those cute, little knuckles. It is a beautiful day for football, 72 degrees, little or no airstream. Raider fans can hardly stand the wait as they make their way through the stadium cata-combs to reserved seats. Most are certifiable, many have had a drink, some are out on bail, a few are off their medication.

And, like an autumn wind, they are howling.

FIRST THINGS FIRST

Neophytes, nabobs, and novices will tell you that football is a "game of inches." But that rhetoric is as tired as referee Walt Coleman's libido. The Oakland Raider's shellacking of the Tennessee Titans cannot fairly be measured in inches. This win was much more.

It was a game of firsts.

With a total team effort releasing the ghosts of Youell Field, the Raiders dismantled the Tennessee Titans, 52–25. More than just victory, it was a multiplicity, a blowout, a thunder strike. To appre-ciate what transpired on the field, consider these foremost accom-plishments:

- The Raiders are 3–0 for the first time since 1990—a year they made the playoffs.
- Oakland's 52 equaled the most franchise points scored in a single game, matching the 52–9 pasting of Carolina on Christmas Eve, 2000, and tying the 52–49 win over (guess who?) Houston at Youell Field in 1963.[5]
- Before their second offensive play, which came with 2:34 left in the first quarter, the team had scored 21 points and led 21–7.
- This was the first time in Raider history where the Silver and Black ran back two punt returns for touchdowns; they both came in the first quarter. With yardage totaling 157 yards, the Raiders established a punt return average of 78.5.[6]
- The 113 cumulative points in their first three games is are the most ever scored by a Raider team in franchise history, eclipsing the 109 points of 1967.[7]
- Oakland has scored at least 30 points in their first three games for the first time in Raider history.[8]
- The Raiders' win over the Titans was their first since returning to Oakland in 1995.
- There are now only two undefeated teams in the National Football League, and they both reside in the AFC West (San Diego).

And those are only the team achievements.

- Jerry Rice caught 7 passes for 144 yards and became the first player in NFL history to record 21,281 yards from scrimmage (beating Walter Payton). Of course, he will be the first to record 21,282, 21,283, etc.—all as a Raider. "This is the ultimate right here, it's one I'll have to sit down and give some serious thought," Rice said. "The majority of the time when I break a record, it's just another day at work. But Walter, this is an all-timer here, man. It means a lot to me."[9] Then, in a testament to his humility as an athlete, Jerry Rice pointed skyward and said, "That was for you, Walter."[10]

- Rod Woodson became the first Raider to recover three fumbles in one game followed by three interceptions in the next, both wins. Thus far, the Raiders have 9 takeaways—Woodson has six of those. Said teammate Charles Woodson, "It's crazy how balls just seem to find him." Phillip Buchanon seemed mystified by the numbers: "He's lucky," Buchanon said. "That's not normal."[11] As if to answer the charge, Woodson offered, "Just because you're 21 doesn't mean you're a better player than (someone who is) 35."[12]

- Woodson became the first player in NFL history to return eleven career interceptions for touchdowns. He has also returned interceptions for more yardage (1,339) than any player in NFL history.[13] Tennessee's Steve McNair, who had just given up 100 of those interception yards on a spin-cycle Sunday, had this assessment: "He's always there when the ball is in the air," McNair added, "I said earlier this week, Woodson is a guy who has a knack for the football. He's always going to be there, at the right place at the right time."[14]

- Tim Brown caught 6 passes for 90 yards; the 954 receptions in his illustrious career moved him past Buffalo's Andre Reed into third place on the all-time list, behind Chris Carter (1,093) and the incomparable Jerry Rice (1,384).[15]

- Coach Bill Callahan became the first rookie coach of the Raiders to go 3–0 since John Madden in 1969.

- With 11:30 left in the first quarter and Oakland leading 7–0, rookie Phillip Buchanon gathered in the Titans' punt at the Raiders' 17-yard line. He started left but changed directions quicker than Dick Cheney left town after 9/11. Now heading up the middle of the field with a burst of speed as fast as male foreplay, Buchanon angled left at the Raider 35; by the 50-yard line, it was all over except for the six points posted on the scoreboard. "It was just a wide-open hole, and I hit it," Buchanon said. "I mean, nobody touched me, and then I just outran them."[16] Play of the Game.

The speed with which this game unfolded left us wondering: who are these guys?

We are Raider fans, not Butch and Sundance. We pretend to know who these guys are. They're the Silver and Black Gang. And they will gang-tackle as soon as look at you.

And we know what they're after. They want an AFC West Division title with home-field advantage throughout the playoffs. And the East, North, and South be damned.

There is something about these 2002 Raiders that is different. It's like they are looking for something. I can tell you: it's been forever since I saw Oakland pull a double-reverse with the wide receiver showing pass as he scampered ahead for 7 yards. I can't put my finger on it yet, so I will guess at the possibilities of what this Raider team seeks:

Trouble: Like the guy in the movie *Swingers* said: "In my neighborhood, you don't look for trouble; trouble finds you." With the toughest competition in the NFL coming from San Diego, Denver, and Kansas City, Oakland will be hard-pressed to stay on top of their game and division. They also bash helmets with the entire AFC East (Raiders lead the series 21–15 over the last twenty years) and NFC West (12–4 lead since 1983).[17]

Perfection: If they are looking for perfection, Oakland is finding it in flashes. Over three games, they are scoring twenty-five points before halftime; and in the second half the Raiders tack a respectable twelve more onto the scoreboard. The rush defense has faced Shaun Alexander, Jerome Bettis, and Eddie George. Their combined total rushing? 103 yards, and they wouldn't have crossed Century Boulevard except that the entire Raider front line was tying their shoelaces during one run. Oakland is at plus-five in takeaways, Gannon has been sacked 9 times in 132 pass attempts (which is 3 sacks every 44 drop backs) and Garner is averaging 7½ yards a try on the ground. Sebastian Janikowski is 5 for 6 in field goal attempts, and touchdowns from punt returns and kickoffs fly across the field like comets streaking through the sky.

Respect: Oakland has it from their peers, but they won't find it elsewhere. A churlish CBS affiliate bought the television rights (thereby negating NFL Direct) and proceeded to show only 50% of the game. They hung on until the last handshake of the edge-of-your-seat Kansas City-Miami game (a 48–30 Chiefs win), brought on the Raider game with five minutes gone in the first quarter, and then pulled the plug with ten minutes left in the third. First in the hearts of their drunken men, the Raiders will always have the respect of their fans, and they could very well find it from the rest of America during the post-Super Bowl victory parade down Hegenberger Boulevard—if they cared to.

Now it is time for Oakland to shuffle off to Buffalo, a highly preferable time to visit versus the minus-90 degree Celsius temperature sure to await them in winter. As I wait for Sunday, I consider the possibilities. Maybe the television wizards will air the entire game this time. Maybe the Raiders will continue to get better as they work through their robust learning curve. Maybe they will reach the pinnacle of their craft and replace the 1972 Miami Dolphins as the new century's icon of unbeaten seasons.

That would be a first indeed.

REFERENCES
1. "Autumn Wind: Music to Pillage By"; Mark Emmons; *Mercury News*; January 24, 2003.
2. *Hey, Wait a Minute (I Wrote a Book)*; John Madden with Dave Anderson; New York: Ballantine Books; 1984; pg. 152–153.
3. "By George, Titans Off on Wrong Foot"; Nancy Gay; *San Francisco Chronicle*; September 27, 2002.
4. "Raiders Take First Steps Toward Better Run Defense"; Bill Soliday; *Oakland Tribune*; September 10, 2002.
5. *The Team of the Decades 2002*; Oakland Raiders Media Guide.

6. "Raiders Explode with Two TDs on Punts"; Jerry McDonald; *Oakland Tribune;* September 30, 2002.

7. Oakland Raiders Media Guide, op. cit.

8. "Calm Smile Hides a Killer Style"; Carl Steward; *Oakland Tribune;* September 30, 2002.

9. "Rice, Woodson Keep Rewriting Record Book"; Jerry McDonald; *Oakland Tribune;* September 30, 2002.

10. "Raider Old and Young Dogs Energize Coliseum in Romp"; Monte Poole; *Oakland Tribune;* September 30, 2002.

11. "Raiders Steamroll Titans on Runbacks"; Bill Soliday; *Oakland Tribune;* September 30, 2002.

12. Poole, op. cit.

13. "A Victory in Return"; Nancy Gay; *San Francisco Chronicle;* September 30, 2002.

14. "Rice, Woodson Keep Rewriting Record Book"; Jerry McDonald; *Oakland Tribune;* September 30, 2002.

15. ibid.

16. "Raiders Explode with Two TDs on Punts"; Jerry McDonald; *Oakland Tribune;* September 30, 2002.

17. Oakland Raiders Media Guide, op. cit.

WEEK 5
Oakland at Buffalo
October 6, 2002

When he introduced the former understudy as the Raiders' thirteenth
head coach, Al Davis summed up his choice's orders in three phrases:
"To win, to win, to win."[1] With a 3–0 Raider start out of the blocks,
it is now time to take stock of the new Oakland head coach, Bill
Callahan. After serving four years as an offensive line coach, Callahan
was the handpicked successor to replace the departed trade-bait, Jon
Gruden. While Gruden was often an inferno of hyper kinetic emotion on the sideline, Callahan seems more like a mild-mannered Rain
Man with contacts.

But looks can be deceiving: beneath that placid demeanor of tran-
quility lies the heart of a merciless mountain climber. "He's so aggressive. You see it on our offense, but you also see it in our defense and
all aspects of our play," said Raiders' tight end Roland Williams.[2]
Indeed, while the 45-year-old Callahan's game-day deportment could
be mistaken for the art of Zen and transcendental meditation, his
Raiders' playbook conduct more closely resembles that of a pitiless
monarch. Consider these highlights:

- "We wanted to establish a physical presence up front, on
  both the offensive and defense," said Callahan.[3] This was
  after Oakland began the 2002 season by running the football
  40 times for 221 yards while amassing 423 yards in total
  offense; allowed 186 yards to the opposing team; and ran the
  no-huddle as if it were a birthright in a 31–17 victory over
  Seattle;
- "Well, we thought that a pass was as good as a run in this
  game."[4] Ever-pious to the understatement, Callahan was
  referring to the Pittsburgh game—where the Raiders threw a
  franchise-record 65 passes and accumulated 464 total yards
  along the way to defeating the Steelers, 30–17;[5]

- "Like I've told the offense numerous times, we're going to continue to work the ball until it gets down under three minutes or so."[6] In defeating Tennessee, Oakland jumped out to an incredible 38–7 lead before allowing the Titans to creep within 13 points at 38–25. The offense then completed seven of eight passes for 123 yards and two fourth-quarter touchdowns in just over six minutes to put the game to rest, 52–25. The last touchdown came with 5:21 left in the game.

Coach Callahan understands the business of professional football. "The expectation level is always high in this league. It's where you always have to win."[7] That was a rule as true for John Madden as it was for Jon Gruden. To win, to win, to win; such is the prime directive, the supreme edict, the bugler's call. Why? Because the only alternative is to lose. Oakland travels to Buffalo this Sunday to play the 2–2 Bills, and the question (how?) contains its own answer.

One win at a time.

EMBRACING ADVERSITY

It was a most unpredictable answer to a predictable question. As he left the field amid a 21–21 halftime tie, Bill Callahan was asked what he thought of the first half. Matter-of-factly, Callahan answered: "We knew coming in here that we would face adversity. And, if we can just embrace that adversity, we should do fine the rest of the game."

It's a good thing that his players listen to Coach.

Playing with a panache for victory and utilizing more marquee performances than a Robert Altman film, the Oakland Raiders survived nearly 1,000 yards in total offense to defeat the Buffalo Bills Sunday, 49–31. For awhile in the second quarter—with 35 points scored—the two teams were turning possessions into points faster than George W. turns surpluses into deficits. To understand the final outcome requires an extensive list of contributors who embraced adversity:

Jerry Porter. There was a time when the word "porter" was only used if it had a "re" in front of it. Raider fans have been grumbling for the last two years about Porter's lack of realized potential, but there is nary a mumble about his ability in Oaktown tonight. "Jerry is really coming on," said quarterback Rich Gannon. "He is a go-to receiver who is big and physical and is very athletic running after the catch."[8] The 6 feet-2 inch, 220 pound Porter led all Raider receivers with seven catches (a career high) for 117 yards and started the offensive onslaught with a sweet 29-yard touchdown grab in the first quarter off a pump-fake from Gannon. He also had an excellent 25-yard drag-your-foot catch in the second quarter on third-and-short.

Sebastian Janikowski. Putting aside his legal distractions (he was busted for drunk driving last week when he couldn't recite the alphabet), Janikowski—as he has all year—brought his lunch pail and game face to Buffalo this weekend. He has made five of six field goal attempts this season and converted all fourteen PATs. Most importantly, when other kickers are landing their kickoffs at the opponent's 12-yard line, Sea Bass consistently frustrates teams with his league-leading fourteen kickoffs for no return (four against Buffalo).

Jerry Rice. Yes, even 'The Best' is human after all. Perhaps a Buffalo witch doctor put a hex on him, possibly it was the hardened Astroturf combined with an aggressive Bill defense, maybe it was the pop he took over the middle after a 33-yard gain in the second quarter, but Jerry Rice dropped four catchable balls. "I had a couple of plays I just lost focus on," he said. "I was just in a funk today."[9] To his credit Rice stayed with the program, catching the last (twenty-yard) touchdown of the game.

Zack Crockett. Less than a month after lying prone on the Network Coliseum turf for ten agonizing minutes on opening day against Seattle, Crockett scored from the 1-yard line and gave Oakland its fourth lead of the game, 28–24 in the third quarter.

Charlie Garner. Garner nearly reached 100 yards rushing on only eight attempts (he finished with 94 and one rushing TD). Oh, and he catches too (4 receptions for 83 yards, one receiving TD). In a game where the lead changed hands more times than Clinton clarifications of definable sex (five), it was Garner's 69-yard catch-and-sprint that put Oakland ahead to stay in the fourth quarter.

Tory James. James fell down on a pair of pass plays, which totaled 93 Buffalo reception yards, and the Bills capitalized by scoring two of their three first-half touchdowns. But his third quarter interception of Bills' QB Drew Bledsoe led to a Raider go-ahead score, and his second pick was the final toss in Bledsoe's nightmare.

Phillip Buchanon. Burned for a touchdown and assessed a 35-yard pass interference call in the first half, Buchanon redeemed himself in grand fourth-quarter fashion Sunday. With the Raiders nursing a scant 35–31 lead and Buffalo knocking at the Oakland 27-yard line, Buchanon—after barely letting an interception go through his hands the play before—closed his grip (and the Bills' door) on the next pass. Chased to his right by a fearsome four-man Raider rush, Bledsoe threw on the run. Ten yards up field, leaning to his left like the Tower of Pisa with hands extended skyward, Buchanon made a leaping interception. Adjusting to the looming sideline, he kept his balance, shook off Bledsoe's pathetic upper-body tackle attempt, and then raced at warp-factor-nine speed 81 yards up the sideline for a touchdown. It looked more like VHS fast forward than regular running. "When the score is that tight, in the kind of tight ballgame that we had today, it's pivotal when you come up with a big play on defense," said Raiders coach Bill Callahan."[10] "Before that drive, I had a vision I would make a play." Buchanon said, although he freely admitted, "I wasn't thinking it would be an 80-yard touchdown."[11]
Play of the Game.

Certainly, there were the usual Raider mistakes which kill drives and turn Coach Callahan's hair prematurely white—including ten penalties for 120 yards. But the biggest obstacle to be overcome on this bright Niagara Falls Sunday was created by the Raider tackling defense. I counted twelve missed upper-body tackles on nine different plays. This dirty dozen was more painful to watch than a high school production of *Kiss Me Kate*.

Coming from a natural grass home field, the Raiders have never liked playing on Astroturf.[12] Hard as concrete, it burns the body, punishes limbs, and endangers careers. But that doesn't mean Oakland tacklers can ride piggyback or throw an arm at the passing shoulder pad, hoping to stop the ball carrier.

Only a leg tackle brings an open-field runner down. Sure, it hurts when the opposing runner uses a Raider head as a hackey-sack against his pumping thighs, but—like rock-a-bye baby—the cradle will—must—fall. Yes, the leg tackle is painful, yes the pain is interminable, and yes it is effective.

That is the two-track lesson from the Bills game: not only must the Raiders embrace adversity; they must also embrace the ball carrier.

There exists a huge chasm between undefeated and simply first place, and presently Oakland is the NFL's sole proprietor of the former distinction. That means everybody in the NFL will be bringing their best game against the Raiders, starting with their next opponent.

The St. Louis Rams: recently mighty, lately vanquished, still dangerous. It can be argued the Sheep are the most dangerous team in the NFL right now. With nothing to lose but the wool on their backs, they will play with all their heart to break into the elusive win column.

The Raiders will have to methodically shear their hides.

In today's America, looking at war and fighting for our jobs in a moribund economy, it is good to be a Raiders fan. Oakland has an effective mix of veterans, yeomen, and protégés making big plays. The general manager is focused, ruthless, and obsessed with bringing a world championship back to the East Bay Area.

Their coach is levelheaded, sees the positive in adversity and has his players understanding that a game is sixty minutes long, which must be played to the last tick.

At 4–0, that is a winning combination all Raider fans can embrace.

REFERENCES

1. "Al Davis Proves Again He Has a Lot on the Ball"; Art Spander; *Oakland Tribune;* March 22, 2002.
2. "Calm Smile Hides a Killer Style"; Carl Steward; *Oakland Tribune;* September 30, 2002.
3. "Callahan, Raiders Can"; Nancy Gay; *San Francisco Chronicle;* September 9, 2002.
4. "Head Coach Bill Callahan's Quotes of the Week"; *Oakland Tribune;* September 26, 2002.
5. "Diverse Attack Keeps Opponents—and Raiders—Guessing"; Nancy Gay; *San Francisco Chronicle;* September 29, 2002.
6. Steward, op. cit.
7. "Davis Right in Tabbing Callahan"; Art Spander; *Oakland Tribune;* September 22, 2002.
8. "Porter Is Catching On as Club's Third Receiver"; Mitch Pritchard; *Oakland Tribune;* October 7, 2002.
9. ibid.
10. "High-Octane Raiders Outlast Bills to Stay Unbeaten"; Nancy Gay; *San Francisco Chronicle;* October 7, 2002.
11. "Buchanon Supplies Game-Breaker Again"; Mitch Pritchard; *Oakland Tribune;* October 7, 2002.
12. *Snake;* Ken Stabler and Barry Stainback; Garden City, NY: Doubleday & Company, Inc.; 1986; pg. 229.

CHAPTER FIVE

2002: Second Quarter

WEEK 6
Oakland at St. Louis
October 13, 2002

They were a force, a juggernaut, the greatest show on turf. They were the only team to both win and lose a Super Bowl on the last play of the game. In three seasons, 1999–2001, their running back (whose initials, M.F., stand for an expletive in the hearts of all opposing spectators) gained 6,785 total yards from scrimmage and scored an NFL-record 26 touchdowns in 2000. In one season, the team gained almost as many yards as the number of arrests at Oakland home games.

No wonder a supposedly knowledgeable sportswriter, in a fit of lustful prediction before the 2002 season began, wrote:

> They have the most dominant quarterback. The most dangerous running back. The premier offensive mind. The best set of receivers.... It almost isn't fair.[1]

Never in the history of sports conflict was so much written with so little value by so few in the name of so many.

Today, the St. Louis Rams are 0–5 and without the services of three marquee starters: Kurt Warner, Orlando Pace, and Aeneas Williams. You would think that a 4–0 Raider team walking onto the Astroturf carpet against the winless Rams would be generate a "no contest" rating from the experts on NFL Gameday. But that prediction would be as unwise as a tax cut passed on the eve of recession.

Oakland can hardly field a team these days: Charles Woodson is out and six starters (four on offense) are questionable. With linebackers Napoleon Harris and Eric Barton ailing, Mike Jones was re-signed and Kick-em Ted Hendricks was offered a tryout. "Right now we are really banged up on both sides of the ball," said Coach Callahan.[2]

Fortunately, the Raiders enjoy a sizable margin that should allow them to play with depleted staff and still walk away with a victory

Sunday in their last appearance on artificial turf this season.[3] Currently, Oakland leads the NFL in total yardage per game at 461.5, turnover ratio (twelve takeaways, five turnovers) at plus-7, and third-down conversions at 51.9% (28-for-54). QB Rich Gannon is completing 67.5 of his throws and the team is scoring 40.5 points a game.[4]

Still, Callahan is all caution when discussing the cellar-dwelling Rams. "No one wants to play a team that's on the ropes like this in their home environment," Callahan said. "They're still loaded on offense, and defensively, they're made for the carpet.[5] Earlier in the season, when a star player went down with a broken shoulder, linebacker Bill Romanowski said, "All the winning teams I have been on always had the attitude that the guy coming in has to play as good if not better." When it was pointed out that a rookie playing better than an All Pro was a tall order, Romanowski replied, "Yes it is. But that is the order."[6]

Callahan seemed to echo this sentiment when he stated, "Heading into St. Louis it's going to be important that a lot of guys—especially in the backfield—step up."[7]

Just how many Raider players was Callahan referring to?
Never so many.

THE FACTS OF LOSS

They lost to St. Louis 28–13. Fact.
They lost as a team. Fact.
They were flat. Fact.
The defense played less than satisfactorily. Fact.
Today the Oakland Raiders and Rams met in St. Louis. Two football franchises, heading in different directions. One going up, the other down. One living a dream, the other a nightmare. One derided pre-season as the "Gray and Black," "Social Security haven," and "old age in pads." The other hailed as the "Second Coming of Innovation" and "Dominant Team of the 21st Century." One undefeated, the other winless.

When it was over, the Raiders had made a third-rate quarterback look like John Unitas/Elway/Hadl. And it made me want to run to my own john and expel.

How did it happen? How did Oakland, down 28–6, find itself out of the competition with over eleven minutes left in the fourth quarter?

They lost as a team: There was no shortage of poor Raider performances on this day. From Rich Gannon passing the football like his right thumb was broken, to losing the turnover margin three-to-one. From an offensive line executing at a 1991 level, to dropped passes, 14 penalties for an inopportune c-note of yardage, and ridiculous special teams coverage. From bad field goal snaps, to impatient fourth-down gambles, and an ineffective East-West game. From pathetic shovel-pass ploys, to grimacing screen pass attempts—the list could be longer and easily more damning. The result was a total team effort that would prove fatal even against a hapless team like the Cincinnati Bengals. Said Rich Gannon, "When you make mistakes, don't convert on third down, turn the ball over and make a bunch of penalties, it doesn't matter who you play."[8] The way it looked, had Osama bin Laden run out to midfield and exploded a dirty bomb, only those wearing silver helmets would have toppled over.

They were flat: Maybe the Buffalo game took it all out of them. Perhaps Jupiter aligned with Mars. Could be they all stayed up late watching *Apocalypse Now Redux*. Whatever the reason, Oakland was not up to this competitive struggle. When they fell behind 14-goose, the television announcers lauded the Raiders for not panicking. Of course not; that's because they were asleep.

Other than Birthday-Boy Jerry Rice (seven catches for 133 yards) and Charlie Garner, who played a solid game (61 rushing yards) and still cannot get more than fifteen rushes a game, nobody ran up to the line and made the big play. A plethora of penalties (24 in two games, 48 for 451 yards this season), inexplicable mental lapses, third-down pass completions short of the stick—this is not the stuff of winning streaks.[9] It is warm, stale backwash in the carbonated world of X's and O's.

How ironic that Oakland played this subpar game against a team that, until now, had perfected deficient performance. Conceivably, the Raiders lost their mental edge. With four straight wins, success may have bred a familiarity ill-suited for a gridiron game where the difference between first down and punt, between tackle and touch-down, is often no more than mental preparation. Nowhere would this seem more apparent than in the defensive realm.

The defense played less than satisfactorily: It is time to say it. The Raiders are not playing Raider defense. After dominating the opposition in the first two games, holding each to less than 200 yards total offense, Oakland's defense has turned into a sieve. In the last three games, they have allowed an average of 410 yards and 26 points. On this particular Sunday:

They did not pressure. The reason Marc Bulger could throw the long-ball was he was standing back in the pocket, smoking a cigarette while waiting for his receivers to get open. If the Raiders give Tom Brady that kind of time, it is going to be a black-eyed November 17.

They did not swarm or pursue. There were far too many instances where only one or two Raiders made the tackle. That's assuming they made the tackle.

They did not tackle. This is the most flagrant foul of the Oakland defense. Too many arm tackles, shoulder-pad grabs and out-of-posi-tion misses. In the NFL, athletes are too good to play against while executing below one's potential. And there were plenty of Silver and Black at that level today.

Nearly one-third of the way through the season, the Oakland Raiders are in prime position for a streak run. At four-and-one, they now face a character-defining, five-game stretch of three AFC West games and another two playoff-caliber opponents (the Raiders' first five opponents have a combined 9–18 record this season and none of the five have a winning record; Oakland's next six opponents possess a 21–12 record; none have a losing record).[10] If they play like they have shown this year in sustained and stunning fashion, they will go 4–1. If they play like they did today, they could go 3–2 or 2–3. They could begin the nowhere-treadmill of win one, lose one. Or worse, they could return to last year's form when they couldn't remember how to win.

This is not negativity. Such talk is not a threat.

It's a fact.

REFERENCES

1. "Unfinished Business"; Dan Pompeii; *The Sporting News: Pro Football*; September 2002.
2. "Raiders Pay Price for Buffalo Win"; Jerry McDonald; *Oakland Tribune*; October 8, 2002.
3. "Stop Faulk, Stop the Rams"; Nancy Gay; *San Francisco Chronicle*; October 11, 2002.
4. "Callahan Defends Substitution Policy"; Jerry McDonald; *Oakland Tribune*; October 8, 2002.
5. "Hard Times for the Rams"; Jerry McDonald; *Oakland Tribune*; October 10, 2002.
6. "All-Pro Lost for Weeks"; Bill Soliday; *Oakland Tribune*; September 19, 2002.
7. "Raiders Pay Price for Buffalo Win"; Jerry McDonald; *Oakland Tribune*; October 8, 2002.
8. "Nobody's Perfect"; Jerry McDonald; *Oakland Tribune*; October 14, 2002.
9. "Raiders Notebook"; Nancy Gay and Ira Miller; *San Francisco Chronicle*; October 14, 2002.
10. "There Was Nothing Special About Raiders Special Teams"; Jerry McDonald; *Oakland Tribune*; October 14, 2002.

WEEK 7
San Diego at Oakland
October 20, 2002

Stretching back five decades, they are the Raiders' oldest nemesis. With 85 games already decided between them, the 5–1 San Diego Chargers now stand atop the NFL's toughest class. In its first division game, Oakland kicks off their defense of the AFC West crown against a dangerous opponent. That can mean only one thing.

Trot out the rhetoric.

Speaking about his old team, which was 6–26 over the past two seasons, John Parrella says: "They're obviously improved. It's going to be a battle."[1]

Jerry Rice offers, "Hey, we're focused. It's on. We're getting ready to get into our division now and this is a pretty big game for us."[2]

Not to be outdone, Tim Brown gives his assessment: "It could come down to a shootout. We'll just try to win the game any way we can. We'll see what happens."[3]

Speaking of San Diego's LaDanian Tomlinson, the second-leading rusher in the NFL after six weeks (632 yards), Trace Armstrong says, "He will be one of the better backs we will see all season."[4]

Frank Middleton predicted, "Whoever has the least amount of bad days is gonna win all of it."[5]

Randy Jordan sees matters in this light: "It's a division game and right now the Chargers are beating the pack . . . we want to take over that spot."[6]

This sounds like fun. As a loyal Raiders fan, let me take a shot at this rhetoric thing:

It's "The Days of our Lives" vs. "The Young and the Restless." Both teams will play hard. If you don't play your game, you're going to lose. That's the way it is. Players may not be 100%, but they'll fight through it. A key factor will be who can run the ball. Just ram it down their throat. Defenses need to swarm the ball carrier, fly around out there, take no prisoners. The offense needs to play smart.

One thing is certain. Both teams will play to win.

To coin a phrase.

HEADS UP

For better or worse, the two teams have battled to a standstill over sixty minutes. Oakland's John Parrella walks out to midfield for the ceremonial coin toss to determine which team gets the football first. But it is San Diego's Donnie Edwards who gets to make the call, on account of they are the lesser team.

The disk is thrown into the air, traveling up skyward toward the klieg lights, spinning in symmetrical fashion, it reaches the apex then descends to terra firma and its just reward.

It was a simple coin toss, yet on that spherical journey rested the green-light hopes of Raider fans. How many times have we seen a penny lying there in the parking lot and never bothered to take note of whether heads or tails looked up at us? The 61,000 Oakland faithful held their collective breaths, and their fears were realized as the referee said:

"It is heads. San Diego wins the toss."

It was that kind of contest, the San Diego Chargers' 27–21 victory over the Oakland Raiders. A game of great passion, so many missed opportunities, such ebb-and-flow, it is unfortunate that its outcome was influenced by a single cylinder resting on the ground.

And, if Oakland isn't careful, their playoff chances will one day rest in the ground, not on it.

It's official. The Raiders are on a losing streak. Last week was an anomaly but this week was an aberration. They've been here before, 52 times in the 43-year franchise. And ten of those 2-game losing streaks occurred during seasons the Raiders made the playoffs. So Raider fans have nothing to fear but fear itself.

Unless, of course, they watched the game Sunday.

Offense: Is it just me, or has anyone else noticed that Oakland has stopped scoring touchdowns? For the second straight game, the

Silver and Black did not cross the vaunted pylon in the first half. And this was against a Charger team that, in its two previous AFC West games, gave up slightly less points (60) than there are un-indicted Enron millionaires. Tim Brown had it right when he said, "We're horrible right now in the red zone...."[7]

The low point came one minute into the second quarter with the Raiders at San Diego's eleven-yard line. On second-and-goal, Gannon attempted a shovel-pass to Charlie Garner, which was laughable except for its drive-killing result. The play was probably Garner's fault but Gannon's responsibility. Taking the snap and back-pedaling, Gannon looked to his right but Garner had gone left. Still back-pedaling, Gannon looked down then found Garner in the no-man's land middle. By this time, on his sixth step backwards, he executed a ridiculous push-pass that belonged more on a shuffleboard rail than a football field. Caroming off Garner's shoulder pad, the football was intercepted by linebacker Donnie Edwards, negating a promising ten-play drive to tie the game at 7–7. In theory, it was a good play call. As executed, it was as ill-advised as having sex in St. Patrick's Cathedral, heeding Martha Stewart's advice on ethics, or assuming Lizzie Grubman will look in her rear-view mirror.

Injuries: The loss of Phillip Buchanon and Terry Kirby was particularly gruesome. First, Buchanon broke his left wrist with 7:23 left in the first half. On a sideline pass pattern at the Oakland nine-yard line, Phillip launched skyward as if thrown by an Eskimo blanket toss; unfortunately, the rookie plummeted to earth like a coin flip, sticking out his left arm as he landed on his head. Kirby simply ran into a pile of tacklers and failed to emerge. These two guys came in and made plays, and now they are both out. To say they will be missed is like saying the D.C. populace want police to catch the Washington sniper.

Kicking: Enough said. After scoring first in their initial four games, Oakland wasted an excellent chance to light the bulbs when Sebastian Janikowski kicked a chip-shot 27-yard field goal attempt directly into the right stanchion. Then, with the scored knotted at 14–14, Janikowski's second attempt—a 48-yarder—was about as close to finding its target as the Mars probe mistakenly programmed for centimeters instead of inches. "It bothers me a lot," Janikowski said. "You saw the scoreboard. We lost the game, and that's six points right there."[8] At least he can add.

Rushing: Is it just me, or do you find it strange that the second leading rusher (not counting three QB scrambles) is a player (Kirby) who left with a broken leg midway through the third quarter after rushing twice for 2 yards? Did I dream that at the beginning of the year the Raiders talked about returning to the running game? Twelve rushes for 37 total yards? You've got to be kidding me. Oakland is currently throwing on 64% of its snaps—a two-to-one margin. That play-calling imbalance makes as much sense as instituting a tax-cut to raise government revenues.

Defense: Let's see. First four games, opposition's leading rush total: 153 yards (38-yard average), all Raider wins. Last two games, leading rush total: 313 yards (157-yard average), both Oakland losses. What is wrong with this picture?

It's like listening to The Beatles; sometimes you just have to get back to basics. Since Earl Campbell's time, Raider D has always stuffed the run. Yet there I was, witnessing some ridiculous defensive scheme with outside linebackers shadowing defensive ends. It looked like an extended Maginot Line with a hole up the middle marked "Ardennes Forest." No wonder Charger Coach Marty Schottenheimer called his favorite football running play—40 or 50 power (make up your mind), a draw play—no less than fifteen times.[9]

San Diego's LaDanian Tomlinson gained 153 yards on 39 carries. In their plus-column, the Oakland defense stopped him at or behind the line of scrimmage 13 times for minus-23 yards.[10] Of course, that means Tomlinson gained close to seven yards each of the other 26 times he carried. And what about pass rush? Six games into a 16-game season, the Raiders have a measly 5½ sacks from their defensive line.[11] I finally did see a defensive end with some stick marks on his helmet; unfortunately, I saw him earlier on the sideline bench, gouging those marks himself with a nail. I would say 'Bring back Bob Buczkowski' (No. 1 DE draft pick in 1986), but I don't think that name appendage (Owski) is very popular this week with Raider fans.

And then there was outside linebacker Bill Romanowski (another 'Owski'), I bet he blitzed eight times. He must have thought he had on Bilbo Baggins' invisible ring, but he was alone in this delusion. Every single time someone picked him up; he never got close enough to blow sweet nothings ('My Precious') in Drew Brees' ear. "We missed tackles, gap assignments, you name it," Romanowski said after the game.[12] His five tackles were low among Raider line-backers.

There was a lot of good that happened in the contest, like the Terrible Trio—Jerry Rice, Jerry Porter and Tim Brown—combining for twenty catches totaling 236 yards and two touchdown receptions (Rice and Porter). And the two-minute drill at the end of regulation—culminating in the excellent play call to Jon Ritchie that tied the game—was particularly sweet.

Heads up, Raider fans. Time to put this loss behind us. Oakland is about to walk the tunnel of Arrowhead to face a nemesis that has surrendered 71 points in their last two (losing) AFC West games. History is not on the Raiders' side: six times before, they have traveled to Kansas City while caught in the throes of a two-game skid. Four of those visits (66%) resulted in a third loss.

Perhaps Oakland teammates would do well to enter their hotel Saturday night expressing their commitment to teamwork, solidarity and sacrifice by holding hands and singing "We Shall Overcome." But come Sunday, their play had better be anything but nonviolent.

Battling the devils of their own miscues and the ghost of Deron Cherry, the Raiders are fortunately led by a QB hired specifically for the purpose of beating KC. During his three-year tenure against the Chiefs, Rich Gannon has guided the Silver and Black to victory in five of the last six meetings. Gannon has saved some of his finest performances for Arrowhead Stadium. In 2000, he completed 28 of 33 passes, and in 2001 Gannon was 31 for 46 for 341 yards and two TDs.

In these efforts, he was helped by another Raider whose positive team contributions began in the flatlands against the Chief flatheads: our own Sebastian Janikowski.

In 2000, the Polish Sausage had Raider fans spitting nails with two missed field goals before drilling a 43-yard late-game winner. In 2001, Sea Bass went 4–4, including the 31-yard game winner with fifteen seconds remaining.

In both game-winning kicks, as his foot squarely met the ball, Janikowski's head was correctly down. Here's hoping he won't have his head up a certain part of his anatomy come Sunday against the Chiefs.

It is best to put the San Diego game into the woulda-coulda-shoulda pile. The Raiders played well enough to emerge victorious; they just didn't win the coin toss. In this game we love, at the professional level, the margin for victory can be as thin as a dime.

Players are huge, emotions run high, and reaction times are immediate. When a team is competing in this hyper-speed environment, the difference between winners and losers can be as small as the orbital change of an electron.

Sometimes a first down is decided by the head of a football.

Sometimes a win is decided by seizing momentum and forging ahead at the last second.

And sometimes, a game is just decided by a head.

REFERENCES

1. "Raiders' Parrella Hopes to Ground Chargers"; David Bush; *San Francisco Chronicle*; October 17, 2002.
2. "Raiders Aiming to Start Another Winning Streak"; Nancy Gay; *San Francisco Chronicle*; October 20, 2002.
3. "Raiders' Air Attack is Passing by Brown"; Bill Soliday; *Oakland Tribune*; October 17, 2002.

4. "Parrella Set for Raider-Charger Duel"; Bill Soliday; *Oakland Tribune;* October 20, 2002.

5. Gay, op. cit.

6. ibid.

7. "Another Loss Puts Damper on 4–0 Start"; Carl Steward; *Oakland Tribune;* October 21, 2002.

8. "Janikowski Takes Two Missed Kicks Hard"; Jerry McDonald; *Oakland Tribune;* October 21, 2002.

9. "Tomlinson Has San Diego Fully in Charge"; David Bush; *San Francisco Chronicle;* October 21, 2002.

10. "Raiders Waste Chances as Hopes for Win Run Aground"; Bill Soliday; *Oakland Tribune;* October 21, 2002.

11. McDonald, op. cit.

12. "Raiders Suddenly Sinking"; Nancy Gay; *San Francisco Chronicle;* October 21, 2002.

WEEK 8
Oakland at Kansas City
October 27, 2002

There is nothing more dangerous than playing a team which is on a losing streak. Unless it is two teams on losing streaks playing each other. This latter scenario occurs Sunday as Oakland and Kansas City, both in the throes of two-game skids, key off against each other in historic Arrowhead Stadium. When the contest is over, one team will continue its headlong tumble down the embankment of league standings while the other will resume its deliberate attempt to push the boulder up the hillside.

Oakland is reeling from the loss of its special teams return-yardage producers: Phillip Buchanon and Terry Kirby. Both were lost for the season in the preceding week after suffering left wrist and right leg fractures. "That's tough to watch, seeing your teammates go down like that," defensive end Tony Bryant said. "But this is when you see what you're made of."[1]

The Raiders defense is chastened from surrendering 312 yards in the last two weeks of competition to a pair of premier running backs. In both games, Oakland defenders were guilty of overpursuing, leaving an open field when the runner cut back against the grain. "It's one of those things you can correct," said cornerback Tory James. "You have to have faith in the scheme and know your teammates are doing their job—that keeps you where you need to be."[2]

The Silver and Black will need to be at the top of their game Sunday, getting no rest as they face the Chiefs' Priest Holmes. Holmes currently leads the National Football League with 766 yards in 167 rushes (4.6 yards per attempt). In contrast, Charlie Garner has one-third as many rushes this year (57), but his average is much better: 7.4 yards per rush.

Much is made of the Raiders' offense, ranked first in the NFL in total yards (2,603), passing yards (1,953), first downs (148) and total points (196).[3] Add to these impressive numbers the fact that Oakland is going up against a team whose rank in the NFL's defensive category matches the number of points it gives up per game (32), and one might be permitted a grin of anticipation. But before the proselytized start sharpening their swords, remember that this is one of the oldest and bitterest rivalries in professional football.

In the 39 years of on-again hatred between the good guys in black and the double-digit IQs in red, the Raiders have come up short in Kansas City 21 times. On the plus side, we are led by a quarterback who has yet to lose an away game to the Chiefs in three outings. A victory will allow Raider fans to draw the veil of defeat from their eyes. The last two games for Raider fans have been about as much fun as reading a commemorative issue of 9/11. So we are permitted to ask: what if Oakland wins?

Then the Raiders are 5–2 and a step up on going 11–5 or better.

And what if they lose?

We'll cross that bridge when we come to it.

BRIDGE OF SIGHS

Why so unforgiving? And why so cold?
Been a long time crossing Bridge of Sighs.

—ROBIN TROWER[4]

The young lad, dressed in solitary silver and black, staggered away exhausted from Arrowhead Stadium. Alone, forlorn and chagrined, each step shuffled in deliberate effort, he came upon a bridge over a famous river.

Halfway across, a pack of Kansas City rednecks taunted the man to throw himself into the abyss and get it over with. Soon a sea of red surrounded him, chanting, "Jump. Jump. Jump." The young Raider hesitated, then thrust both arms into the air in obscene defiance before grabbing the railing with his left hand and vaulting into the icy waters of the Missouri River.

Which is where the 4–3 Oakland Raiders find themselves after losing to the Kansas City Chiefs 20–10: surrounded by the freezing environs of their own incompetence. Floundering away opportunities as if they played a 160-game season, Oakland willed a loss from another winnable game Sunday. Playing against a KC defense which had previously surrendered enough points and yardage to guarantee safe passage to Baghdad, the Raiders managed a mere ten points in their most meager offensive showing of this rapidly deteriorating season.

In doing so, Oakland squandered the season's best performance of Tim Brown. The KC game saw the return of Timmy: 13 receptions for 144 yards, the forty-second 100+ yard game of his career. "I'm going to always press and make sure everybody realizes that 81 is still over there, trying to put in a little work."[5] Because this was the first time all season that he visited the century corral, let's revisit the Raider playbook: Brown to the left, Brown to the right, Brown down the middle. Eight yards, nine yards, twelve yards. The 25-yard pass play in the first quarter was a thing of beauty, and the third-and-8 juke move on the hapless Chief defensive tackle to pick up a first down was a guffaw.

But the only real laugh is on Oakland. Sure, they racked up 417 total yards—but that means little unless you visit the house. "Moving the ball doesn't mean anything unless you're getting in the end zone," said Raider guard Mo Collins.[6] Tackle Lincoln Kennedy agreed: "The correlation is only in the end result. How many touchdowns did you score ... did you outscore the other team?"[7] And, right now, the Raiders score less than a broke gambler visiting a brothel.

Forget the end zone; the new Raider world order can't even make it to the red zone (inside the opponent's twenty-yard line). On four separate non-scoring occasions, Oakland crossed the midfield stripe, yet the closest they came to pay dirt was the 26-yard line early in the game. On third-and-two, QB Rich Gannon threw an out-pattern to rookie Madre Hill that was predictably incomplete. With three clutch receivers in Silver and Black against the worst defense in the NFL, calling that play made about as much sense as a fat man suing a fast-food chain because he's obese. Sebastian Janikowski then attempted a 43-yard field goal that was blocked. For the third loss in a row, the Raiders failed to score points on their opening drive. "We need to do a better job finishing drives," Gannon said, and Callahan agreed that the key might be in using more familiar plays.[8] Putting a rookie in such an unfamiliar role in pressure-packed Arrowhead is simply a predictable road to fourth down.

Oakland is playing way too tight. The team is playing not to lose, which is antipathy to the Raider "play to win" style of football. "That fifth win is just kicking our ass," admitted guard Frank Middleton. "If we can ever get past five wins, I feel we can probably do something."[9] The team needs more antics like Roland Williams' (provided he catches the pass) pointing down field after a chain-moving reception. Right now, the only one pointing fingers is Rich Gannon. Like the average Raider fan can't understand who's at fault when a pass bounces off a receiver's fingertips or a field goal attempt rises just high enough to hit a teammate's ass.

Strangely enough, Gannon never points the finger at himself. This next game, after every play that doesn't work, Gannon should point the finger directly toward his own chest. Maybe then he'd realize how absurd he looks. Play for the love of the game, erase the finger pointing, and get on with the controlled insanity. The wins will follow.

Perhaps Gannon feels the self-imposed pressure of his own hype. Brought to Oakland four years ago with the goal of delivering Raider fans from their eighteen-year desert-exile, on Sunday last, White Moses No. 12 was unable to part the Red Sea.

Too much attention is paid to Gannon's current consecutive 300+ yard passing streak (now at six games—half of them wins). Here's a suggestion: take all those 300-yard game stats and ludicrous Pro Bowl nods and put them in an attic shoe box along with lottery ticket non-winners, because that is all they are worth. Statistics are for voyeurs, sportswriters, and spectators. While suffering a losing streak, quoting categories in which the Raiders lead is a bit like citing promising unemployment figures without acknowledging a median hourly wage increase of only 6% in twenty years.[10]

Speaking of statistics: only four times before in the 43-year history of the Raider franchise has a receiver gained 127 yards or more and the team scored as few as ten points (Art Powell, 1966; Bob Chandler, 1981; Mervyn Fernandez, 1988; and Tim Brown, 1997).[11] Why, why, why can't these picturesque efforts be turned into Raider points? Perhaps—revisiting the fourth quarter interception, fourth quarter fumble, and fourth quarter defensive screw up—the more pertinent question is: weren't the veterans on the team supposed to help win ball games because of their experience?

It was a trio of veterans who offered insight into this sad state of affairs:

- **Rich Gannon:** "We're making too many mistakes, and in division games like this, mistakes are magnified. . . . It's not one guy. It's one guy on each play, and it just so happens they're coming at critical times."[12]
- **Jerry Rice:** "To be honest with you, no, I was not in a rhythm. It was one of those games. You try and stay focused and wait on opportunities and it just didn't happen for me today."[13]
- **Rod Woodson:** "Things happen for a reason. Fate is fate, even in sports. If it is for us to lose three games and wake everybody up—the front office, the players, the coaches, the trainers—to say 'Yeah, we're great on paper, but you have to play the football game.'"[14]

Maybe it was fate, in the form of a hostile Arrowhead crowd. After all, this was Callahan's first journey into Kansas City as head coach—and John Madden, Tom Flores, Art Shell, and Jon Gruden all failed to obtain a win in their initial appearance.[15]

Or perhaps this is just flailing about looking for any balm to heal the scab of defeat.

Surprisingly, there were plenty of good points in the Arrowhead debacle: Tony Bryant running down a lumbering Priest Holmes from behind; a swarming defense dominating at times; a plus turnover margin; over 75 yards rushing and actual leg tackling. Terrance Shaw had his first interception of the year, Mo Collins returned to the playing field for the first time this season, and Bill Romanowski not only showed good coverage in obtaining an interception just before halftime—he showed real class by not pointing fingers after the game when explaining the blown coverage ("It wasn't my guy, but it's my fault.... I take responsibility.").[16] With nine games remaining in the schedule, the good news is that Oakland is only two games behind the San Diego Chargers. The bad news, however, is that Oakland's record is only two games better than the Seattle Seahawks'.

And here comes the San Francisco 49ers, 5–2, alone atop their division—ready for "The Brouhaha by the Bay." If the Raiders come to play, I am confident they will win. If they show up flat, they should start up a slush fund now, because there are going to be plenty of rowdy fans that will need bail money come Monday morn.

So what happened to the Raider lad, the one who replicated Billy Joe MacAllister's dive off the Tallahatchie Bridge? Unlike Billy Joe, he survived, of course. C'mon, he's a Raider. When he pulled himself up on shore and was asked why he jumped, the young boy echoed the words of Lincoln Kennedy: "It's just that this season offered so much promise to start with."[17] Raider fans will endure to tell the tale. We have lived through Jessie Hester, Rusty Hilger and Joe Bugel, innumerable losses to Kansas City and Denver, and a franchise move motivated by greed.

But the franchise was has now returned to its rightful city. And on Sunday, the seats will be (almost) filled. Raider fans will watch in judgment. Oakland teeters on the precipice. The truth hangs in the balance. And we all stand atop the rail of a bridge.

Bridge of sighs.

REFERENCES

1. "Injuries Leave Return Teams' Ranks Dangerously Thin"; Nancy Gay, David Bush, David Steele; *San Francisco Chronicle*; October 21, 2002.

2. "Defenses on Spot in Raiders Game"; Nancy Gay; *San Francisco Chronicle*; October 27, 2002.

3. "Brown's Competitive Fire Fuels Angst"; Nancy Gay; *San Francisco Chronicle*; October 25, 2002.

4. "Bridge of Sighs"; Robin Trower; 1974; Chrysalis Records.

5. "Woodson to Get Tough Workout"; Bill Soliday; *Oakland Tribune*; October 24, 2002.

6. "Yet Another Troublesome Trip to Arrowhead"; Monte Poole; *Oakland Tribune*; October 28, 2002.

7. "Raiders Try to Pick Up Pieces"; Bill Soliday; *Oakland Tribune*; October 29, 2002.

8. "Raiders, Chiefs Match Up Unevenly"; Jerry McDonald; *Oakland Tribune*; October 27, 2002.

9. "Only One TD Means a Third Straight Loss"; Nancy Gay; *San Francisco Chronicle*; October 28, 2002.

10. "Out of a Job and No Longer Looking"; David Leonhardt; *New York Times*; September 29, 2002.

11. *The Team of the Decades 2002; Oakland Raiders Media Guide.*

12. "Loss at KC Has Raiders' Skid at Three"; Jerry McDonald; *Oakland Tribune*; October 28, 2002.

13. "Raiders Catch More Grief"; Jerry McDonald; *Oakland Tribune*; October 28, 2002.

14. Poole, *op. cit.*

15. "Nerves Frayed by Lapse on TD"; Nancy Gay; *San Francisco Chronicle*; October 28, 2002.

16. "Loss at KC Has Raiders' Skid at Three"; Jerry McDonald; *Oakland Tribune*; October 28, 2002.

17. "Raiders Try to Pick Up Pieces"; Bill Soliday; *Oakland Tribune*; October 29, 2002.

San Francisco at Oakland
November 3, 2002

To win or not to win, that is the question.

With three straight losses, the Oakland Raiders have already suffered more than their share of the slings and arrows which befall mortal men. It remains to be seen whether the defeats have steeled their resolve or weakened them to the further challenge. Will the Silver and Black sail off into the sunset of victory this Sunday against San Francisco, or continue their death spiral into the awaiting sea of ignominy? The Raider players themselves seemed no closer to providing answers to these central questions.

"We have a great football team, with a lot of great individual athletes," observes veteran Rod Woodson. "But we have to come together as a football team. . . . And every man, to a man, needs to look in the mirror and just pick it up—and say 'I'm going to be there for my teammates.'"[1]

Woodson must know something. After the first four games, he must have overheard a few of his teammates asking their mirrors 'Who's the fairest of them all?,' confident of an ego-swelling reply. Lately though, the Raiders have turned into a bunch of ugly stepsisters.

Starting with the defense. Over the first four wins, Oakland's defense stuffed opposing rushers to the tune of 238 total rushing yards, less than 60 yards per game. In the last three losses, they have allowed 463 yards rushing, more than 154 yards a game on the ground. When asked if criticism of their effort was warranted, Sam Adams was blunt. "Yeah, of course," Adams said. "Because when you give up 100 yards on the ground, you suck. That's it in a nutshell. You are terrible."[2]

Special team problems flared up in a unique and demoralizing fashion against Kansas City when Sebastian Janikowski's first field goal attempt, a 32-yarder, was mishandled and blocked. The Chiefs gained 89 yards on three kickoff returns. There were no Oakland yards gained on four punt returns.[3] And Shane Lechler's 28-yard average on three attempts would not have won the twelve-year-old division of Punt, Pass and Kick. Special-teams captain Randy Jordan acknowledged, "We haven't helped our team win many ballgames, and we haven't helped create field position, and if you don't do that, you don't do your job."[4]

QB Rich Gannon was more circumspect. "We're in a rut, I don't have to tell you," Gannon said. "But it's not because we're not trying or we're not working hard."[5]

Okay, Raider fans get it: the effort is there and work ethic is there. But, come Sunday evening, will the 'W' be there?

As a team, Oakland knows what it has to do.

Just answer the question.

LOLLYGAGGERS

It is a scene that will not be included in the "Team of the Decades" video.

While Raider players silently took their showers Sunday evening, Coach Bill Callahan suddenly appeared and violently threw a set of first-down markers into the stall area. As the sticks clanged and clamored on the tile floor, Coach launched into a tirade:

"You guys make me sick. You lollygag on pass rush. You lollygag on kickoff coverage. You lollygag on third downs. Do you know what that makes you?"

On cue and without missing a beat, defensive coach Chuck Bresnahan chimed in, "Lollygaggers."[6]

Excuses are all that is left of a once-promising season after the Oakland Raiders lost in overtime to the San Francisco 49ers, 23–20. Because, if history is any indication, this season is finished for the Silver and Black almost as soon as it began.

In their 43-year franchise history, the Raiders have made the playoffs twenty different times. And in how many of those twenty playoff seasons did they lose four games in a row?

Try never. Not a single solitary time.

The last year they lost four in a row this early in the season was 1992, when the Raiders quickly made a shambles of their season by dropping the first four games. Over the final dozen contests, they went 7–5.[7] Laying the 1992 template on this year's star-studded performance, we can safely predict the 2002 season will be 9–7. No 2002 playoffs, no substantive draft choice, and an unforgiving 2003 schedule.

At the end of that 1992 star-crossed season, after Tim Brown spiked the winning touchdown catch against the Washington Redskins, the Raiders faced a rebuilding year. And that is exactly what Oakland faces will face after this disastrous season ends.

For if there is one lesson that rang clear yesterday, it is this: all other things being equal, when youth comes up against age, youth wins. Every time.

Did you see the fine shiver-sack move that SF's Andre Carter made on Rich Gannon? It was a miracle Oakland didn't lose the resulting fumble (recovered by Barry Sims). What made the play so beautiful was it was the first time I had seen it done at a Raider game. Yet Oakland brought over a perennial Pro Bowler last season to execute just such a sack move. Instead, battling age and injuries, so far Trace Armstrong is marginal at best. Said Armstrong, "We need to rise up in certain occasions and make plays to get off the field. We haven't done that—particularly on third down—a turnover, a tipped pass, a sack—anything."[8] May I add another untried Raider defensive maneuver: a tackle.

Age showed itself plainly in this game, and—like Michael Jackson's disfigured nose—it wasn't pretty. How about 28-year-old Terrell Owens (Mr. Owens to the Raider team) laughing in their face? And why shouldn't he? Twelve catches for 191 yards, nearly a sixteen-yard average—the kind of numbers Clifford Branch used to put up. Three of the catches went for 110 yards. On the other side of the field, the best Oakland athlete on this day—Jerry Porter with six catches for 53 yards—had the play of the game with his first-quarter TD catch. How old is JP? Twenty-four and there's so much more.

In contrast, there was Tim Brown, whose one catch at the eight-minute mark in the third quarter, just after the Carter sack, was so telling. Grabbing a short reception over the middle, Brown took off at a slight angle to the left. In years past, a juke and a burst and TB heads up the left sideline. But at age 36, on this day he picked up only ten yards. Moments later, Gannon tossed low and behind Brown, and the Raiders punted.

It was then that San Francisco pleaded the third against Oakland. Over the next 28 minutes, they would convert an incredible 8 for 9—89% of their third-down plays. And the one time they came up short, they converted on fourth down. Third-and-six, third-and-four, third-and-five, third-and-goal: touchdown. On their next series, with a short 52-yard field in front of them (thanks to a 48-yard kickoff runback afforded the 49ers with six minutes to go in a tie game), Jeff Garcia sprinted around No. 93's end to convert on third-and-four to the Raider twenty-yard line.

It has been theorized that Oakland's defense has not found their inner-child identity since bringing in ten new starters over last year's team.[9] After the San Francisco game, I can posit fairly that the Raiders' defense now has an identity. They suck.

After another third-and-short conversion, followed by Jose Cortez's Christmas present to all Hispanic Raiders in the Black Hole, the 49ers took the coin-toss gift and made good on three separate overtime third-and-longs: third-and-eight, Tai Streets over the middle; third-and-eight, Garcia runs right again. But it was the third-and-eleven that will long stick in my craw like a wishbone lodged in the trachea. Flushed out of the pocket, Garcia ran right past (a young) Travian Smith for ten yards.

How ironic that plans are being made to have the Super Bowl XI reunion this year. For that 1977 game featured the immortal words of Phil Villapiano: "We got 'em right where we want 'em."[10] Villapiano. Rod Martin. Monte Johnson. Matt Millen. Ted Hendricks. The history of fine Raider linebacker tacklers is long. Back in 1963, new Coach Al Davis impressed upon the players that Oakland "would be a team of hitters and there would be no slacking off...."[11] I wonder: would Dan Conners have made that tackle? Heck, I think Carl Weathers could have brought down that balding stick figure dressed in prostitute red.

I know who else could have made that tackle: me. Whenever I feel amorous and give my sexy wife the evil eye, and she takes off sprinting for the bedroom door, I run her down and throw the right arm around her pumping thighs. I make that tackle. Every time.

On fourth-and-one, Fred Beasley ran for the first down, leaving behind an immobile Raider—Tony Bryant—to be removed from the field on a cart. It was the third such exit for an Oakland player this home season.

In the end, the game was lost by an Oakland defense that erased any luster from the Raider history of stalwart D. It is laughable to let 65% of your opponents' third-down plays go for first down, yet San Francisco converted 13 of 20 tries in this regard, and that's 65% every time. "We couldn't get off the field," lamented Coach Bill Callahan.[12] Stating the obvious, Charles Woodson said, "I think we're ready to make that play, we're just not making it. It's kind of frustrating as you get a team in third-and-long and the quarterback can scramble for a first down, or scramble to make a throw for a first down." Added Bill Romanowski, "I just knew we were going to fight right down to the end, to come up and make a play. That's how I felt. We didn't do that."[13]

Bill, what was your first clue? Was it when the defense spent more time on the field looking for a stop (fifteen minutes) than George W. does on the podium trying to regain his lost train of thought?

Relying on only four words (The Future Is Now), Al Davis brought in a whole new defensive lineup this year. Impatient for the Vince Lombardi trophy, Mr. Davis chose an older approach in the hopes that experience would win ballgames. He always was the master of personnel and field chemistry—except for this year. I wonder if he ever regrets returning the phone call of a linebacker who called Davis and boldly proclaimed: I want to help you win another Super Bowl. Right now I would settle for ... win another game.

That next game is against the Denver Broncos, a team that has beaten the Raiders as regularly (12 of last 14) as aspen leaves turn gold in autumn. You've got to hand it to this Oakland team: they are entertaining. And I learned from the 2000 Indianapolis game (a game where the Raiders fell behind 24–7 after two quarters before dominating the second half enroute to a 38–31 victory): I'm not leaving my wingman.[14] But I am no longer under any illusions.

They lost the time-of-possession battle (44 minutes to 24). They lost the total yardage measure (434 yards to 239). They lost third-down containment. They lost the coin toss. They lost the game.

Do you know what that makes them?

Do you really want me to answer that question?

REFERENCES

1. "Yet Another Troublesome Trip to Arrowhead"; Monte Poole; *Oakland Tribune;* October 28, 2002.

2. "Raiders Attempt to Plug Holes"; Bill Soliday; *Oakland Tribune;* October 31, 2002.

3. "Special Teams Have Trouble All Over"; Jerry McDonald; *Oakland Tribune;* October 28, 2002.

4. "Charles Woodson Listed as Probable for 49ers game"; Jerry McDonald; *Oakland Tribune;* October 31, 2002.

5. "Only One TD Means a Third Straight Loss"; Nancy Gay; *San Francisco Chronicle;* October 28, 2002.

6. Adapted from *Bull Durham;* written by Ryan Long; directed by Ron Shelton; 1988.

7. *The Team of the Decades 2002; Oakland Raiders Media Guide.*

8. "Raiders Ineffective Defense Gets Overexposed"; Jerry McDonald; *Oakland Tribune;* November 4, 2002.

9. "A Victory ... or Else"; Bill Soliday; *Oakland Tribune;* November 3, 2002.

10. *Hey, Wait a Minute (I Wrote a Book);* John Madden with Dave Anderson; New York: Ballantine Books; 1984; pg. 203–204.

11. *The Pain of Glory;* Jim Otto and Dave Newhouse; Champaign, IL: Sports Publishing Inc.; 1999; pg. 111.

12. "Home Wreckers"; Bill Soliday; *Oakland Tribune;* November 4, 2002.

13. "Raiders Ineffective Defense Gets Overexposed"; Jerry McDonald; *Oakland Tribune;* November 4, 2002.

14. "They Never Say Die"; Bill Soliday; *Oakland Tribune;* September 11, 2000.

CHAPTER SIX

2002: Third Quarter

WEEK 10
Oakland at Denver
November 11, 2002

The criteria for a good lifeboat are: buoyancy; self-righting when capsized; stability; a self-bailing capacity; and the ability to progress in stormy waters. After their first four games of idyllic flying aboard Sinbad's magic carpet, the Oakland Raiders suddenly crash landed. They now find themselves in a lifeboat—adrift in their own inability to win and threatened by a Mile High storm. Their only distraction at this point is a strange sound which no one can quite identify.

Tossed about by the fury of the AFC West—where they have fallen from first place to last in three short weeks—Raider players found solace in rhetoric and work ethic:

- Rich Gannon: "It's a mind-set. You have to have a passion for what you're doing. It's the belief that, 'Every time we get the ball we're going to be effective with it—we're going to get some points some way, somehow.'"[1] **Buoyancy**
- Bill Romanowski: "I'd say we have to get better on third down, and the only way I know how to get better is to work—work hard," Romanowski said. "The only thing that has ever worked since I've been playing in the NFL is showing up and busting your ass."[2] **Self-righting when capsized**
- Jerry Rice: "It boils down to playing football. We came out and we did some great things and we put a lot of points on the board. And now it's not happening. It's going to be interesting to see if the older guys step up and somehow turn this around."[3] **Stability**
- Charles Woodson: "When we look at it during the week, it feels like it's going to work," Woodson said. "When we get out there and the real bullets start to fly, it breaks down."[4] **Self-bailing capacity**
- Jerry Porter: "I'd prefer to pass the ball and let the short passes be our running game, and then to change up off that

and run draws, lead plays ... this is a passing offense that
will throw a changeup at you with the running game."5
Ability to progress in stormy waters

Now Oakland must guide its lifeboat through the treacherous
shoals and into safer waters. "I look at it like that movie, *The Perfect
Storm*, Callahan said. "We're in that storm, and we've got to find a
way to pull out of it."6 As they approach shore, the team hears that
same strange sound. Is it a foghorn? A horny humpback whale bid-
ding them safe passage? The Raiders will need an auspicious force of
nature to overcome history. In their last ten visits to the Mile High
city, they are 2–8—and Gannon has yet to taste victory in three
Denver tries while wearing the Silver and Black.

Finally, the team can see the stadium, bathed in the bright lights
of Monday Night Football. They hear the roar of the crowd, feel the
pre-game jitters. Now they know what that strange sound was, the
soulful resonance that comes every eight years to those willing to
accept it.

It's destiny calling.

VETERANS DAY

It is a day of reflection. A day when the President stands solemnly
before a tomb for thirty seconds, and the lucky man sleeps peacefully before the tube for thirty minutes. It is Veterans Day, commemorating that fateful morning the guns fell silent on the Western
Front 84 years ago.

There is something special about Veterans Day and the game of
football. Perhaps it is the month of November that ushers in the promise of December playoffs. Perhaps it is the autumn wind that blows
through the trees and focuses our mind on what is to be. Regardless
of the reason, this combination of two cultural bastions seems so very
American. As American as donuts and fat, Starsky and Hutch, death
and taxes, tropical passion love oil and ... well, you get the idea.

For all of us, 11/11 provides an extra day to consider the blessing of freedom and the price of peace.

And for Raider fans, Veterans Day bestowed a resurgent football team and newfound win streak.

The Oakland Raiders defeated the Denver Broncos 34–10 on the 500th telecast of Monday Night Football. No, make that throttled, dominated, bedazzled, and outplayed the Broncos. "We had guys making plays all over the field," said Jerry Rice.[7] They made those plays in Denver, they did it on Monday Night and they did it with veterans.

In a special place, at a special time, three players came up big on a special day.

Rod Woodson: The Donkeys were driving, down 3–0, intent on outscoring their opponent for the seventh time in nine games with three minutes left in the first quarter. On second-and-goal from the four, Denver quarterback Brian Griese willed a pass into the middle toward his running back. Following Griese's eyes like a security guard watches the clock, the wily-crafty Woodson stepped into the pass. But he didn't just knock it down and slam the turf in frustration. He made the INT and took off at a gallop toward the end zone far, far away.

"He was just looking, just looking," said the father of five (children) and leader of one (team). "I don't know if he was throwing to the fullback or the running back. I don't know which one. But he looked the whole way. He didn't even see me—I looked like I was going the other way. He just stood there and I went right by him."[8]

No doubt, the sight of Woodson's prowess stunned Griese. I guarantee: every Raider fan was shocked by Woodson's snatch-and-dash panache. True, his age began to catch up to this Dorian Gray at about the twenty-yard line, when he was carrying the leather with all the speed of a Sherpa guide hauling a load to Base Camp One. But Woodson felt Rod Smith closing on him from behind, and he found the strength to get into the end zone. "I saw Rod Smith closing on me from way across the field and didn't know if I was going to make it."[9] Instead of trailing 7–3, the Raiders led 10–0. There, surrounded by hostile fans in the first quarter's early going, was Play of the Game. And there, amid the Rocky Mountains in the rarified air, was the Play of the Season.

Please take note, Rod Woodson is 37 years old. In his sixteenth season, Woodson now has 65 interceptions, twelve of which have been returned for touchdowns. In that illustrious dozen, his two longest returns have come this year, against Tennessee and Denver. His return yardage from INTs now stands at 1,438 yards—approaching one mile—another NFL record. "I'm a reverted corner playing safety. I'm in it for interceptions and knockdowns, then a hit," said Woodson. "I'm the opposite of most safeties."[10] He certainly has taken it the opposite way enough times. And never was there a more important interception than at Mile High.

Rich Gannon: In a fiery display of execution and leadership, Gannihan (as ESPN kept calling him after the game) was as near to perfection as any QB can come in victory. The 21 straight completions (a single-game NFL record) were amazing enough, but it was the points on the board produced through such efforts that impressed me the most. During the twelve-play, 96-yard drive which culminated in a 27–7 third-quarter lead, Gannihan was 11 out of 11 for 94 yards. And most satisfying were the 22+-yard tosses: one to Garner, one to Rice, two to Porter. All on the money, all thrown with fearless delivery in the face of a relentless Bronco cavalry two-man rush, all completed, all led leading to Raider points. And who was the Raiders' leading rusher with twelve yards? Rich Gannon. Referring to the 38 passes thrown versus 14 rushes, Gannon acknowledged that "our aggressiveness was there and we got back to our style of football."[11] The numbers tell the tale: three touchdowns, seven different Oakland receivers, 34 completions, no interceptions, one win.

Jerry Rice: I can still remember, back in 1989, when the Seattle Seahawk Steve Largent, in his fourteenth season, caught his 100th touchdown pass, breaking the 54-year-old record of 99 TDs set by Green Bay's Don Hutson (1935–45).[12] By the way people reacted, you'd have thought Largent had caught Osama bin Laden. Now, in his eighteenth season, the 1985 first-round draft pick from Mississippi Valley State caught his 200th touchdown pass. Who did the Raiders draft in the first round of the 1985 draft? Jessie Hester. Nine catches for 103 yards, two touchdowns, the second a sweet over-the-shoulder 34-yard grab in the fourth quarter; the man definitely brought his ink game to Invesco Field (Rice, not Hester). And we are all so very glad that he brought his suitcase to Oakland.

It has been a long four weeks. Economic meltdown, massive layoffs, tumbling stocks, Bali bombing, sniper shootings. Oh yeah, and a four-game losing streak. The players who brought Oakland out of that losing streak were veterans. "We were stale bread, a sinking ship," pointed out Rod Woodson.[13] After paying tribute to the veteran leadership displayed in this game, Coach Callahan echoed the sentiment for all Silver and Black followers: "This puts us right back in the race in the AFC West."[14] Indeed, there is no AFC team today with less than three losses—and the Raiders' 5–4 record places them directly on track with the league leaders.

And, down the track, Raider fans can almost see the train in the distance, a train that left the East Coast last January 19. During this week, as we patiently wait for Sunday, Raider fans carry the same (blurry) vision: it is the first time we viewed the Stalingrad-like snow falling on a Foxboro field. Nearly ten months later, November 17 portends to be a special evening—a celebration of reckoning and commitment.

It is time to follow through.

Veterans Day is a special holiday. It provides an extra 24 hours to pause and reflect on what others' sacrifice means to us. We remember Omaha Beach, Antietem, Ia Drang Valley, Hiroshima. We worry for the young and poor who will fight the next war.

Raider football provides the opportunity to divert painful attention, cheer athletic ability and see the larger whole in a contest with rules. Together, a holiday and a game allow us to consider what is important in each of our lives.

Honey, where is that tropical passion love oil?

REFERENCES

1. "Team Appears Less Than Confident"; Nancy Gay; *San Francisco Chronicle*; November 5, 2002.

2. "Raiders Ineffective Defense Gets Overexposed"; Jerry McDonald; *Oakland Tribune*; November 4, 2002.

3. "Rice Mostly Watching, not Catching, in Second Half"; David Bush; *San Francisco Chronicle*; November 4, 2002.

4. "Raiders at a Loss to Explain Four-Game Skid"; Monte Poole; *Oakland Tribune*; November 4, 2002.

5. "Bryant in Hospital with a Spinal Injury"; Jerry McDonald; *Oakland Tribune*; November 4, 2002.

6. "Raiders Have Tough Climb at Mile High"; Jerry McDonald; *Oakland Tribune*; November 11, 2002.

7. "Milestones at Mile High"; Nancy Gay; *San Francisco Chronicle*; November 12, 2002.

8. ibid.

9. "Woodson Extends NFL Mark with TD Return"; Jerry McDonald; *Oakland Tribune*; November 12, 2002.

10. "Rod Woodson's Hands—Where Passes Go to Die"; Nancy Gay; *San Francisco Chronicle*; October 6, 2002.

11. "Milestones at Mile High"; Nancy Gay; *San Francisco Chronicle*; November 12, 2002.

12. *2002 Seattle Seahawks Media Guide.*

13. "Woodson Extends NFL Mark with TD Return"; Jerry McDonald; *Oakland Tribune*; November 12, 2002.

14. "Raiders Reborn"; Jerry McDonald; *Oakland Tribune*; November 12, 2002.

WEEK 11
New England at Oakland
November 17, 2002

All right, Dave, this time you've gone too far.

The warning is to Dave Newhouse, who wrote a scathing critique of Raider fan behavior at the San Francisco game November 3. "Oakland Raiders fans," wrote Dave, "you've gone and done it. You've finally topped yourselves in terms of crudeness, vulgarity and general incivility."[1] As if a beat reporter is the final arbiter in the rules of decorum and proper behavior.

I have the greatest respect for newspaper reporters. The way they turn out two and three articles following a football game is as wondrous as cotton candy to a kid. And Dave was simply trying to make a point before things really got out of hand—like at the New England game coming up. Dave was very aware of a stadium full of Cleveland fans hurling batteries out onto the field, and a few unruly Denver fans throwing snowballs at Raider players. After the Denver game, Raider Lincoln Kennedy punched a Bronco fan.[2] It was altogether fitting and proper for Dave to express his views as he did.

But in other ways, he was the one out of bounds. First off, Raider fans threw plastic water bottles and snarled vulgarities at 49ers coach Steve Mariucci. That is no different from the way Raider fathers deal with their own boys at home. So, in one sense, they were just treating the visitors like family. On this day, Mariucci happened to be the favorite son. In Raiderland, it's all about the love—sometimes it's tough love.

Newhouse claims that the percentage of out-of-control fans is "under twenty percent." That estimation is far too high—twenty percent of 60,000 is (uh) 12,000. I would put the number of maniacally, moronic psychopaths that attend Raider games at no more than 10,000. Plus the two thousand that sneak into the game. And these guys are tough. When Kennedy slugged the Denver heckler, that fan went to the hospital. If an opposing lineman smashed one of these Raider fans, they'd just go on eating their baloney sandwich.

One should not forget that some Oakland fans have always displayed unruly behavior. Ed Podolak of the Kansas City Chiefs (1969–1977) told Ken Stabler that he never removed his helmet on the sidelines in the Coliseum due to flying debris.[3] And when I attended the last game of the 1979 season, a home loss to the Seattle Seahawks, by the fourth quarter there was a steady stream of drunken Raider fans being led away to the clink; every last one of these boy scouts took the time to deliver a vulgarity-laced soliloquy to the visiting fans. Ya gotta love these guys. But only if they're in handcuffs.

Sunday evening, New England comes to town, and the gloves (and handcuffs) come off. The Patriots are in the fight for their Super Bowl-defending lives and, when the two teams square off with identical "5 win-4 loss" records, the game will have all the passion and fervor of a playoff game. If I were the Patriots coach, I would tell the players to keep their heads clear and their helmets on. I can say this because I think the Raiders are going to win. I always think the Raiders are going to win. Even when the phantom tuck rule is manifesting in the Foxboro snow before unbelieving eyes.

And now I believe this beyond a trace of doubt.

BEYOND A TRACE OF DOUBT

For the record, the Oakland Raiders defeated the New England Patriots 27–20 on Sunday night at Network Associates Coliseum.

In doing so, they eviscerated the snow-blown Tuck Bowl like the exploding football helmets on television. They separated themselves from .500 clubs like wheat from the chaff. They proved they are ready to make a run for the playoffs.

How conclusive was this proof?

Beyond a trace of doubt.

The Oakland defense won this game. It is that simple. The great shootout anticipated by New England fans never materialized, mainly because QB Tom Brady never got time to load. After throwing seven completions in as many pass attempts for 27 measly yards and walking off the field with only 3 points on his first possession, Brady never again completed more than four passes in a row—and that coming in a 5-of-6 string which resulted in a turnover on downs at the Raider 43 with just under ten minutes left in the fourth quarter and Oakland leading 24–13.

In contrast, it was the numerous Oakland defensive gems throughout the game that shone in the moonlight for Raider fans: a seven-swarm sea of black tackling the ball carrier for a one-yard gain, a Travian Smith sack; an uncharacteristic long throw by a shook Brady over the middle. On second-and-12 in the second quarter, nine Raiders set up on the line of scrimmage, resulting in a DeLawrence Grant sack. They did the same thing in the fourth quarter, leading to a Rod Coleman sack. Whatever the situation—whether traversing the field to make a tackle or recovering fumbles which were prematurely blown dead—the defensive eleven spent much of the night boarding the USS Constitution and taking prisoners. And a good deal of credit goes to No. 93, Old Ironsides, Trace Armstrong.

Trace Armstrong has had a rough fourteen months as a Raider. Helped off the field in Game 3 of the 2001 season against Seattle with a torn Achilles tendon, he vowed that would not be his last play. But in the first half of the season, too often he was a bystander on the sidelines. When he did get in for limited action, his lack of playing time was apparent, and I began saying out loud that he was no longer a point of impact.[4]

Against New England, Armstrong played a gutsy and impacting game. Needing disruptive defensive performances to throw off Brady's rhythm, Trace was all that and more. He turned in a sweep for a three-yard gain. He forced Brady with pressure to throw the ball away, then came back the next play and forced Brady under threat of bodily harm to throw into the ground. On the next play, Rod Coleman blacktopped Troy Brown for no gain while being bear-hugged by the opposing lineman. Said Armstrong, "My playing time and practice time have increased, and that's really what I needed. I'm starting to feel good back out there again."[5] Belying the one-tackle statistics that show on paper, Armstrong was a vector of violent nature on a field of turf surrounded by love.

But it was Armstrong's hustle on one particular play that would shine brightly on this mid-November night. With 1:46 showing on the first-half clock, on first-and-ten from New England's own thirteen-yard line with a tight 10–6 Raider lead, Brady brought the Patriots to the line of scrimmage. A moment later, as moved to his left, not only was Brady dropping back to pass—he was also dropping the ball, thanks to a beautiful strip-hit from No. 75 Howie Lon..., I mean Chris Cooper. The ball lay on the green tundra, soon to be covered body-and-soul by Trace Armstrong as 62,000 Raider fans sang Halleluiah praises. "I was double-teamed on that play, so I was just trying to stay alive and I saw it there. A guy who was a better athlete would probably have picked it up and run with it. But I thought it was better just to secure it," said Armstrong.[6]

Play of the Game.

Two plays later, QB Rich Gannon scampered left for two yards and secured the touchdown pylon to put Oakland ahead 17–6 at the half.

For the game, Patriots gained a pathetic 48 yards rushing on seventeen attempts. With only four first downs in the second half, New England's third-down conversion ratio was 33% (4-for-12), compared to the Raiders' 50% (7-for-14)—and the Patriots came up empty on two fourth-down attempts. Tellingly, the Patriot offense was unable to score a touchdown against the Silver and Black. "Coach Callahan challenged the defensive line to get after Brady," said defensive line coach Mike Waufle. "They came through."[7] On 18 completions in 30 attempts, Brady could gain just 147 yards. "It's the first time in a while we had seen a classic dropback passer like that," said tackle Sam Adams. "We knew going in we were going to be all over him."[8] The D racked up 7 hurries, 3 hits, 7 knockdowns, 4 sacks (three by defensive linemen) for 25 yards, in every Raider fan's mind, another journalist was hauled off to jail for hurling vulgar epithets toward Tom Brady about his family.

And finally, on fourth-and-six with 3:46 left in the game, Brady received his final sack at the kinetic hands of ... Trace Armstrong.

There is no doubt: a healthy No. 93 gives the Oakland Raiders more powers to detain opponents than the U.S. Patriot Act.

You would think the game would be over, and at 27–13 with 1:13 to go, you would usually be correct. But now we must witness the most vile and ungrateful creatures to wear the Silver and Black, a unit whose slogan is not "Pride and Poise" nor is it "Commitment to Excellence"; rather, their motto is "Let the Other Guy Do It." On the road to the last Super Bowl, unfortunately the "other" guys, the ones dressed like Paul Revere, did.

The kickoff return coverage cannot let a guy run the ball back all the way just because his last name is Faulk. The pawing and hand-holding exhibited during that debacle runback is better suited for a drive-in movie. Ten grown men have to tackle one runner; the eleventh man—the kicker—has already done his job. Now, I don't wish to cast aspersions, but I believe that nine of those Silver and Black imposters played with dolls as children, wet the bed as adolescents, and now sleep with the light on. Dog another kickoff like that last one and I am going to start talking about your mothers.

It is called the "Nut Squad" for a reason. You don't need talent to be nuts.

I must admit: I got a kick out of watching Sebastian Janikowski run after Faulk down the left sideline. That was some of the best kicker antics since Garo Yepremian lofted his helium pass in Super Bowl VII. Sea Bass gave it a good try; he almost caught him. Unfortunately, Jano took his tackle-angle tutelage from Anthony Dorsett. It is something to work on in the coming days.

The Raider players were quite reserved about such a big victory. Lincoln Kennedy, for one, seemed unimpressed by the New England win. "So we're headed in the right direction. We've got a long way to go. We're going up against some talented teams. I don't think we can take Arizona for granted. . . . We damn sure can't take San Diego for granted, because they beat us and we have to go play them at their house. We've still got Denver and Kansas City. It's going to be a race to the end. We can ill afford to look back, or look ahead, for that matter."

Rich Gannon echoed the same sentiment. "We're going to be on probation for the rest of the year, that's just the way it is," Gannon said. "We've got to play like this every week, against every team."[9]

And, given the fine performance, Bill Romanowski's assessment of the defensive effort was surprising: "The guys know that how we played tonight is not good enough for next week. We have to continue to get better."[10]

To me, that seems like a pretty tall order. Right now, with back-to-back wins, Raider intensity and performance is are sky-high. They have shown character and professionalism of the utmost level. They have stared into the abyss and met the challenge head-on. They have been tested. They have come away with a passing (.600) grade. They believe they belong in the upper echelon of NFL teams.

And they have proven it beyond a trace of doubt.

REFERENCES

1. "Raiders Fans Gone Wild"; Dave Newhouse; *Oakland Tribune*; November 7, 2002.
2. "Raiders Hope Ideas for Revenge Melt Away"; Monte Poole; *Oakland Tribune*; November 24, 1999.
3. *Snake*; Ken Stabler and Berry Stainback; Garden City, NY: Doubleday & Company, Inc.; 1986; pg. 92.
4. "Quest for Conviction"; Michael Wagaman; *Silver & Black Illustrated*; Vol. 14, #15; December 2, 2002.
5. "He's Appearing with Very Much a Trace"; Jerry McDonald; *Oakland Tribune*; November 18, 2002.
6. "Defense Tightens its Grip"; David Bush; *San Francisco Chronicle*; November 18, 2002.
7. "Raiders Leave No Doubt"; Bill Soliday; *Oakland Tribune*; November 18, 2002.
8. "Memorable Win for Raiders"; Nancy Gay; *San Francisco Chronicle*; November 18, 2002.
9. "Great Then Awful"; Carl Steward; *Oakland Tribune*; November 18, 2002.
10. Bush, op. cit.

Oakland at Arizona
November 24, 2002

*And I thought our special teams really need
to improve and upgrade.*

—Coach Bill Callahan, August 10, 2002[1]

Is it just me, or are the special teams starting to get on Raider fans' nerves? What is with the schizophrenic nature of these guys? I'll start with the manic personality phase. In the opening game, kickoff coverage gave up a 66-yard return, but then Zack Crockett redressed the balance by sacrificing his body on a punt return. Terry Kirby blew the Pittsburgh game open with a 96-yard kickoff return, and Phillip Buchanon and TK each got touchdown runs on punt returns against Tennessee. Sebastian Janikowski was five for six in field goals over the first four games. Shane Lechler averaged 43.8 yards on his first 26 punts and Janikowski made kicking 16 touchbacks look as easy as licking an ice cream cone.

Then, along with infrequent glimmers of light, special teams assignments began to break down as the Raiders slid into depression. Against St. Louis, there were six penalties on special teams, while kickoff and punt coverage allowed 149 yards in returns, including a 55-yarder off a punt which resulted in a touchdown on the next play; at home against the Chargers, Janikowski missed two FGs and coverage surrendered a 39-yard kickoff return; in Kansas City, a field goal was blocked and 89 yards on three kickoff returns were permitted; San Francisco was given six points on a fumbled Raider kickoff return as well as gratis on a 48-yard 49er kickoff return near the end of regulation.

The special teams' mental state reached a low against New England. The Raiders were assessed a fifteen-yard penalty on a punt that gave the Patriots the ball again—and they scored. The Raiders averaged sixteen yards on five kickoff returns and were outgained in this category for the seventh time in ten games. A third-quarter

Raider kickoff return was fumbled (but fortunately recovered by Oakland). A Raider field goal attempt was blocked. And New England ran back a kickoff 86 yards for a touchdown with under a minute left in the game. "We were fortunate that our defense played well and our offense played well enough, where we did not need to win the special teams battle," admitted Coach Bill Callahan.[2]

Bob Casullo has done a good job as special teams coach in some areas, but kickoff return coverage has far too often been mediocre. Special teams are very much on Coach Callahan's mind, as evidenced when he said, "It's an area that, if we don't upgrade, it will cost us a game."[3] And now, Oakland travels to Arizona to play the Cardinals, winless in their last four attempts after a 4–2 start. As both the Rams and Raiders have shown, a team with four or five losses is itching to break out of its slump. It was a fumbled fair catch in overtime last December 2 that allowed Arizona to defeat Oakland, 34–31—starting the December slide that resulted in four Raider losses in six weeks.

Word gets around about a team's weaknesses and, when the Raiders go out as a team to eat in Phoenix, don't be surprised if the hired help gives them a hard time. Putting her right hand on her hip and shifting the weight to a left-leg slouch, the waitress may hold the order pad up and ask innocently:

"So. Will you be ordering the special today?"

The Cardinals certainly will.

RUSH TO JUDGMENT

From the Oakland 30-yard line, the player takes the fourth-quarter pitch and heads left with velocity and vigor. Carrying the leather like an eighteen-wheeler carries a load of furniture, he protectively shifts the ball to his left arm, races past the Jerry Porter block and lumbers up the sideline for 36 yards to the Arizona 34-yard line before being pushed out of bounds.

For those 40,000 Raider fans awake in the stands and equal number not asleep on their living room couch, you know who the player was.

For the unenlightened few, consider these stellar individual statistics in the Oakland Raiders' trouncing of the Arizona Cardinals, 41–20, and decide which information gives you the most satisfaction:

Rich Gannon	27 completions in 45 attempts, 340 yards. 3 TDs;
Charlie Garner	16 rushes, 100 yards. 1 TD;
Charlie Garner	5 receptions, 82 yards.
Jerry Porter	5 receptions, 67 yards. 2 TDs;
Jerry Rice	7 receptions, 110 yards. 1 TD;
Tyrone Wheatley	13 rushes, 82 yards. 1 TD.

My money says 80% of Raider fans answer with one word. Tyrone.

Against the Cardinals, in the stadium where he won his starting job three years ago, Tyrone Wheatley showed a form not seen since the opening game of the season, when he gained 65 yards on 18 carries. This past Sunday, Wheatley gained more yardage in a single game than he did in the previous nine (23 rushes for 65 yards since September 9). Does Sun Devil Stadium bring out the stride in Wheatley? "Statistically and sentimentally, I guess you can say that," Wheatley said. "But when it's time for me to roll, I roll, regardless of what stadium I am in. Some places are tougher than others. But if you look at it that way, yeah, it's pretty fun to run here."[4]

It could be that the opposing defense was lackluster. While Arizona was ranked 7th seventh in the NFC against the rush coming into the game, it now has yielded 594 rushing yards in three of its last four games. Still, the Raider success at running the ball was an added weapon to an already-potent arsenal and an exciting validation to a team goal to rush up the field at will. "You see how it really benefits your football team, not only from a time-of-possession standpoint but for ball control, for keeping our defense off the field and giving us the confidence we can do it," Gannon said. "We're going to need that down the stretch."[5]

It is certainly an apropos time to pull-start that lawnmower. In the last six contests, Oakland has averaged 65 rushing yards per game that contributed to a whopping twenty-one percent of Raider first downs. In those games, the run had less of a chance than the Islamic Jihad opening a nightclub in Manhattan. Now, with Garner and Wheatley healthy, Oakland can rush against defenses. At least, that is the plan—and, in this game (as opposed to game 8 against San Francisco), the plan worked. "We needed that," Garner said, "to get back and establish again that we can run the football. A lot of teams are coming in against us, just running zones on us and dropping back and letting us throw these routine passes ... we definitely showed tonight that we can still run the football." Almost as an afterthought, Garner added, "The playoffs are the payoff, and you have to run the football. The run-and-shoot is not going to work."[6] Not without Charlie Garner rushing for daylight, anyway.

What does work is Rich Gannon finding Jerry Rice open for touchdown passes. For the sixth time this season (and third time for 20+ yards), the tandem hooked through flight to produce six points. Taking the snap on third-and-seven from the Arizona 37-yard line, Gannon—behind incredible offensive line protection—looked first to Jerry Porter cutting toward the middle, stopped, saw Rice running a post pattern, reset his feet and let fly the floater that Jerry took in stride over his left shoulder as he crossed the goal line. Coming at 28–14 with five minutes to go in the third quarter, the pass inflicted mortal damage on Arizona's comeback aspirations. Play of the Game.

There are two other Raider players who are also beginning to wreak havoc on opposing teams:

Jerry Porter: Porter's first-quarter seven-yard touchdown grab for a 7–0 Raider lead may not have been "Play of the Game." But Porter's first TD set the tone for the whitewash to follow, and his subsequent dunk over the crossbar was an adrenaline joy to behold.

"I had to show the ultra-vertical with the left hand. It's powerful."[7] Porter has already caught 42 receptions for 586 yards and eight TDs in this career-breakout season. Three of those six-pointers have been the team's first score. "He wants everybody to know that he can make plays and that he can be the go-to guy," said Jerry Rice.[8] And it's only a matter of time before he embarks on a successful end-around.

Sebastian Janikowski: To make a run for the playoffs, you need a good kicker—and the Raiders have theirs in the number one draft choice of 2000. He is 16 for 22 in field goal attempts this season, and while his 40+-yard attempts against AFC opponents (3 for 7) could be improved, Sea Bass's season-best 51-yard field goal against Arizona was long and true. The word is that, following the Kansas City game, SJ shortened his field-goal move toward the ball to just over one stride. "I feel like I've got more control of the ball," Janikowski said, adding that the new approach doesn't detract from his distance. "If I take three or four steps, then I'm kind of off-balance. You take one-and-a-half steps, it's more secure."[9] Coach Callahan echoed the kicker's new method: "His approach has changed. He's one-step kicking as opposed to three-stepping it. That's a big modification in his play."[10]

On his new effort, that was one small step for Jan, one giant hope for the Raider Nation.

The game certainly was not without its shortcomings. After stopping two powerful running games (Denver and New England), Oakland gave up 122 yards rushing to Marcel Shipp (who?) in the first half alone.[11] Penalty flags against the Raiders flew for a C-note of yardage for the fifth time this season. "We did what we needed to do," wideout Tim Brown said. "We obviously didn't play a perfect game."[12] A perfect game would first of all entail learning how to count. Like a Goldilocks plot, the Raiders one time had too few defensive players on the field (10), and another time too many (12).

The most outrageous play came when Oakland got the ball at its fifteen-yard line with just 1:03 remaining in the first half. Gannon moved the team down the field with marching precision, using the

Raiders' last timeout along the way. With seconds ticking down and Oakland poised at the Cardinals' 23-yard line, Gannon was set to spike the ball and stop the clock with two seconds left. But someone sent in the field goal unit; suddenly, there were more Raider players on the field than Raider fans attending a pay-what-you-can evening at the Mustang Ranch. Perhaps players were simply eager to make a contribution. Whatever their motives, confusion is not a virtue on the football field.

Oakland will need all of its athletes ready to play the game and willing to make positive contributions this coming Sunday. For the New York Jets come to town—the same franchise that derailed Oakland in its regular-season finale last year, 24–22.

It is a little-known scientific fact that the Raiders only lose to NFL cities that have two names (St. Louis, San Diego, Kansas City, San Francisco). Luckily, this rule does not apply to two-name regional teams (New England) and cannot be repeated by an AFC team already blessed with a win (Chargers).

That leaves the New York Jets as the final hurdle in this double-jeopardy theory.

Announcers with too much ego about their brain, too much coffee in their system and too much time on their hands have already started speculating who Oakland might face in the Super Bowl. Will it be Tampa Bay? Green Bay? San Francisco? Seattle?

For Raider fans, though, there can be only one goal:

8–4.

Anything else would be a rush to judgment.

REFERENCES

1. "A Rough Beginning to Callahan Regime"; Nancy Gay; *San Francisco Chronicle*; August 10, 2002.
2. "Raiders Aren't So Special"; Nancy Gay; *San Francisco Chronicle*; November 19, 2002.
3. "Special Teams Concern Callahan"; Bill Soliday; *Oakland Tribune*; November 19, 2002.

4. "Raiders Roar On in Desert"; Bill Soliday; *Oakland Tribune;* November 25, 2002.

5. "Good Day for Raiders to Add Some Run to Their Gun"; Monte Poole; *Oakland Tribune;* November 24, 2002.

6. "Garner Running in Right Direction"; Nancy Gay; *San Francisco Chronicle;* November 25, 2002.

7. "Porter Adds Post-TD Dunk to his Repertoire"; Monte Poole; *Oakland Tribune;* November 25, 2002.

8. ibid.

9. "Gannon Not Content with Win at Denver"; Jerry McDonald; *Oakland Tribune;* November 14, 2002.

10. "Gannon Also Did Great Job with Audibles"; Bill Soliday; *Oakland Tribune;* November 13, 2002.

11. "Feeling Right at Home"; Nancy Gay; *San Francisco Chronicle;* November 25, 2002.

12. "Good Time to Play Bad Opponent"; Monte Poole; *Oakland Tribune;* November 25, 2002.

WEEK 13
New York Jets at Oakland
December 2, 2002

It's enough to make a grownup cry.

It was the 1991 AFC Wild Card playoff game in Kansas City against the Marty Schottenheimer Chiefs. Down 10–6 with four minutes to play, the Raiders were driving at the opponent's 24-yard line when disaster gonged four times. On second-and-one, the Raider right tackle was called for a fifteen-yard face mask penalty. On the very next play, the same player was charged with a false start; the football now rested at the Chief 44-yard line. After a five-yard defensive holding call moved the ball to the 39-yard line, an offensive holding call on the tight end moved it back ten yards to the Chief 49. Then, incredibly, an offensive pass interference call against a Raider wide receiver moved the football back to the Raiders' 41-yard line. Without hardly running a play, the Raiders had moved backward 35 yards near the end of a playoff game.[1]

What is it with the love affair between the Raiders and penalties?

They certainly have chased their prize with lustful purpose. The Raiders led the NFL in number of penalties five out of six years from 1991 to 1996; that last year, they were called for miscues 156 times. In 2000, there were 118 flags for 940 yards; in 2001, Oakland was fifth in number of penalties (107) and sixth in yardage assessed (897 yards). This year, with 93 penalties and 829 yards punitively levied after only eleven games, the Silver and Black is guaranteed to surpass last year's dubious totals. I wonder if there is a rehabilitation clinic for repeat penalty offenders?

It is not the number of penalties but the type of infraction that creates a twitch and rash on this Raider fan's backside. I have never had a problem with Silver- and- Black roughness penalties: face mask, roughing the passer, unnecessary roughness, kicking Marty Schottenheimer in the groin out of bounds. Football is a violent game of extreme emotion and passion. I figure the offending player will make a big play later on in the game.

It is the non-contact errors that drive me up the wall like a scurrying spider. False start, illegal motion, offside, encroachment—these are the penalties that should be stricken from the Raider playbook, because there is no contact with the opposing player. "When you get backed up in the down and distance by penalties, it is really difficult to overcome the third-down element," Coach Callahan said after the first loss of the year. "Of the 46 penalties we have right now, 13 were mental penalties both offensively and defensively. You're going to have physical penalties but the mental penalties are what you try to eliminate."[2] If a Raider player smashes somebody and hears the referee's whistle—fine, huddle up and we'll get them next play. But if an Oakland player starts before the snap, Raider fans know what that means. We know because John Madden told us:

> Third-and-two down near the goal line, that's when you can't make a mistake. But that's just when some teams jump offside. Now it's third-and-seven, a big difference. The players on that team might all wear ties and sportcoats, they might look good on the airplane and look good in the lobby of the hotel. But they're not a disciplined football team.[3]

In fairness, it is important to consider the offensive lineman's point of view. Explaining the new emphasis on lineman alignment versus responsibility, seven-year Raider veteran Lincoln Kennedy said, "As a tackle, if I see a Jevon Kearse sitting out there next to me, do you think I'm gonna sit there and be worried about alignment? I've got to get back." And what happens if Kennedy doesn't get back? "Some good defensive end is gonna come along and take the quarterback's head off. And then the quarterback's gonna be out for the season."[4]

The defense's explanation on penalties is also instructive, especially when it comes from two grizzled veterans like Rod Woodson and Bill Romanowski. Said Woodson: "Today if you hit the quarterback too high, it's called; too low, it's called. To me, they're trying to take the physicalness out of the NFL, and that's hard to do when guys are getting bigger and stronger and faster. If you don't want to get hit, you better go play flag football or powder-puff or something like that."[5] When asked if the Raiders' reputation for rough play preceded them, Romanowski held firm: "I think the proof is in the pudding," he said. "That is what has been happening most of the season. But that is the way it is and we have to overcome that . . . being a Raider. We truly feel it is us against the world. I kind of like that challenge."[6] While such talk lacks the tenacity of George Atkinson—"I treat pass receivers the way you would treat a burglar in your home"—Raider fans still like Romanowski's attitude.[7]

Against the New York Jets, Raider players need to continue to cut down on the mental mistakes and play with all the controlled attitude, emotion and passion they can muster.

Just don't make the referee so teary-eyed that he pulls out his handkerchief.

FOURTH QUARTER

Raider fans across the nation share a common experience these days. Only the timing varies. Whether it is upon opening one's eyes in the morning, or coming after the initial cup of coffee, or occurring when the first onslaught of daily sports section mathematics permeates consciousness, the Oakland faithful all experience that anxiety of the closet numerologist presented with the following repetitive pattern:

4–0, 0–4, 4–0. . . .

And then?

Then we realize we have stopped breathing and need to begin again soon before the heart stops.

The Oakland Raiders defeated the New York Jets 26–20 on Monday Night Football and placed a unique footprint on a franchise landscape already well-trodden in history. Sure, there have been 12–4 Raider teams (four), one 11–5 year and a pair of 10–6 seasons.

But never has a Raider franchise put together three separate and equal streaks of favor and misfortune. There have been years when the Raiders won everything and years they lost whole highways of games, but this team is special—and the numerological proof of it is in the various multiples or dividends of the number four.

Like his forerunner, Coach Callahan likes to split a football season into manageable four-by-four segments.[8] It was Jon Gruden who coined the four-quarter strategy, a strategy he no doubt stole from someone else. I am fairly certain that, originally, it was Al Davis' brainchild, and this season it is an idea as appealing as it is relevant.

For in the eight years the Raiders have made the playoffs since the 16-game season was instituted in 1983, the Silver and Black have gone 21–11 over their final four games. That is basically two victories for every loss, a .667 winning percentage. Which is the current Oakland percentage at 8–4, a record made more remarkable by the .333 division record against teams which make up three of its final four games.

Another unique facet to this season is that Oakland has already avenged five of six regular-season losses from last year, tucked a W into the win column against New England and still plays Miami (who beat half a team in 2001's second game of the season, 18–15) in two weeks.

The revenge theory would have the Raiders win three of their last four, with the sole loss coming at home against Denver on Dec. 22. Not surprisingly, this is contrary to the aforementioned numerological theory, which posits that if the Raiders win the next game, they will win the remaining four. Or if they lose the next game, they will lose all four. But this latter scenario is simply unacceptable and has as much chance for fan approval as the possibility of the next Miss World pageant being peacefully held in Nigeria. Better that Oakland just keeps winning. That's the best theory of all.

With each win, the Raiders draw the veil over the eyes of the 0–4 stretch that once looked as bad as a school lunch menu. The first half of the Monday Night game saw Oakland move the ball well but wipe out promising drives even better, and they trailed 10–6 at halftime. "We were just a little antsy, a little jittery," offensive tackle Lincoln Kennedy said. "We all felt the pressure of this game and wanted to put on a great performance." Penalties (10 this game for 83 yards), pratfalls, and incomplete passes against a team with four straight wins to its credit was a dangerous proposition—and Tim Brown knew the antidote: "The veterans had to lead."[9]

And lead they did. Brown caught eight passes for 90 yards; Rod Woodson blocked a field goal in the second quarter; Rich Gannon fought his way through a pesky Jets defense to complete 31 passes in 42 attempts and one touchdown. John Parrella and Sam Adams, with a lot of help from their friends, stuffed Curtis Martin like a pork chop for a nondescript 26 yards on 11 attempts; Jerry Rice's 66 yards pushed him over 1,000-receiving yards for the fourteenth time, an ongoing NFL record, and Charlie Garner had 113 yards in total yardage. "This is just a great team with a lot of phenomenal players," assessed Parrella. "You can say what you want about age, but this is the hardest-working group of guys I've ever been associated with."[10]

Not to be outshone in the national television light, Raider youth got into the mix as well. Doug Jolley had a career-high five catches for 58 yards (including a nice nineteen-yarder, most of which was gained by breaking tackles) and Sebastian Janikowski kicked four field goals in the six-point win.

The number three also had significance in this game. It was in the third quarter that Tim Brown lazed over the middle for a six-yard gain, his 1,000th catch. Who can name their favorite Tim Brown moment, this single-team marquee player whose career has spanned over one-third of Raider franchise history? TB led the Raiders in pass receptions in eleven of fourteen seasons (the last ten in a row), plus led the team in punt returns seven straight seasons and in kick-off returns in 1988, his rookie year, when he amassed 1,098 yards for a 26.8 average. And the classy way he handled the introduction of legend Jerry Rice to the team reminds us that you do not gauge the measure of a man in statistics alone. It may be arguable, but it can safely be said: in a world of Art Powell, Fred Biletnikoff, Clifford

Branch, Dave Casper, and Todd Christensen, Tim Brown is the greatest receiver to wear the Silver and Black.

But it was the next play that proved to be the Play of the Game. After a 22-minute delay following Brown's 1,000th catch, during which Tim smooched everyone in sight like he was working a kissing booth at the county fair (and Jerry Porter told a Jets player, "Now we're fixin' to score"), Gannon took the snap with eleven minutes left in the third quarter.[11] He quickly found Jerry Rice splitting the seam, running right to left across the middle of the field, hit him in stride at the 12-yard line, and Rice raced into the end zone. Oakland now led 13–10 and they would never trail again, although the game was far from over. "That's Jerry Rice," Brown said. "Any time he catches the ball, he'll steal your thunder. It doesn't bother me. I'm just happy to have him here."[12] Raider fans are equally glad to have them both here. Especially heading into the fourth quarter.

Since the Raiders have played three quarters of the season with one four-game stretch still ahead, it is timely to speak of their third-down conversions. Currently, they are 65 for 145, a 45% conversion clip. It was on third-and-10 that Gannon hooked up with Jerry Rice for the 26-yard touchdown. On third-and-1 on the next series, Gannon pitter-patted for a scramble first-down—giving the Raiders 11/11 this year on third-and-1. That perfect record was broken in the Jets game; it is time to start a new third-and-1 streak and continue winning.

Three-quarters of the way through the season with one-quarter remaining, Oakland stands on a plateau and enjoys the vista of its successful season. There are only four places in the AFC West and, twelve games into the season, the Raiders have symbolically visited them all—more than once. Technically, the only position they have not yet held outright is first place. That opportunity avails itself this Sunday against the San Diego Chargers. Appreciating the debris of twelve teams with losing records across the league (9 NFC, 3 AFC), the Silver and Black know the titanic struggle that floats on the Brees ahead. You can be sure that someone is going down with San Diego's ship.

And you can bet these certainties are not lost on the many. The faithful followers understand numerology. We know who we are (Raider fans). We know what to do (drink heavily). We know how many Super Bowl rings the Raiders have, and we know how many more it takes to make four.

And we know what quarter it is.

Fourth quarter.

REFERENCES

1. "Raiders Get Cherry-Picked"; Chris Dufresne; *Los Angeles Times*; December 29, 1991.
2. "Raiders Are Seeing Red Over Yellow Flags"; Bill Soliday; *Oakland Tribune*; October 15, 2002.
3. *One Knee Equals Two Feet*; John Madden with Dave Anderson; New York: Villard Books; 1986; pg. 195.
4. "Raiders Anything but Neutral"; Nancy Gay; *San Francisco Chronicle*; August 14, 2002.
5. "Rod Woodson Sounds Off on Crackdown"; Nancy Gay; *San Francisco Chronicle*; November 1, 2002.
6. Soliday, *op. cit.*
7. "The Raiders Were Suped Up"; Dan Jenkins; *Sports Illustrated*; Vol. 46, #3; January 17, 1977; pg. 16.
8. "Raiders Back Tied for First in AFC West"; Bill Soliday; *Oakland Tribune*; November 26, 2002.
9. "Opportunity Knocks, Oakland Answers Door"; Ira Miller; *San Francisco Chronicle*; December 3, 2002.
10. "Graybeards Deliver for the Silver and Black"; Carl Steward; *Oakland Tribune*; December 3, 2002.
11. "Old-Timers Day"; Bill Soliday; *Oakland Tribune*; December 3, 2002.
12. "Brown's Major Milestone Was No Time for a Party"; Gwen Knapp; *San Francisco Chronicle*; December 3, 2002.

CHAPTER SEVEN

2002: Fourth Quarter

WEEK 14
Oakland at San Diego
December 8, 2002

It is the thirteenth game of a 16-game season. Undisputed first place is on the line in the AFC West. Fifty-three men dressed in Silver and Black will test whether that team, or any team so conceived and so dedicated, can first endure. They will meet their foe on a great playing field of that rivalry. And the thought in the narrow minds of all Raider fans is the same.

Will the real Oakland Raiders defense please stand up?

It is not a simple question to answer. This Silver and Black eleven has pulled more personality changes than Al Gore trying to reinvent himself. They stuffed their first four leading ground gainers for 161 cumulative yards, prompting their rookie sensation Phillip Buchanon to effuse, "We haven't had our best game yet. So that is kind of scary."[1]

Scary came in the following four games, as the rushing defense gave up 402 yards to the next three opponent plowhorses, then allowed Jeff Garcia to twitter for 46 first-down, back-breaking, anus-puckering yards. Oakland stopped Denver's and New England's running game like INS agents detaining bearded Arab clerics. But then they let an Arizona Cardinal rush for the third-highest individual total this season (Charles Woodson observed, "We made him look like a star."[2]). Finally, they silenced Curtis Martin with a gag order to the tune of 26 yards.

In the air, the Raiders have kept the opponent's passing game under 280 yards no fewer than nine times this season—winning six of them. Yet they allowed San Diego's snot-nosed Drew Brees far too much time to stand in the pocket and throw completions back on October 20. Their obsession for turnovers has been amazing, fourteen interceptions and nine recovered fumbles. During the wins, they have forced many opponents to run their offense about as well as Robert Reid lit his shoe. Amid the losses, the defense has been as porous as trickle-down logic—and just as devastating.

The list of new defensive personnel to the Raider stop-shop is long: Sam Adams, Trace Armstrong, Eric Barton, Chris Cooper, Derrick Gibson, DeLawrence Grant, Napoleon Harris, Tory James, Brandon Jennings, Clarence Love, John Parrella, Bill Romanowski, Terrance Shaw, Travian Smith, and Rod Woodson.

"We have a great football team, with a lot of great individual athletes," said Rod Woodson. "But we have to come together as a football team."[3]

Defensive tackle Sam Adams echoed his words: "That's what we have to do here—come together and play for each other."[4]

Raider D, enough of the toe-jam football. It's time to put together the game of your season. I know you, and you know me. All I've got to tell you is you've got to be mean.

Come together. Right now.

Over Brees.

THE DEFENSE FINALLY RESTED

The buses wait patiently, there in the darkness. Implacable night mixed with light iridescent, waiting to take the ballplayers toward home. Qualcomm Stadium lies quietly vacant, the roar for first downs now but a memory. The buses run rhythmically, exhaust pipes fuming; they have no idea what transpired this day.

What transpired this day in the Oakland Raiders' 27–7 shellacking of the San Diego Chargers was a clinic of how to play defense. The Raiders beat them down like Missouri's late Governor Carnahan, already in his grave, defeated the current U.S. Attorney General: decisively. More than mere stoppage, it was a torrent, a flood, a veritable cyclone of denial.

The tale of the tape tells only part of the story. Where once the Raiders contained, now they controlled: the San Diego offense held the ball seven minutes less in this game than in their first contest in October (29 mins. vs. 36 mins.). Where once Oakland D allowed, now they rejected: the Chargers were 6 for 13 (46%) in third and fourth-down conversions in game one, 5 for 16 (31%) in this contest.

And where once he ran, now he ... what did LaDanian Tomlinson do, exactly? First game: 39 carries for 153 yards; second game: 18 rushes for 57 yards. I get more yardage than that going back and forth to the bathroom after drinking coffee all day at work. "This was a heated, physical game. You talk about rivalries? We had one today," coach Bill Callahan said. "It was a fistfight throughout the game."[5] I saw Tomlinson's jaw flapping quite a bit after he picked himself up yet again from under a pile of white jerseys, usually for little gain. "Don't go out now, I'm not backing down," Tomlinson shouted at Bill Romanowski after getting pounded by the linebacker.[6] Maybe he wasn't backing down, but No. 21 spent much of this game getting knocked down.

It was the onslaught unleashed by the Raider defense on San Diego QB Drew Brees that was so impressive. Brees chewed on the Oakland D for 16 completions in 25 attempts for 170 yards and two touchdowns in the first game, standing in a halo of protection for much of that time. After the first Raider contest, Brees cracked that the hardest hit he took all day was when he was hit with a bottle while leaving the field. He was not so lucky this game. Harried, pursued, and threatened with bodily harm nearly every time he took a four-step drop, Brees looked every bit the youngster under fire. By game's end, his quarterback rating was an abysmal 40.6—only slightly higher than the average Charger IQ.

From the first series when he took an opening hit on third down, Brees was a man harassed. If DeLawrence Grant wasn't after him, Rod Coleman was hitting him, or Travian Smith was chasing him. When he finally got decent offensive line protection, Brees was so flustered that he overthrew his intended receiver and Terrance Shaw intercepted him (14:10 left, second quarter). After throwing a second INT, this time to Rod Woodson that led to three Raider points and a 13–7 halftime lead, Brees was 9–20 for 83 yards. Based on the first thirty minutes of play, I will say there are three things in this world that are highly overrated: smart bombs, artificial limbs, and the San Diego Chargers.

But it was the second half where the Raider defensive eleven shined. After two rushes into the middle for five yards and a quick pass right for four, SD faced fourth-and-1 at the 10:45 mark of the third quarter. Tomlinson headed left and just kept going laterally, tackled by Anthony Dorsett (who took a fine angle) and hunted by Eric Barton and DeLawrence Grant amid a white-jersey contingent that looked like your mother's laundry hung out to dry. "I know I had some games last year where I missed some critical tackles, and it seems that's all people remember," Dorsett said. "I know I can play ball, and that's what it's all about."[7] Play of the Game.

But the D wasn't done yet with Drew. After LT ripped off his long run of the day (fifteen yards) to the Oakland 30 with 8:30 left in the third quarter amid a 13–7 Raider lead, Brees called timeout. He then promptly air-mailed a dying quail to a perfectly positioned Tory James for Brees' third INT—his highest single-game interception total of the season. By the time the fourth quarter began with San Diego at their own 41-yard line facing a third-and-3, Brees had been sacked twice, hurried ten times and knocked down another five. With five minutes left in the game and trailing 27–7, Brees had the Chargers first-and-ten at the Raider eleven-yard line. First down: pass batted down by Chris Cooper; second down: Tomlinson tackled by Eric Barton for a three-yard gain; third down: Brees open-field tackled by Anthony Dorsett; fourth down: pass batted down at the line by Rod Coleman. It was now official: San Diego was done.

The Chargers were finished but the Raider D was not. In Callahan's view, "It was one of those games where it was physical and guys weren't going to relent."[8] Ahead 27–7, the game no longer in doubt, the Alameda Eleven made one last statement. With first-and-goal from the four-yard line and only fifteen seconds showing on the game clock, San Diego ran an incredible five more plays and failed to get into the end zone. Red zone, gold zone, no zone.

After a spike stopped the clock, Brees tossed into the left end zone where Rod Woodson knocked the pass away. Only after doing so did Woodson realize he could have taken that pick all the way back for a 98-yard runback. That would have been his third TD-returned pick of this season. Woodson looked like a pirate who had dropped a treasure overboard. Eleven ticks remained in the game. Travian Smith tipped away the next pass into the end zone. And when Sam Adams was called for unnecessary roughness, he proceeded to tell the referee which way was the best route to leave town. With seven seconds left, yet another Brees pass into the end zone was broken up. And, with one second remaining and the football on the two-yard mark, the Raider D—refusing to rest on their well-earned laurels—denied the Chargers one last time on a run left.

The Oakland defense.

They never gave up.

They never gave in.

They never gave ground.

There, in the shadow and silence of darkness, the buses awaited. Oakland Raider players calmly made their way out of the locker room, through the tunnel and out into the open environs of the parking lot. A few defensive players strayed off to receive well wishes from family and friends. The remaining players slowly boarded the buses, maneuvered their aching bodies down the aisle and gingerly slid into their seats. When all were aboard, the buses shifted into gear and began the caterpillar-trek through the shadows and home to Oakland.

Finally, the defense rested.

REFERENCES

1. "Buchanon Supplies Game-Breaker Again"; Mitch Pritchard" *Oakland Tribune;* October 7, 2002.
2. "Raiders Roar On in Desert"; Bill Soliday; *Oakland Tribune;* November 25, 2002.
3. "Yet Another Troublesome Trip to Arrowhead"; Monte Poole; *Oakland Tribune;* October 28, 2002.

4. "Raiders Attempt to Plug Holes"; Bill Soliday; *Oakland Tribune;* November 25, 2002.

5. "Raiders Begin Playoff Run by Winning the Hard-Nosed Way"; Nancy Gay; *San Francisco Chronicle;* December 9, 2002.

6. "Simply Smashing"; Bill Soliday; *Oakland Tribune;* December 9, 2002.

7. "Suspect Secondary Stifles Chargers"; Jerry McDonald; *Oakland Tribune;* December 9, 2002.

8. Gay, op. cit.

WEEK 15
Oakland at Miami
December 15, 2002

It was a great game if you like line play and you like 'backer play,
if you like all those things about the game of football.

—COACH BILL CALLAHAN[1]

If you love the game of football, then it is a safe bet—at some point
in your life—you wanted to be a linebacker. Surrounded by teammates in front and in back, the linebacker is the solitary bastion of
refusal—a dissenter who votes with his body, reads with his eyes,
and metes out punishment with all the compassion of a collection
agency. And, in a linebacker's world, the bill comes due with each
snap of the football.

The Raider list of notable linebackers is long and illustrious. Each
athlete brought his own body type, longevity, and style of reprimand
to the game. All probably agreed with the sheer ferocity of Phil
Villapiano (1971–1979): "When I hit people, I knew I could hurt
them. . . . I just couldn't wait to hit somebody hard."[2] In the Raider
scheme of things, the wait was never long.

This year, the triumvirate of Silver and Black stoppers consists
of Eric Barton, Bill Romanowski, and Napoleon Harris.

Eric Barton: In the San Diego game, Barton flew to the ball carrier like Maynard G Krebs to a welfare check, collecting ten unas-
sisted tackles. "He has such a feel for the inside, and the running
game especially," coach Bill Callahan said. "He has really emerged
into one of the top linebackers in our division." Barton gives the
credit to John Parrella and Sam Adams—who stop the double-
teams—as well as increased playing time. "My anticipation is getting a little better just from having more experience," he said. "And
when you guess right, it is good.'[3]

Bill Romanowski: "I always had a certain passion, a drive," Romanowski said. "I don't think it's something that's coached into you. I think it comes from within, and it's something I've always had." This passion can find expression in extracurricular activity, as Tim Brown related in this LaDanian Tomlinson-Romanowski encounter: "We told the ref, 'Aw, he just twisted his neck a little bit. Let it go.'"[4] With 232 consecutive games and 72 tackles this season, Romanowski seems in no hurry to go anywhere soon.

Napoleon Harris: Taken as the twenty-third player in the 2002 draft, Harris has adapted to the middle linebacker position with all the confidence of an egocentric actor serving as a lightning rod in a violent orgy of action. "I expected to come right in and play.... In the middle, you are dealing with tight ends, backs, centers, guards, tackles. You are really in the mix." Added Bill Callahan, "I think sometimes he gets a little confused, but he has studied very hard, and if he makes a mistake he'll correct himself."[5] Correct me if I'm wrong, but I think the Raiders made a good draft in this young man.

Seeking to improve on a defensive standing of 17th best in the NFL (2000) followed by 18th (2001), Al Davis brought in ten new defensive starters for the 2002 season. Three of these athletes were linebackers. With helmets, pads and abandon, they were unleashed on an unsuspecting league.

And it was good.

WAITING FOR THE TIDE

There the Oakland Raiders were, aboard a Silver and Black yacht amply powered by Teameffort engine, cruising steadily up the Winthemall River toward safe haven in the halcyon harbor of First Round Bye-Home Field Advantage.

Then a funny thing happened.

They got stuck on a sandbar.

More to the point: they were mooned over Miami.

The Miami Dolphins edged the Oakland Raiders 23–17 in the state known for its orange juice, Daytona race-cars and Apollo rockets. It was a game every bit as close as the final score indicates. A game Oakland played for revenge but Miami played for survival. An AFC match against a desperate team led by an insomniac coach who looked like he had more fat in his head than the Pillsbury Doughboy. It was a contest entirely winnable but ultimately sacrificed at the altar of dropped balls, sacks, and turnovers. Thankfully, it was the last road game for the Raiders, who went a respectable 5–3. And hopefully, it will be the last regular-season loss surrendered by the 2002 Raiders.

Overall, the loss was more a minor irritant than a major cataclysm. One of two division leaders to taste defeat this last Sunday (San Francisco still cannot get by Green Bay), Oakland remains on top of the AFC West, courtesy of a San Diego team that has cast off its winning ways and now embraces defeat in a twenty-first century rendition of the infamous "Marty Molt." Just keep running them in pads on Wednesday, Marty.

Ignoring the 62%–38% discrepancy in time of possession, there was much to praise in the Raiders' losing effort.

Rush defense: It was yeoman work; Oakland held Miami's Ricky Williams to his sixth lowest total-yard effort (101 yards) and fifth lowest yards-per-carry (3.7). The ferocity with which Eric Barton ripped the football out of Williams' arm in the first quarter (recovered by Anthony Dorsett) was alarming. Had the time-of-possession been a little more in balance, Williams' totals would have assuredly been less; he picked up seventeen yards in the final two minutes, after the game-clinching Miami interception. "For the most part we had him under control," said defensive tackle John Parrella.[6]

Cornerbacks: At the beginning of the season, the names Brandon Jennings and Clarence Love would seem more likely to be heard at one's front door as an introduction to the First Order of Jehovah.

Yet their effort was impressive as they ran stride for stride with Dolphins' receivers in general. Unfortunately, they spent too much time chasing after one receiver in particular: Chris Chambers, who caught seven passes for 138 yards. In the first half alone, Chambers gathered in five of those catches for 117 yards. In the second half, though, the long Miami gain through the air was fourteen yards, hardly the stuff of vertical dominance. Speaking of Jennings, Love and Terrance Shaw, Charles Woodson said, "Those guys fought hard," adding "For the most part, they held up pretty good."[7]

Sebastian Janikowski: He changed his approach after the October 20 San Diego game and over the last six games the Polish Pound has been amazing, connecting on 15 of 17 field goal attempts. "To his credit he was willing to change in midseason," Callahan said. "He's comfortable one-stepping it, and there's more consistency with the range and obviously with the motion of his kicks." Added holder Shane Lechler: "There is less room for error when you shorten up like that. Not only is he making everything, he's making better contact. He's hitting the ball excellent."[8] Three for three against the Dolphins, the field goals were the only points scored by Oakland until Jerry Porter's twenty-yard touchdown catch on the first play of the fourth quarter.

Unfortunately, not every Raider had a good day. One example will suffice., With five minutes to go in a 20–17 game and the Dolphins punting, the Raiders were in fine position to take the lead and escape Miami with a win. But then they experienced a most unusual event, something Californians once felt in their gluteus maximus and characterized as annoying, uncertain, and inconvenient.

Oakland suffered a Brownout.

Tim Brown took the Miami punt and angled right. The subsequent tackle by Miami defender Trent Gamble caused Brown to fumble, which the Dolphins recovered. "Obviously I am not there to take it 90 yards even though on that play once I caught it, all I saw was green grass," Brown said. "I never saw (Gamble) until the last second. That guy is supposed to be in the middle of the field. I wasn't expecting him to be where he was. . . . My guys on the punt return want to take responsibility for the fumble, but the only reason I am returning punts is to be sure we have the ball at the end of the play."[9]

To say Tim Brown had a tough game is like saying Trent Lott had a bad week. There is no need to go over the dropped passes and elusive touchdown miss. To err is human, and Timmy showed himself only too much so against the Dolphins. On the bright side, there is probably no receiver in Raider history who has caught more passes against the Broncos and Chiefs than Tim Brown. Come Sunday, he will be ready; great players always are. Tim will bounce back; true champions always do. Cliches are greatly overused to finish thoughts; sportswriters always will.

Over fifty years ago, Eddy Duchin penned the lines:

Moon over Miami
Shine on as we begin
A dream or two that may come true
When the tide comes in.[10]

Today, that stanza stands testament to Raider hopes and wishes. For Denver and Kansas City come to Oakland to close out the regular season over the next two Sundays. Ahh, to beat the Donkeys and Chiefs—sending them to non-playoff Purgatory while clinching the AFC West—now that would be a dream (or two) come true.

December 22 and 29 are marked on our calendars and, oh yeah, an encounter with Santa Claus is sandwiched in between.

Yet the Miami loss lingers like a scabbed-over mosquito bite, and a stigma borne that has not been felt since the dog days of November 2. Let the call go forth: 11–5 will be a successful season; anything less is a disappointment. What can never be a disappointment is this 2002 Raider football season.

So, over the next few days, Raider fans will fill the time with Christmas parties, revelry, gift exchanges, gluttony, tree decorations, lechery, wrapping presents, and screaming at children. And, in a corner of our mind, we stand on a Silver and Black yacht and share one common anticipation: an AFC Championship.

Supreme in our goal, confident in our future, happy with our Raiders. Our ship has come in.

But, until Sunday, it's stuck on the sandbar, so we're waiting for the tide to rise.

REFERENCES

1. "Raiders Begin Playoff Run by Winning the Hard-Nosed Way"; Nancy Gay; *San Francisco Chronicle;* December 9, 2002.
2. *Raiders Forever;* John Lombardo; Lincolnwood, IL: Contemporary Books; 2001; pg. 192.
3. "Barton Making Pro Bowl Waves"; David Bush; *San Francisco Chronicle;* December 13, 2002.
4. "Call Him Crazy, But 'Romo' Keeps Getting in his Licks"; Jerry McDonald; *Oakland Tribune;* November 11, 2002.
5. "Harris Starting Fast, but He's Still a Rookie"; David Bush; *San Francisco Chronicle;* October 3, 2002.
6. "Communication Breakdown Hurts"; Bill Soliday; *Oakland Tribune;* December 16, 2002.
7. "Charles Woodson Plans to Play with Broken Leg"; David Bush; *San Francisco Chronicle;* December 17, 2002.
8. "Janikowski Living Up to Billing"; David Bush; *San Francisco Chronicle;* December 14, 2002.
9. Soliday, op. cit.
10. www.leoslyrics.com

WEEK 16
Denver at Oakland
December 22, 2002

Hegenberger Boulevard. Network Associates Coliseum. Sitting against a concourse slab of cement. Two Raider fans grousing, waiting for the ticket office to open.

RaiderX: Never shoulda lost.

RaiderPal: Seems pointless.

RaiderX: Were you at that one game? Napoleon Kaufman rushes 28 times for 227 yards, an all-time Raider record, had an 83-yarder on third down. Jeff George threw twelve passes. Eric Turner had a 65-yard touchdown fumble return.[1]

RaiderPal: Who won that game?

RaiderX: Haven't the foggiest.

RaiderPal: How about the game when Oakland had 63 yards in penalties during a 92-yard Denver touchdown drive. John Elway leaves with a hamstring injury and in trots Bubby Brister . . .

RaiderX: Did you just make that name up?

RaiderPal: Nah. Brister comes in and promptly throws an interception to Eric Turner, who returns it for a 94-yard touchdown. The Brickster then goes 10 for 16 with two TD passes while a panic-stricken Jeff George throws three interceptions.[2]

RaiderX: And the final score was?

RaiderPal: It wouldn't change things.

RaiderX: I was at one Denver game: a third-string punk named Brian Griese completes 17 of 29 passes for 234 yards and a touchdown. Gannon drives the team down to the Denver 23 but his pass is grabbed by guess who . . . Denver's Tory James.[3]

RaiderPal: Who intercepted?

RaiderX: Never heard of him.

RaiderPal: There was this one game, Rich Gannon fumbled the first snap he took and a Denver defender ran it in for a score. On the next Oakland play, Tyrone Wheatley fumbles and Denver recovers.

Mike Anderson runs for 187 yards on 32 carries against the Raider defense and Denver dominates time-of-possession.[4]

RaiderX: How'd the game turn out?

RaiderPal: I can't recall.

RaiderX: It's all ridiculous.

RaiderPal: What's the use?

RaiderX: Who can forget the time Gannon went 25-for-34 and three touchdown passes, with Tim Brown catching two.[5]

RaiderPal: Who got the W?

RaiderX: It doesn't matter.

RaiderPal: Whatever.

RaiderX: Beyond my comprehension.

RaiderPal: Why bother?

RaiderX: I'm gonna go.

RaiderPal: Go where?

RaiderX: I gotta pee.

Raider X stood up and walked a half-block away before turning around to look back. RaiderPal was still sitting in the same spot; he had taken off his shoes and was peering inside them. RaiderX understood his brother's motive. If death was eternity and life was a moment, what better way than to use the available blink of time in a manner that seemed natural. Which was waiting. Waiting, like forever, in purgatory for that damn game . . . after game.

Waiting for Denver.

MAKING IT LOOK (HALF) EASY

The Oakland Raiders defeated the Denver Broncos at Network Associates Coliseum Sunday, 28–16. In doing so, they secured the AFC West division title for the third consecutive year. The Raiders also stayed in the hunt to have a first-round bye, home-field advantage throughout the playoffs. But it was the manner in which victory was secured that was of most interest here, coming against a foe they had fought some 84 times before. Because Oakland made it look easy.

Well, they made it look half-easy.

In the first half, the Raiders could do no wrong. Playing with a fervor previously exhibited only by young Republicans at a Jerry Falwell picnic, Oakland took no prisoners and offered little quarter. Capitalizing on Denver mistakes, forcing Bronco turnovers and executing their offense at will, the Silver and Black systematically jumped out to a 21–0 lead with nearly thirteen minutes left in the second quarter. But in the second half—perhaps like the world around them—the Raiders' future more closely resembled a balance between promise and peril. In that second half, their fortunes changed faster than a dot-com bust.

Initially, a victory appeared as effortless as a sunrise. After holding Denver for a three-and-out series, Oakland found itself on the Denver 46-yard line after a booming 25-yard Broncos punt. 6 Six plays later, divided equally between run and pass but hardly equal in yardage—pass 43, rush 3—Zack Crockett plunged in from the one-yard line.

Denver took over and quickly ran into the Raider D buzzsaw. After an initial first down, QB Brian Griese's pass to the left side was tipped at the line by John Parrella and nearly intercepted by Bill Romanowski. Then, on third-and-ten against a four-man rush, Griese took the snap. Make that a six-man rush. In came blitzing linebacker Travian Smith on the left and safety Derrick Gibson on the right. Gibson was picked up but had a six-yard push and deflected Griese's pass into the air where Trace Armstrong made a nice look-what-I-found grab for his first career interception.

Oakland took their time with this opportunity, using 4:13 to go 38 yards for the score. Wheatley ran twice for 21 yards and Garner caught two for 16 more. Then, on third-and-three, Rich Gannon made a beautiful S-curve scramble up the middle to score when it seemed a sack was assured. Said Gannon, "I felt like I could run and make some plays."6

On the next Denver series, it became apparent that the only team making plays were dressed in Silver and Black. On first-and-five from their own 35, all three Raider linebackers stacked the right side. Eric Barton had his shifty eyes glancing left but he was coming right. There was nobody in the middle of the field. Romanowski took the running back in motion and middle linebacker Napoleon Harris got a running jump on the snap as perfect as Pamela Anderson's implants. At the same instant, defensive end Chris Cooper fell back to help out in the middle. Griese tried a quick toss to Ed McCaffrey in the middle but, delivered in haste, the football was off-target. Who was there to make the proper anticipation to intercept? No. 26, Rod Woodson. It was interception No. 7 on the season for Woodson, No. 68 in his career and No. 2 in a hat-trick of Raider interceptions this fine day.

From there, the Raiders scored faster than Howard Stern says "Hey now." On third-and-five from the eight-yard line, Rich Gannon correctly read the Denver blitz coming from the left side. "The truth is that Charlie ran the wrong route," Gannon said. As Garner ran left toward the sideline (while looking back over his left shoulder), Gannon retreated seven steps to give his running back time to adjust his route. Garner did adjust, breaking straight down the sideline toward the left corner of the end zone. Now Garner was looking over his right shoulder, and Gannon floated a lazy spiral that Charlie gathered in unmolested before falling out-of-bounds. "I just thought I'd take a shot in the back of the end zone where nobody could get it. I was basically throwing it away."[7] Play of the Game.

Three touchdowns over twenty-five plays covering 109 yards. Not a bad (half) day's work.

Meanwhile, the Oakland defense was playing madder than Raider tailgate fans without beer. On the subsequent possession, Denver's Shannon Sharpe caught a seven-yard pass on second down. An instant later, Napoleon Harris hit Sharpe so hard his shadow actually shriveled up. "I think guys came out assertive and hungry to hit," said Harris. "What better way to do it than to come out and get big hits and get guys intimidated?"[8] Harris stood up and howled at the moon even though the field was bathed in bright sunshine. Sharpe stayed on the ground, trying to comprehend the black shadows in his mind. He has been the bane of Raider existence on innumerable plays in the past. On this day, however, Harris cleaned his receptacle like a pumice stone on a toilet ring.

The next big play came with 4:40 left in the first half and Oakland still leading 21–0. Denver had a first-and-ten from their own thirty-yard line. The Raiders were set up in a four-man rush, but who was that body sneaking up on the upper-left side of the line? Why, it was No. 53 Bill Romanowski. At the snap, the left guard pulled to get over and block Romanowski, but he couldn't intercept the charging linebacker. Griese dropped back five yards, which gave Romo time to build up speed. WHAM! All those memories of the Grieses'—father and son—superb play burying the Raiders over the years were not erased by this hit, but at least they were smudged.

When he stood up after making the tackle—looking directly at the Black Hole—Romanowski was animated and raised his arms in triumph before imitating a rousing right-uppercut. As if to say: that was for you. "Bodies were everywhere on the field," crowed Bill Romanowski. "But you know what? They weren't our guys."[9] Griese limped from the field with a gimpy left knee. In a contest he admitted beforehand was a defining game in his career, Griese had 7 completions in 15 attempts for 48 yards, two interceptions and no touchdowns.

But the game is sixty minutes long, not thirty. And, in the span of 15:05, Denver crawled back to within five points at 21–16. With 10:36 and the ball at their own 44-yard line following a taunting call against Denver, Oakland went back to work. Rather, they went back to rush. "Hey, two years ago, we had the No. 1 rushing attack in the whole league," reminded guard Mo Collins. "So it was like old times."[10] First up was Charlie Garner, who initially appeared stopped behind the line of scrimmage. But appearances with Charlie are as deceiving as CIA disinformation. By the time he was done juking, Garner had moved the ball forward 19 yards to the Denver 37. Next, Tyrone Wheatley steamrolled for 17 yards through a hole as large as any budget deficit. Garner followed suit with 19 yards through another hole large enough to drive a Humvee through. Zack Crockett's second 1-yard run behind the block of Jon Ritchie made the score 28–16.

Denver's subsequent drive ended when Eric Barton picked off the third Bronco pass at the Oakland 45-yard line. This interception with 5:49 left in the game effectively ended the Broncos' comeback chances.

So the Oakland Raiders are AFC West champs for the third year in a row, the first time such an honor has been earned in twenty-one years.[11] The Silver and Black swept Denver for the first time in eight years.[12] And they accomplished both noteworthy events in spite of a four-game losing streak. "You don't appreciate something unless you work for it, right?" reasoned Tyrone Wheatley. "Hopefully we'll savor this, knowing that we worked really, really hard for it."[13]

As the seconds ticked down to 0:00 in this significant victory, Raiders coach Bill Callahan and the Broncos' Mike Shanahan walked out to shake hands at the end of the game.

Like two ships passing, but not in the night, Raiders past and Raiders present met halfway.

REFERENCES

1. "Kaufman, Raiders Bust Broncos' Streak"; Ron Kroichick; *San Francisco Chronicle*; October 20, 1997.

2. "Broncos Frustrate Raiders"; Ron Kroichick; *San Francisco Chronicle*; September 21, 1998.

3. "JV Broncos Steer Raiders Toward Cliff"; Brian Murphy; *San Francisco Chronicle*; October 11, 1999.

4. "Raiders' Comeback Fails"; David Bush; *San Francisco Chronicle*; September 18, 2000.

5. "Loss Streak to Denver Ends at Seven"; David Bush; *San Francisco Chronicle*; November 6, 2001.

6. "Gannon the Master of All He Sees"; David Bush; *San Francisco Chronicle*; December 23, 2002.

7. ibid.

8. "Broncos Take Tough Lesson in Hard Knocks"; Ira Miller; *San Francisco Chronicle*; December 23, 2002.

9. "Champs by KO"; Nancy Gay; *San Francisco Chronicle*; December 23, 2002.

10. "Raiders Can Play Smashmouth Ball, Too"; Carl Steward; *Oakland Tribune*; December 23, 2002.

11. "Back in the Saddle"; Jerry McDonald; *Oakland Tribune*; December 23, 2002.

12. "Callahan Gets It Done for Davis"; Carl Steward; *Oakland Tribune*; December 23, 2002.

13. Gay, op. cit.

Kansas City at Oakland
December 28, 2002

When I was just a youngster, I first heard the term, "Block out the sun." In my mind's eye, it applied to gigantic defensive linemen like Ben Davidson, or linebackers like Ted Hendricks who used his height advantage and athletic ability to block twenty-five field goals and point-after-touchdowns (PATs) in his career.

This year, though, the term has taken on a new meaning—pirated away to the other side of the line by an anonymous group of five teammates whose positions form the fulcrum for the number one offense in the NFL. They are the offensive line of the Oakland Raiders.

And they are a team force of violent persuasion. When Rich Gannon is standing back in the pocket for five, six, and seven seconds—checking off his primary, second, and third receivers—that is because the purveyors of pain up front are doing their job. Barry Sims calls it "'leadership by committee.' I think that everybody on the offensive line has a purpose to lead this team because it begins up front for the championship."[1]

It is quite a committee. From 'Smurf' Sims at 300 pounds to Langston Walker at 345, the eight front linemen who start and substitute total an incredible 2,565 pounds (average weight: 320). That's more than my family weighs combined after a hungry night out at King's Table. Sims and Walker—along with Matt Stinchcomb, Barret Robbins, Frank Middleton, Lincoln Kennedy, Mo Collins, and Adam Treu—all these players provide flexibility and depth to a multiplicity of positions due to the philosophy of their current (and former line) coach: Bill Callahan.

"I always have thought that if you were an offensive linemen you really had to have the ability to play guard and tackle and be trained at center," said Callahan. "I never looked at a lineman as just a guard or a tackle. I really wanted to educate them on every position and give them an awareness of everything that was happening up front."[2]

Playing a position in which having their name called is a sign of error, the front line has honorably held up the Raider tradition that an efficient set of blockers is necessary to give the QB time to throw downfield. And the offense has responded: Oakland has led the NFL in offense practically since game one. Each game they average 99 yards rushing, 293 yards passing and 28 points.

But the front line is not sitting back on their laurels going into the regular season-ending game against Kansas City—not with a possible first-round bye, home-field advantage at stake. As they stand in possession of a third straight AFC West crown, this team is more cautious, more focused, and more detail-oriented than past years. "We have to critique every little thing," tackle Lincoln Kennedy said.[3]

Spurred to greater effort by the offensive line coach, Aaron Kromer, and guided under the watchful eye of Bill Callahan, the Oakland Raiders have solidified into a unit stronger than the sum of its parts. Said Frank Middleton: "Lincoln brings the big brother-type attitude to the team. B. Sims brings the quietness to the team. [Barret Robbins] sometimes brings knowledge, and Mo and I bring the 'physicalness' to the game."[4]

With a setup like they currently have, the offensive line has every reason to be successful.

Heck, one day they might even block out the sun.

RUNNING IN THE RAIN

It was a fitting end to an amazing regular season.

In a game as wacky as the American dream amid a rivalry as old as Kennedy-Nixon, the Oakland Raiders met the Kansas City Chiefs on an unusual day (Saturday) and unique time (2 P.M.). What followed in the 24–0 shutout was an extraordinary spectacle in both process and result.

For Oakland, the game presented a marvelous opportunity: the best record in the AFC. For Kansas City, the contest posed an enticing possibility: win, they might rise to the plateau of 9–7 wild card;

lose, they would doubtless fall on the trash heap of 8–8 ignominy. Raider fans who remember 1999 (the last 8-win, 8-loss season for the Silver and Black) can relate.

When the game was over and the Chiefs closed their eyes to sleep, their thoughts did not conjure visions of sugar plums and eggnog. Instead, they saw Oakland Raiders galore, more Raiders than orcs at Helm's Deep, more Oakland nemeses than return gift-shopping sycophants on December 26. And the Silver and Black hordes were all doing the same thing.

Running in the rain.

And, oh, how it rained. John Steinbeck was right. It rained an abundance. It rained a cataclysm. It rained an avalanche. The rain began falling with serious intensity about 12:30 P.M. on Saturday and it never stopped. It rained constantly, forcefully, inevitably. It rained straight down, straight up, diagonally, and sideways. The one foot of precipitation that fell on Hegenberger Boulevard in the two weeks preceding this game strongly implies that El Niño is simply a Hispanic term for "The Pirate."

The field was a swamp, a bog, a marsh. Parts of the surface more closely resembled a wading pool or catch basin than a place for athletic competition. It was so bad that Al Davis need not have turned on the sprinklers the day before.

The rain was relentless, unyielding and immovable. And the Raider response? "We went to the bad weather plan," quarterback Rich Gannon said.[5] Offensive coordinator Marc Trestman said that the Raiders began making rain-day revisions to the game plan on Friday night. "We wanted to see how the game went early, and we were going to adjust."[6] Oakland was ready through and through for the contingencies of the skies above. "I was certainly excited about it, because we knew the game was going to be in our hands," said center Barret Robbins.[7] Through the mud, through the slop, through it all—matching step for step what nature offered drop for drop—there was the Oakland Raider rushing game.

The game ball undeniably goes to the offensive line. "The offensive line was just phenomenal," Rich Gannon said. "It was their type of game."[8] "The credit goes to the guys up front," offered Tyrone Wheatley. "My guys were happier than pigs in mud."[9] Coach Bill Callahan, who mentored the behemoths as offensive line coach, echoed the sentiment. "This was a classic mudder, and our linemen really enjoyed it," Callahan said. "To finish the game in this style, and run the ball effectively in the conditions we faced, was a classic December outing."[10] "This is what you pray for," said guard Frank Middleton, referring to knocking opponents around in inclement surroundings. "That's when it gets fun. It's one of those things, where they've got to go straight and we've got to go straight, and whoever has the most power wins."

Then Middleton added, "I'm going home and praying for rain throughout the playoffs."[11]

What a difference nine weeks makes.

In the ill-fated 20–10 loss in Kansas City October 27, the Raider rushing game was extremely one-dimensional. Four reverses for nineteen yards, two Gannon scrambles for sixteen more, one Crockett plunge for a single yard, and the other ten were Garner runs for 47 yards. The Raiders never ran two rushing plays consecutively. What was most disturbing was that one hundred percent of Charlie's runs were up the middle.

Things were vastly different in Saturday's slip n' slide torrent of revenge. Oakland ran more running plays than passes for only the third time this season. Sixty rushes for 280 yards? It used to be sixty passes. In Callahan's view, "Our running backs-by-committee, they ran the ball physically. Garner had some darting runs, Wheatley came in there and had some violent runs and Zack Crockett came in and had some finishing runs."[12] Such prodigious production deserves closer examination by reviewing the performances of The Three Rapscallions:

Charlie Garner (29 rushes, 135 yards): Taking the handoff at the 10, Garner hits a hole up the middle big enough to drive a space shuttle through, slams into the safety head-on at the four going full blast and drives to the one. On the next play, Garner scores the game's first TD.

At the 21, Garner hits a huge hole up the middle, adjusts left while guard Frank Middleton takes out two defenders by himself, jukes those little quick steps in rapid succession while continuing up field to the 34—first down. "I pride myself on being able to run in any conditions," said Garner.

At the 45, Garner takes the hand-off up the middle, gets to the line of scrimmage, completely stops, leaves DE Dwayne Clemons grasping for air like Democrats searching for original ideas, then races straight downfield for ten more yards.

"Under normal conditions he is quicker than anybody in the National Football League," Barret Robbins said. "He can move so well it enables us to hold our blocks longer." Tackle Barry Sims agreed. "He is just so elusive and so quick, and he's a punisher," Sims said. "That makes him a great player."[13]

"He can catch, he can run, he can block—he can do anything we ask him to do," Middleton said of Garner.[14]

Garner rushes: 13 up the middle; 2 left end; 1 left side; 3 right end; 10 right side.

Tyrone Wheatley (17 rushes, 69 yards): "There were big holes, and it was a pleasure to run through them," said Wheatley.[15] From the 47, Wheatley takes the hand-off up the middle, begins to shed tacklers just past the line, then drags the remaining defenders like the winner in a tractor pulling contest. Eight-yard gain on first down.

At the 25, Wheatley is stopped behind the line of scrimmage, bolts left and breaks a tackle, then bulls forward for five yards.

Wheatley rushes: 9 up the middle; 1 left end; 2 left side; 1 right end; 4 right side.

Zack Crockett (11 rushes, 72 yards): "We had the cutback lanes, the holes just opened up and once you have open field it's off to the races."[16] With eight minutes left in the game and the ball at the Raider 30, Crockett goes into the middle at full speed, hits a corner and safety, performs a lumbering spin and heads toward the right sideline for a 33-yard gain. "It felt good, just to get out in the open field and put on a burst of speed."[17] Play of the Game. After going out of bounds, Crockett rushes to the sideline to breathe deeply from the oxygen machine.

From the eight-yard line, Crockett performs exactly the same play, meeting the same corner and safety at the 6, performs an identical lumbering spin and races into the end zone with the Raiders' final score.

Crockett rushes: 11 up the middle.

As they exited the stadium, Oakland fans were beside themselves with joy. The past now forgotten, feeling no pain. What a glorious feeling, they're happy again. Yelling out loud, dismissing the clouds. Still dampened and cold, the sun in their soul. Though darkened above, it's all about love. Each in the place has a smile on their face. In their mind, one refrain:

The Raiders are running.

Just running in the rain.

REFERENCES

1. "A Force to be Reckoned With"; Erin Leigh O'Brien; Raider Newsroom; Official Web Site of the Oakland Raiders; September 23, 2002.

2. ibid.

3. "Raiders' Goal: March Through December"; Monte Poole; *Oakland Tribune*; December 1, 2002.

4. "Let's Be Frank"; Frank Middleton; Raider Newsroom; Official Web Site of the Oakland Raiders; December 12, 2002.

5. "Raider Running Jells in Rain"; David Bush; *San Francisco Chronicle*; December 29, 2002.

6. "In the Rain, Raiders Go Retro to Run All Over Chiefs"; Art Spander; *Oakland Tribune*; December 29, 2002.

7. "Raiders' Supporting Cast Takes Over Starring Role"; Monte Poole; *Oakland Tribune*; December 29, 2002.

8. "Home-Field Edge Goes to Oakland"; Nancy Gay; *San Francisco Chronicle*; December 29, 2002.

9. Bush, op. cit.

10. "Rompin' in the Rain"; Jerry McDonald; *Oakland Tribune;* December 29, 2002.

11. "Unheralded, Slop-Loving O-Line is Best in the NFL"; Gwen Knapp; *San Francisco Chronicle;* December 29, 2002.

12. Poole, op. cit.

13. Bush, op. cit.

14. Poole, op. cit.

15. Bush, op. cit.

16. "James' Play Solidifies Secondary"; Jerry McDonald; *Oakland Tribune;* December 29, 2002.

17. Bush, op. cit.

CHAPTER EIGHT

2002 Playoffs

WEEK 18
First-Round Bye
January 5, 2003

It is the second season, the long-awaited incentive gift awarded to an Oakland team that showed up for all of its games, winning 69% of them. Keeping in mind that none of what came before matters if the Raiders don't advance—recognizing that nothing is worse than a first-round playoff loss—how successful was this year's AFC West crowning effort? How does one gauge the regular season's performance of a team with a freshman coach, a myriad of new defensive players and a multitude of fans as dysfunctional as they are loyal? Perhaps we can be permitted to refer to one writer's pre-season article that spoke of attitude, efficiency and competitive solidarity as criteria for evaluation.[1]

Attitude: Highs and lows in this regard. The Raider defense had the proper attitude. Rod Woodson, Sam Adams, and Bill Romanowski all said things during the four-game losing streak that were severe without blaming anyone. When he was introduced as a Raider, Romanowski said: "To me, defense is about attitude and desire. It's about flying around and putting your helmet on somebody, OK? And if you're afraid to do that, you don't belong out on the field."[2]

The offense did not fare as well during the four weeks from hell. First, Charlie Garner spoke out about "touches" following the St. Louis loss.[3] Then Tim Brown was attributed the philosophy of "I got mine" after the Kansas City loss.[4] Rich Gannon insisted the whole issue of football distribution was media-driven.[5] As a Raider fan for twenty-six years, I don't ever remember hearing the term "touches" until recently. I find the term a bit swishy, and it's my hunch that it was introduced here like a virus by a 49er fan from across the Bay. Raider players make tackles, blocks, interceptions, rushes, grabs, catches, first downs, and field goals; they don't make touches. From here on out, anyone using the term 'touches' will be sent directly to the office where they will have to answer to Run Run Jones.

On a positive note, the best comment on attitude was provided by an offensive lineman. "We are old," 31-year-old tackle Lincoln Kennedy said. "But we find a way to play with youth on game day."[6]

Efficiency: The statistics on 2002 Raider efficiency have been banged on an amount equal to Led Zeppelin's Jon Bonham's drums and more times than Ken Stabler took it to Wonderful Wanda. Concerning wins, this year's Raider team (11–5) did better than last year's AFC West winner (10–6) but not as well as the year before (12–4). Using an arbitrary number of six points difference in scoring to signify a close game, Oakland had seven close games (four wins, three losses) in 2000, six close games (two wins, four losses) in 2001, and four close games (one win, three losses) in 2002. The average point differential in games was: 13.3 points (2000); 7.5 (2001); and 14.8 points (2002). It would seem that, while this year's Raider team has a greater likelihood to lose the close games, they are also more likely to win the games they should by a greater margin.

Competitive Solidarity: To their credit, when Oakland was in the throes of the four-game losing streak, they never turned on each other. Instead, for the most part they talked of coming together and getting on the same page and not pointing fingers. Bill Romanowski took heat for the late Kansas City touchdown in October even though it was rookie Napoleon Harris who missed the assignment. "Every week is a challenge for us," Rich Gannon said. "That's just the way it has always been. But we are a very competitive team, and we are going to be in every game with a chance to win it."[7] John Parrella expressed it most succinctly: "It's when you win that you feel good. That's what's good about being here, an opportunity to win every week."[8]

Regardless of whom the Raiders play, it is the playoff season. Now is the time to answer the door when opportunity knocks.

OPPORTUNITY KNOCKS

If once it be neglected, ten to one
We shall not find like opportunity.
—WILLIAM SHAKESPEARE, *HENRY VI*, PART ONE[9]

You are in the kitchen—doing the dishes or putzing around, scuffling your slippers on the floor as you walk—when you hear a sound coming from the other room. Your teenage daughter is sitting in front of the TV or computer monitor, and she yells out to no one in particular, "Someone's at the do-oo-r." Like she has now done her part.

You walk past her thinking: once you were the hopeful gleam in my eye, now you are the loving bane of my existence. You get to the door and look out the peephole. An old man is standing there. He looks vaguely familiar—as if you'd seen him before, but can't quite place him. Then you unlock the doorknob, release the dead bolt, slide back the surface bolt, detach the chain guard, and unhinge the balled arm. You open the door and greet the man standing there. "Yeah, wadda ya want?"

He smiles broadly and replies, "Sir, people call me Mr. Opportunity, and do I have a deal for you."

You turn your head and yell out to your spouse: "Honey. Opportunity's here!"

Opportunity—with a first round bye and home field advantage—is what the Oakland Raiders have in the current playoffs. But what is opportunity? And what makes the current Oakland team more likely than seven Raider playoff predecessors to profit by it?

We do not really understand opportunity's amorphous nature, so we speak of what we do with it instead. We make the most of opportunity, we take advantage of it. For Raider fans, that means if we mistakenly receive two checks from an insurance company, we cash them both. And the 2002 Oakland Raiders have taken this same approach all season.

Much is made of the turnover (takeaway/giveaway) ratio in pro football. In this category, the Raiders are a takeaway +12. They were +7 in their first four wins, −3 during the four-game hiatus from victory, and +8 over their last eight games.

Each takeaway stops an opponent's drive, but I would argue that it is what a team does AFTER the turnover that counts. And it is in the POT (points off turnover) ratio that Oakland excels, scoring 114 of their 450 points (24%) after defensively taking the football away.

Pittsburgh: 2nd quarter fumble recovered by Rod Woodson;
Oakland 17, Pittsburgh 7.
4th quarter fumble recovered by Rod Woodson;

Drive: 7 plays, 2:56; 45-yard field goal;
Oakland 30, Pittsburgh 17.

Tennessee: 1st quarter interception by Rod Woodson;
Drive: 1 play, 0:17; Charlie Garner 17-yard reception;
Oakland 7, Tennessee 0.

3rd quarter interception by Rod Woodson;
Drive: same play, 0:16; Rod Woodson 82-yard TD
return;
Oakland 38, Tennessee 7.

"When I came here from Pennsylvania, it was to win football games," Woodson said. "If I don't get any more turnovers in the rest of our games and we still win, I'm the happiest guy in the world."[10]

4th quarter interception by Phillip Buchanon;
Drive: 3 plays, 1:08; Tim Brown 41-yard TD
reception;
Oakland 52, Tennessee 25.

Buffalo: 3rd quarter interception by Tory James;
Drive: 4 plays, 2:12; Zack Crockett 1-yard TD run;
Oakland 28, Buffalo 24.

4th quarter interception by Phillip Buchanon;
Drive: same play, 0:16; Phillip Buchanon 81-yard TD
   return;
Oakland 42, Buffalo 31.

"I didn't think I was going to get it after I let one get away on the play," said Buchanon. "But he came right back to me."[11]

San Fran: 1st quarter fumble recovered by Charles Woodson;
Drive: 5 plays, 2:30; Jerry Porter 1-yard TD
   reception;
Oakland 7, San Francisco 0.

Denver: 1st quarter interception by Rod Woodson;
Drive: same play, 0:20; Rod Woodson 98-yard TD
   return;
Oakland 10, Denver 0.

"I don't think he ever saw me," Woodson said. "I looked the other way for half a second and he just threw it. I was glad it wasn't 101 yards. It's hard to play at this altitude—I was pretty gassed."[12]

New Engl.:   2nd quarter fumble recovered by Trace Armstrong
Drive: 2 plays, 0:44; Rich Gannon 2-yard TD run;
Oakland 17, New England 6.

"We had a lot of guys play well," said Armstrong. The defensive backs had great coverage. The linebackers were outstanding. And that was the best pressure we've had all year."[13]

Arizona: 1st quarter fumble recovered by DeLawrence Grant;
Drive: 6 plays, 2:49; Jerry Porter 7-yard TD
   reception;
Oakland 7, Arizona 0.

"He has cat-quick leverage where he can come out and strike and he can get off blocks well," Coach Callahan said of Grant. "The other thing I've seen is his uncanny ability to come up the field and secure the pocket and contain the quarterback on the bootleg or the naked bootleg or even the reverse."[14]

> 1st quarter interception by Eric Barton;
> Drive: 3 plays, 1:12; Charlie Garner 8-yard TD run;
> Oakland 14, Arizona 0.

NY Jets: 3rd quarter fumble recovered by Adam Treu;
Drive: 4 plays, 2:03; Zack Crockett 1-yard TD run;
Oakland 20, New York Jets 10.

"I got there kind of late and saw it popping around and fell into the pile, " Treu said. "I actually was able to get it away from one of their guys, I don't know who it was. He had it underneath him and my arms were on it, too. I was able to pull and roll my body toward him and pry him away from it."[15]

San Diego: 2nd quarter interception by Rod Woodson;
Drive: 10 plays, 1:50; 20-yard field goal;
Oakland 13, San Diego 7.

"I've had some good teachers who've taught me to understand the fundamentals of the game," said Woodson. "How to take angles, how to read patterns, and how to play within the system. That lets you make up for the inevitable in life. Everybody gets older."[16]

> 3rd quarter interception by Tory James;
> Drive: 8 plays, 5:02; Zack Crockett 1-yard TD run;
> Oakland 20, San Diego 7.

"It felt like it was broken," James said. "They asked me if I wanted to get a shot. I knew this was a real big game. I didn't want to let my teammates down so I got the shot and came out and was able to play on it."[17]

Miami: 1st quarter fumble recovered by Anthony Dorsett;
Drive: 6 plays, 2:35; 26-yard field goal;
Oakland 3, Miami 3.

Denver: 1st quarter interception by Trace Armstrong;
Drive: 8 plays, 4:13; Rich Gannon 3-yard TD run;
Oakland 14, Denver 0.

Kansas City: 2nd quarter interception by Rod Woodson;
Drive: 14 plays, 6:42; Doug Jolley 15-yard TD
reception;
Oakland 14, Kansas City 0.

"I got a little excited on the first one," Woodson said, referring to an earlier missed pick. "The second one, I was very cool—thinking about putting the fingers together, all the fundamentals of catching the football."[18]

Of the eighteen opponent turnovers (7 fumble recoveries, 11 INTs) resulting in Oakland points, fifteen were turned into touchdowns. Clearly, the 2002 Raiders feel the two swords on their team insignia stand for "takeaway and score."

What sets this Raider team apart from its seven playoff predecessors is necessity. Something happened last year that changed the Silver and Black. It is not talked about among the athletes in any outward fashion. Rather, each player that participated in that disappointing season carries with him an internal wound that was not allowed to bleed freely and heal. For a year, it has festered and lingered. It is like an itch that cannot be scratched, a void that will not be filled. Good food does not satiate; great sex cannot alleviate. Only victory will suffice.

For Oakland fans, we have adjusted well to the double-edged sword of home field and wait. In the breach, we do the little things to feel better. If the car door is not quite shut after being locked, we give it a shoulder to finish the job. If the door to our home is stuck and our arms are full, we kick it open with the ball of our foot. As we remain in abeyance, we hold to the things we know:

We know who the NFL's most valuable player is;

We know who the team's most valuable player is;

We know who the coach of the year is;

We know who the defensive player of the year is;

We know who we play this week.

Raider fans think of this and a million other things, until we are interrupted by something or someone.

Wait.

Did you hear that?

Someone's at the door.

It's Opportunity knocking.

REFERENCES

1. "Raiders Provide Answers at Last"; Carl Steward; *Oakland Tribune*; September 8, 2002.

2. "New Raider Romo Ready to Rumble"; Carl Steward; *Oakland Tribune*; February 28, 2002.

3. "Injured Garner Would Feel Better With More 'Touches'"; Nancy Gay; *San Francisco Chronicle*; October 18, 2002.

4. "Losing Puts Star Players at Odds"; David Steele; *San Francisco Chronicle*; October 28, 2002.

5. "A Victory . . . or Else"; Bill Soliday; *Oakland Tribune*; November 3, 2002.

6. "Raider Old and Young Dogs Energize Coliseum in Romp"; Monte Poole; *Oakland Tribune*; September 30, 2002.

7. "Raiders' Glass Half Empty"; Bill Soliday; *Oakland Tribune*; November 6, 2002.

8. "Parrella Loves Being in Trenches with Raiders"; Dave Newhouse; *Oakland Tribune*; August 8, 2002.

9. *Henry VI*, Part One; William Shakespeare; *The Complete Works: The Edition of The Shakespeare Head Press*; New York: Friedman/Fairfax Publishers; 1994.

10. "Rice, Woodson Keep Rewriting Record Book"; Jerry McDonald; *Oakland Tribune*; September 30, 2002.

11. "Alone at the Top"; Michael Wagaman; *Silver & Black Illustrated;* Vol. 14, #8; October 13, 2002.

12. "Veterans Day"; Michael Wagaman; *Silver & Black Illustrated;* Vol. 14, #13; November 17, 2002.

13. "Defense Tightens its Grip"; David Bush; *San Francisco Chronicle;* November 18, 2002.

14. "Drawing the Line"; Michael Wagaman; *Silver & Black Illustrated;* Vol. 14, #18; December 22, 2002.

15. "Center Treu Stays Loyal to Raiders"; David Bush; *San Francisco Chronicle;* December 6, 2002.

16. "Consistency, Longevity Define Woodson"; Dave Newhouse; *Oakland Tribune;* November 27, 2002.

17. "Suspect Secondary Stifles Chargers"; Jerry McDonald; *Oakland Tribune;* December 9, 2002.

18. "Jelling Defense Drives Historic Shutout of Chiefs"; Carl Steward; *Oakland Tribune;* December 29, 2002.

WEEK 19
New York Jets at Oakland
January 12, 2003

Familiarity breeds contempt. How accurate that is.
The reason we hold truth in such respect is because we
have so little opportunity to get familiar with it.

—MARK TWAIN (1835–1910)[1]

The great thing about contempt is that it doesn't have to be accurate; it just has to be heart-felt. Through a quirk of franchise-history and scheduling, the New York Jet visit Oakland's "House of Thrills" for the fourth time in two years. These visits come after a 29-year absence dating back to the nostalgic time (1972) when mini-skirts were still in fashion, napalm was a mainstay of the U.S. arsenal, and the U.N. Secretary General, Kurt Waldheim, still had amnesia about his sordid past serving in the German Army during World War II. The Jets were, as one Raider said, like a division foe that you never played at their park.

Today, the blue-collar Oakland Raiders feel they are being dismissed by the glam-rock New York press. Responding to the stated misconception that the New York Jets are the NFL's hottest team, the Raiders' Tim Brown fired the first salvo across the Jets' bow when he correctly assessed:

> That's funny, because we went 7–1 in the last eight games of the
> year. I think they went 6–2. No one's giving us credit for what we did,
> but that's fine. We want to be the underdogs. We want people to
> think these old guys can't get it done. We feel as if we're a very good
> team, and if we go out and play the type of football we're capable
> of playing, we should win the game.[2]

Oh, the Oakland Raiders are going to do more than just win this playoff game.

Upon reading that Jets quarterback Chad Pennington is being compared to last season's poster child, Tom Brady, and "hailed as the spiritual leader of a team on the rise," Raider fans' reaction is predictable.[3] *Oh yeah? Spiritual leader, huh? Hallelujah brother. How about we introduce you to our Apostles of Pain, Mr. Fist and Mr. Pummel. Eric Barton wants to twist your head like it's an apple on a stem, and then Rod Coleman's going to run you down. And don't' forget: we've got a pretty good quarterback on our team, too.*

The Jets' acolytes in the New York press don't know who they're messing with here.

Then there is Josh Evans, the loud-mouthed defensive end who—after the 26–20 Oakland win on December 2, charged Raider players with dirty tactics: "Dirty hits to the knees, the s—they were doing was uncalled for," he complained, pointing the finger squarely at guards Frank Middleton and Mo Collins. "They aren't too athletic. They're not athletic at all, so they have to do something like that, those cheap shots, just to try to get under your skin."[4]

I'm telling. He said a bad word.

We can go on and on about the East Coast slights, but the plain reality of the matter is this: the New York Jets are a formidable opponent who—when Sunday arrives—will become familiar with truth, Oakland Raiders style. That means quarterback pressures, a stout front four, a suffocating secondary, minus takeaways, a quarterback rating hovering around the average male life span, an offensive yardage disparity, and a flight home where the only football talk is complaints about being so far down in about next year's draft order.

Respect that.

FULL STRIDE

It is said that, in the beginning, there was light.

But for Raider fans watching the 2002 Divisional Playoff, there is a new saying.

In the beginning, there was the pump fake.

And after the pump fake came the vertical launch, the oblong leather spiraling mysteriously on its own trajectory some thirty yards downfield while the faithful held their breath. As it descended, a

Silver and Black streak was seen galloping toward its re-entry point. At the proper moment, No. 84 extended his arms and gathered in the present as gently as if it were the Baby Al himself. Play of the Game.

No. 84 caught it in his hands. He caught it in-bounds.

And he caught it in full stride.

The Oakland Raiders are in full stride after advancing to the AFC Championship game by defeating the New York Jets 30–10 Sunday in Oaktown. Surviving a hideous second-quarter collapse, Oakland returned from the tunnel a team transformed—tormenting and predatory on defense, opportunistic and focused on offense.

Nowhere was this authority more apparent than during a twelve-minute span in the third and fourth quarters. It started with 5:00 left in the third, when the Jets' Santana Moss, out-positioned by Charles Woodson, stood up and made no attempt to go for the pass to his left. Why is it that large men put on pads and helmets, and then whine because referees are not calling fouls like it's a basketball game? As Woodson commented in his post-game interview, "The game is played on Sunday. . . . I have no respect for somebody that talks during the week and then don't come out to show up for the game."[5]

The correct call was made: no pass interference was charged.

Next play, on third-and-8 from the Jets 21, QB Chad Pennington (hailed in New York as the next Joe Montana) lofted a well-intentioned air ball downfield to the left sideline. There, at the Raiders' 45, cornerback Tory James made a spectacular interception after the Jets' Laveranues Coles gave up on the ball. Perfectly positioned on the outside and ahead of Coles, No. 20 made a leaping grab over his right shoulder, then two-stepped the sidelines in a fashion that would have made Mr. Bojangles proud. The interception was as pretty as typical ESPN analysis is stupid.

Oakland wasted no time cashing the Jets' seized money order. After a fifteen-yard completion to Brown, Gannon lofted the aforementioned manna-from-heaven strike to the Raiders' No. 3 receiver. Speaking after the game, Jerry Porter described the play:

The touchdown pass was a cover-2 and I was just supposed to out-side release. Aaron Beasley was giving me a little problem trying to get outside him and he was trying to make a play on Charlie Garner releasing in the flats. And Damien Robinson is supposed to get over the top. And he was responsible for that half of the field and he didn't get there in time. And Rich stuck the ball on me.[6]

Rich Gannon stuck a ball on a lot of receivers in the first ten min-utes of the second half. After completing just 6 of 10 passes for less than a C-note of yardage, "Gannihan" was 11 of 15 and 115 yards. "Well, I tried to take a page after watching Chad Pennington play," deadpanned Gannon, "and do the stuff he was doing."[7]

Suddenly, 36-seconds under the five-minute mark, Oakland had the lead back 17–10—a lead they would never relinquish.

After the Raiders' prevent squib kick was returned to their own 35, the Jets went to work in a deliberate, albeit confused, fashion. After losing a coach's challenge on a juggled sideline reception, the green-and-white got going thanks to an unnecessary roughness call after Pennington was sacked on third down. Pennington then exe-cuted a nifty shovel pass as John Parrella was about to rip the last three letters from his jersey. The Jets got lucky again, fumbling a double-reverse out of bounds after a 7-yard gain. Pennington (who played at times like he was wearing Don Quixote's washbasin for a helmet and looking out through the drain hole) then overthrew a wide-open receiver, and Curtis Martin was stuffed for a no-gain on third-and-3. Finally, Pennington overthrew a harmless out-pass to a slipping Wayne Chrebet on fourth-and-2 from the Oakland 35. "He was rattled," said Oakland defensive end DeLawrence Grant. "We put some good licks on him."[8] Result: Raiders' ball with 1:20 remain-ing in the third quarter.

On the next play, Gannon stuck the ball on Porter for his longest reception in an outstanding 57-catch season. With Garner in motion to the left, Gannon faded back and pump-faked right to Jerry Rice, then rifled a pass in the left seam to Porter, who basket-caught it at the Jets' 40. Porter raced to the middle of the field before he was brought down at the Jets' fifteen-yard line. Said Porter: "Rich pumped to Jerry on the outside and got the safeties' attention and that just opened up the seam for me."9 The completion gave him six catches for 123 yards on the day.

Three plays later (two plays into the fourth quarter), Gannon found Rice in the back of the end zone with a nine-yard TD pass and it was 24–10.

New York still had over 14 minutes on the clock, plenty of time to mount a comeback. They proceeded to commit their third turnover when Richie Anderson dropped the handoff and Bill Romanowski recovered the football. "We beat up that team today," linebacker Bill Romanowski said. "We played harder, more physical football than they did."10 Rising from the pile, No. 53 ran straight into the Black Hole and tossed the trophy gently into the first row. With that toss, Romanowski took another step on his pilgrimage toward becoming a Raider. He will complete his journey when he walks from the field a champion on January 26.

Surprisingly, on the first play following the cough-up, Gannon's ill-advised pass to Rice at the midfield right sideline was picked off by the Jets' Damien Robinson. The Raiders' Eric Barton quickly returned the favor when he stepped into a misdirected Pennington sideline throw at the Raider 38. Charlie Garner immediately ripped off 16 yards to the Jets' 46 on the first play following the turnover. Two plays later, Tyrone Wheatley high-stepped through a nice Jon Ritchie hole and pounded his way for a 25-yard gain to the Jets' eighteen-yard line. Charlie Garner then put a rare fumble on the turf but astutely retrieved his own error. Sebastian Janikowski's 34-yard field goal at 7:55 of the fourth quarter put the Raiders ahead 27–10.

In twelve minutes, Oakland had gone from a deadlocked 10–10 tie to a comfortable 27–10 lead.

So now it is Tennessee, all guts looking for the glory, coming to town. The Oakland Raiders know about guts, and they know the lesson of glory. They know discipline and they know the danger of letdowns. And they will somehow get through this week. As Tim Brown (three catches, 52 yards) said, "The hard part of these games is Monday through Saturdays, because you have to deal so much with the media and people talking."[11]

And Raider fans have a lot to talk about. About how Anthony Dorsett laid down Curtis Martin. About how ESPN post-game talked about the Miami Dolphins' "window of opportunity." And we'll talk about the decisive twelve minutes. That's the time it takes to vacuum a rug, get through a Costco checkout line or pick the hair out of your comb. Raider fans are feeling pretty good these days. The music sounds a little sweeter; the air smells a little cleaner. Any mishaps that may occur this week, we'll just take them in stride.

Full stride.

REFERENCES

1. www.brainyquote.com
2. "Raiders Host Familiar Foe Sunday: Jets"; Jerry McDonald; *Oakland Tribune*; January 6, 2003.
3. "Oakland Should Be Wary of Jets' Daring QB"; Monte Poole; *Oakland Tribune*; January 6, 2003.
4. "Raiders Keep Rolling"; Nancy Gay; *San Francisco Chronicle*; December 3, 2002.
5. Charles Woodson, post-game news conference, ESPN, January 13, 2003.
6. Jerry Porter, post-game news conference, ESPN, January 13, 2003.
7. "Big Pain, Big Gain"; Nancy Gay; *San Francisco Chronicle*; January 13, 2003.
8. "'Next Montana' Pales next to Reigning MVP"; Dave Newhouse; *Oakland Tribune*; January 13, 2003.
9. "Porter's Big Game Outshines Big Names"; David Bush; *San Francisco Chronicle*; January 13, 2003.
10. "Raiders Made Their Points on the Field"; Dave Newhouse; *Oakland Tribune*; January 13, 2003.
11. Tim Brown, post-game news conference, ESPN, January 13, 2003.

WEEK 20
Tennessee at Oakland
January 19, 2003

It is an adage as old as Wayne Newton's hair, as ancient as the world's oldest profession—and followed by the Raiders just as religiously. Run run pass. Run the football to set up the pass. In 1976, the first of two fateful AFC Championships won at home, the percentage of run versus pass for the season was 61%–39%. In 1980, it was 55%–45% and, in 1983, the breakdown was 52%–48%. You could take it to the bank: if the Raiders were going to host playoff football in January, they were going to run to get there.

Until this year.

In a reversal as surprising as it was effective, the Oakland Raiders this season eschewed the run for the pass. Gone were the days of run left, run first, run second. In its place was a playbook featuring a cast of seven receivers, five linemen, and one very productive quarterback. As the season began, new head coach Bill Callahan and offensive coordinator Marc Trestman, concerned that the running game fell from No. 1 in 2000 to No. 24 in 2001, decided to stretch the field through the pass in order to open up the running game.[1] Then, after running the football 57% in an Opening Day win against Seattle, a funny thing happened on the way to the huddle: they fell in love with the pass.

And I don't mean puppy love, either. This was the fervently wild, think-about-you-every-play kind of love. Against Pittsburgh, running plays accounted for 20% of the total; against Tennessee, rushes were 34%; and versus Buffalo, the disparity was 59%–41%. As long as the Raiders were winning, who was to argue with success? The rhetoric certainly was all plum pudding and goodness. "Ideally, at the end of the game you don't want to have a ratio of 80 percent passing and 20 percent running, something that unequal," said running back Randy Jordan. "Maybe 60–40, run or pass."[2] Coach Callahan predicted: "As time moves on, (the passing) will run its course, and defenses will catch up to the no-back attack, and you'll have to have another plan to trump what you're seeing." In Rich Gannon's view, "It's still a big goal of ours to be a balanced football team whether it's against Buffalo or when we get back home."[3]

Then came the St. Louis game, where the defense played a 4-1-6 to force the short pass and converged to tackle the receiver short of the first down. The resultant three-game loss streak saw the running game never crawl out of the 20% range; incredibly, from Pittsburgh through Kansas City, pass attempts accounted for 73% of total plays. Then came the San Francisco debacle, when 21 rushes equaled 42% of total plays and helped contribute to the lowest offensive output of the season. "You can see where that got us," observed Callahan dryly. "It just wasn't our type of game today offensively," added Gannon.[4]

The Raiders' type of game was shown in obvious fashion against the Denver Broncos, when Gannon threw at everything but the rearing mascot in the sky and the ball never hit the ground. According to Coach Callahan:

> We wanted balance. We went into yesterday's game wanting to run the ball. Every game that we play takes on a different set of circumstances. We felt very good about the plan. We had a good mix in our first 15 of run and pass, and when you start getting some no-huddle and you feel a rhythm and you start to become successful with it, you stay with the flow of the game.[5]

Balance between the run and pass did return—in a fashion—for the following four games, all wins. During the New England-San Diego stretch, running plays were 42% of total plays. Then, after the Miami non-ground game (25%), the running game season broke out as it began—in the majority: 54% against Denver and 80% versus the Chiefs in the rain. Over the entire regular season the pass-run split was 61%–39%.

Why the change in Raider philosophy? The biggest factor has to be the quarterback himself: Rich Gannon is like a computer who plays with passion and delivers in spades. In Coach Callahan's words,

"He's responsible for all the switches in the offense, all the audibles—and that can mean four or five checks on a given play depending on the defense. The volume is incredible. Right now we have the most extensive package we've had since I've been here, and he loves it. He wants more."[6] The other factor is the head coach. After stating flatly, "I don't get hung up on not running the ball," Coach Callahan acknowledged that the Raiders were "getting more first and 10 plays that are better than some of the runs that you could possibly get because we spread the field."[7]

Sunday, the Oakland Raiders seek to even their record hosting the AFL/AFC Championship at 3–3. What game plan will they employ in search of the valued trophy? In the eight games in which Oakland ran on at least 40% of their plays, they were 7–1. My best guess would be that the Raiders will come out spreading the field via the passing game, then shift to the run and control the clock while keeping the defense on the field.

But if you asked me to make a prediction, I'd pass.

Pass pass run.

BOTH SIDES NOW

It is an amazing organ, the human heart. It is arguably the most important piece of anatomy in a Raider fan's body—more so than the brain or mouth—since we possess double-digit IQs and display an innate ADD (Attention Deficit Disorder) penchant for Tourette's Syndrome.

It has been purported that the heart is purportedly capable of physically functioning up to 125 years (Al Davis, for one, believes this to be true). The multi-chambered heart performs its rhythmic function in balance, synchronicity and power. Pro football teams attempt to emulate this three-prong efficiency. Ideally, each football player contributes to the team effort in a whirlwind of action that wears down an opponent. The result is a vortex of activity where each unit—offensive and defensive—performs at its peak.

Both sides now.

Of course, football is a mass of athleticism, emotions, play calling, crowd noise and violence. As the Oakland Raiders 41–24 victory over the Tennessee Titans in the AFC Championship attests, the vortex is seldom achieved in totality. Only striven for. Far too often, there is an either/or dichotomy between offense and defense ruling the field.

- The Raiders' opening drive goes the 69-yard distance; Oakland's defense then gives up an 84-yard Tennessee touchdown drive. 7–7 tie.
- The Silver and Black responds by going 90 yards in seven plays, culminating in Charlie Garner's 12-yard catch and scamper; the Titans then drive 62 yards for a field goal. 14–10 lead.
- Oakland fumbles on their own 40-yard line; the Raiders' defense holds and forces a Tennessee punt. 14–10.
- The Titans score on a 55-yard drive and Oakland punts. 17–14 deficit.

Raider fans were tense and apprehensive. Little did we know, with under two minutes left before halftime, that the Raiders had their sails up, the autumn wind was about to blow, and the full moon would soon declare that the time was indeed right.

It was at this juncture, 1:30 left in the second quarter, that Tennessee's Robert Holcombe decided to engage in commerce. He put the football up on EBAD.

Raider fans already had their fill of Robert Holcombe. A 242-yard regular-season ground gainer on 47 carries, in this game he had eight rushes for 22 yards and had caught a critical nine-yard pass to set up the go-ahead Titan score. On second-and-five from the Tennessee sixteen-yard line, Holcombe took the straight-ahead handoff. Almost immediately, a charging Rod Coleman grabbed him in by the right arm, spinning him around to his right about a three-quarter turn where he was creamed by Eric Barton. Barton poked the ball clear onto the Coliseum grass where Anthony Dorsett fell on it in reverence and good form. In Barton's words: "It was a cutback play, so I just sat back and made the play on the ball and it popped out."[8] Eric Barton (EB) and Anthony Dorsett (AD) were plainly EBAD on this critical turnover. Rod Coleman was just himself.

On the first play following the turnover at the 16, Rich Gannon— 13 completions in 17 attempts after starting out 12 for 12—took a three-step drop, pump-faked to Jerry Porter down the right side and rifled a shot that Jerry Rice took in above his eyeballs while striding over the middle. Andre Dyson was hanging on to Rice, trying to make some sort of play, but Jerry had bigger problems: in three quick steps, he was going to be hit by an oncoming train in the form of Tank Williams.

The resultant jarring, head-on collision stunned and flummoxed Rice, and the football fell limply to the turf, a fumble at the one-yard line. But No. 80 never gave up, never forgot, and never gave in— looking for the ball while on his knees like a blind man casting about for his cane. He located and cradled the ball just before the leaping Williams could snare it.

Said Rice: "He got a good shot on me, and in a situation like that, even if you are seeing stars, you want to jump back on your feet and not let him get the gratification."[9] Jerry Rice may have been forty years old when he fell to the ground, but he was 42 when he arose. Play of the Game.

On the next snap, Gannon faked to Zack Crockett and threw to Doug Jolley for a 21–17 Raider lead.

The subsequent deep kickoff was taken by Tennessee's John Simon, but not for long. Simon coughed up the football when hit by Tim Johnson. The Raiders' Eric Johnson then fell on the pigskin but tried to run with it and kicked the ball out his backside like a rup- tured-duck bowel movement; Alvis Whitted eventually fell safely upon the treasure (like one is supposed to) at the Titans' 39-yard line. "We overloaded the right side," Eric Johnson said of the punt play. "We've been watching a lot of film, and we knew that we could get in there, and it happened. It just seemed like everybody was in there. Said Whitted: "I was just in the right place at the right time."[10]

Two fumble recoveries in 39 seconds in an AFC Championship game. A 43-yard field goal by Sebastian Janikowski completed the ten-point turnaround and Oakland led 24–17 at the break.

TV announcers often label a simple lead change "shift in momentum." Everything is shifting momentum in their eyes. But momentum can only occur when the defense and offense are both firing, when everyone is contributing in a positive manner and turnovers lead to points on the board. This the Raiders have done all year.

So, when Tampa Bay lines up this Sunday against the white jerseys with black numerals on their chests and focus in their eyes, they are not just facing a cohesive unit supported by loyal and rabid fans.

They are looking at a potential vortex.

It was so very apropos that the 2002 AFC Championship was played one year to the day after the 2001 New England-Oakland Snow Bowl (for those of you not aware of the tuck rule, please check your pulse; you're probably in a coma). In that unfathomable ending, the Raiders played well enough to win but did not put the Patriots away. Ahead 13–10 when a referee's ruling nullified the frozen-tundra fumble, Oakland could not recover their composure in regulation time. Tied at 13-all with 25 seconds to go and the Raiders on their own side of the field in a faraway state, Rich Gannon took a voluntary knee.

That was the last snap Gannon took in the 2001 season.

So it was with a great deal of irony and satisfaction that the final play of the AFC Championship was again Gannon (29 of 41, 286 yards, 4 touchdowns) taking a voluntary knee. Only this time, it was done in front of 62,000 roaring Oakland fans and the Raiders ahead by 17 points. It was done after 59 minutes of Raider football attacking both offensively and defensively. That knee retrieved the error of former years and sent the Oakland Raiders to Super Bowl XXXVII.

The win also evened Oakland's AFC Championship record in front of the Coliseum faithful at 3 wins, 3 losses. The last time Oakland won the AFC on holy ground was 1976. Who can forget

George Atkinson and Jack Tatum hugging each other at midfield as the 24–7 victory over Pittsburgh wound down?

A nine-year-old child watching cartoons on that December 1976 morning is today old enough to be president (and could probably do a better job). Mr. Wizard may well have been referencing Oakland's newest AFC Championship trophy when he chanted "Trizzle-trazzle, trizzle-trome. Time for this one to come home."

We know that there are two sides to every story. This aphorism applies to each coin tossed and every argument engaged. We are continually urged to listen to both sides of debate on an issue (unless that issue involves Iraq). We understand that people can talk out of both sides of their mouth—and that is what sports announcers will do ad nauseum in the coming days before the Super Bowl.

Raider fans acknowledge that two is better than one. They watch cheerleaders with both eyes, eat food with both hands, drink liquor with both fists and, occasionally—when the mood strikes—they go both ways.

But when the world championship sun rises above the refurbished Qualcomm junkyard, Raider fans can entertain only one course of action. Their path was decided long ago and, like sub-standard genetics, it's for life.

In like manner, the Oakland Raiders do not get the luxury of choice in Super Bowl XXXVII. They have already looked at the game of football through win and lose; they know which outcome they prefer.

The Silver and Black play with heart. The Raiders won the AFC West this year and they secured first-round bye, home field advantage throughout the playoffs. The team won tough division and championship games by an average of 2+ touchdowns. Barring an undefeated season, they have achieved every goal they set for themselves.

Every goal except one.

So, while millions of viewers settle in front of their television sets and illogically choose sides this Sunday, there is just one strategy for the Oakland Raiders.

Both sides now.

REFERENCES

1. "NFL 2002 Raiders Preview"; Nancy Gay; *San Francisco Chronicle;* September 3, 2002.

2. "Diverse Attack Keeps Opponents—and Raiders—Guessing"; Nancy Gay; *San Francisco Chronicle;* September 29, 2002.

3. "These Two Shall Pass: Raiders, Bills"; Jerry McDonald; *Oakland Tribune;* October 6, 2002.

4. "Home Wreckers"; Bill Soliday; *Oakland Tribune;* November 4, 2002.

5. "Raiders Passed on Running, and It Worked"; David Bush; *San Francisco Chronicle;* November 13, 2002.

6. "Gannon Is A Winner Playing Mind Games"; Jerry McDonald; *Oakland Tribune;* September 28, 2002.

7. "Raiders Not Giving Up Ground Game"; Bill Soliday; *Oakland Tribune;* October 22, 2002.

8. "Special Teams Create Pivotal Plays"; Nancy Gay, David Bush, Ron Kroichick, Kevin Lynch, David Steele; *San Francisco Chronicle;* January 20, 2003.

9. "Rice Shakes Off Big Hit by Titans' Williams" Jerry McDonald; *Oakland Tribune;* January 20, 2003.

10. "Raiders' Special Teams Superb"; Roger Phillips; *Oakland Tribune;* January 20, 2003.

WEEK 21
Oakland vs. Tampa Bay
January 26, 2003

In Super Bowl XVIII, Marcus Allen of the Los Angeles Raiders rushed for what was at the time a Super Bowl record 191 yards. Allen could have easily reached the bicentennial bookmark of 200 yards, but he took himself out so teammate Greg Pruitt—who mostly returned punts and kickoffs for the Raiders—could play some. It was in the fourth quarter, and the Raiders had a 35–9 lead. "I really felt at that time that we'd be returning to many more Super Bowls."[1]

Little did he know: Marcus Allen would never again step onto a Super Bowl playing field as a competitor.

The Super Bowl has been around so long (I couldn't tell you exactly how long because I can't figure out those stupid roman numerals) that there are only eight teams who have never been to a Super Bowl. And of those twenty-four franchises that have visited the last real NFL game of the season, seven have never tasted sweet victory: Minnesota, Philadelphia, Cincinnati, Buffalo, San Diego, Atlanta, and Tennessee. There were some good players on those teams—and some pretty bad ones.

What those players share in common—as do all players who step into the stadium on the designated Sunday in January—is that each of them can make a play to help their team to victory. And, as the seven non-winning team owners can tell you, there is no guarantee that your franchise can make it back. 1983 was the last season the Raiders played in the Super Bowl. In today's world, that's ancient history: the El Salvador civil war was raging; the Iran-Contra affair was just beginning; the Russians shot down KAL Flight 007, 279 passengers killed; a truck bomb hit U.S. Marine headquarters in Beirut, Lebanon, 239 Marines killed; Margaret Thatcher led Great Britain; record budget deficits plagued U.S. fiscal policy; and Ronald Reagan was beginning to show signs of Alzheimer's disease.

Now it is the end of the 2002 football season. Incredibly, it has been nineteen years since the Raiders played this late in January. So long, in fact, that you can't think about the past—only the present and future. "You can't jump out of the present in this league," Tim Brown said. "Because of last year, one thing we've been saying all along is stay with the present . . . stay with today, don't worry about tomorrow. So we can't start thinking about Super Bowls. There's a whole lot of football to be played yet."[2]

The impressive thing about the Super Bowl is that it is the last game of the season, and so everything is magnified at least 250 times. On average, there are approximately 129 plays in a football game. The Super Bowl is thus the culmination of over 726,528 individual efforts of professional football athletes over the season.[3] Over 130 million viewers will watch the game, entire households will give up their Sunday to host friends and families in their homes, New Year's resolutions to diet will officially end on this day, and the game will be viewed in more nations than the U.S. runs a trade deficit against. In an effort of this magnitude, an athlete can make a good play (Ray Guy, SB XVIII), a bad play (Scott Norwood, SB XXV), or make no play at all. It's been nineteen NFL seasons since the Raiders have bussed to the Super Bowl stadium as a team.

There's a whole lot of football to be played yet.

NO FLY ZONE

The 7-year-old girl sat on the carpeted floor, near the stain where she had spilled the red soda pop. She still had not heard the end of it. She was making paper dolls. She would carefully draw the doll first—head, neck, shoulder, arms, torso, and legs. Then she would draw the clothes, color them, and cut them out—making sure they had tabs at the shoulders and sides so they could be attached to the doll. Scissors, paper, and pencil were strewn about her on the carpet.

The girl's mother sat in a Lay-Z-Boy near her, calmly crocheting an afghan in silver and black. No. 9 crochet hook in, grab the yarn, and pull it through. The repetitive motion was relaxing and the eventual accomplishment would be a nice gift.

"Can we go upstairs and listen to Daddy read me the book about the friendly giant?" the little girl asked her mother.

"Not yet," the mother answered. "You know we listen each night just before we go to sleep."

"Okay," the girl answered, with a hint of disappointment.

Suddenly, the girl looked up at the television set and called out in plaintive surprise: "Oh nooo, the white team isn't scoring any points."

Out of the mouths of babes comes wisdom beyond their years. Indeed, the white team wasn't scoring any points. In fact, they weren't doing much of anything. Correct that, the Oakland Raiders did do one thing in Super Bowl XXXVII: they let the game slip through their fingers until there were no more chances left. And, against a good team, when you do that you're going to eventually get pummeled—which is exactly what happened, as Oakland lost to Tampa Bay, 48–21.

The game started well enough for the Silver and Black: an interception of an errant Tampa Bay pass gave Oakland the football at the Buccaneer 36-yard line. A first down, a rush, a scramble, and a sack later, the Raiders made it 3–0 with 10:40 left in the first quarter. Readers might want to go over that last sentence again, because the next 34 points were to be scored by Tampa Bay.

Oh, those chances. In the next eight minutes, the Raider defense would have three separate opportunities to intercept a Brad Johnson pass. The possibilities to shake this yeoman quarterback's confidence were there. The first occasion came after a Buc first down put the ball on their 40. Johnson's pass over the middle was bobbled into the air, where it suspended itself like a fly in a web for just a wink of time before falling to the turf. Tampa Bay then put a pass and run together that gained 56 yards, followed by a 39-yard field goal which tied the game at 3–3.

The Oakland possession that followed lasted 47 seconds: completion for six yards, incompletion, sack. Opportunity number two for the defense presented itself almost immediately after the Raider punt: on second down, Johnson's pass over the middle deflected off the receiver's hands and traveled up and forward through the air for another thirteen yards before finally falling to the ground. Four Raiders were in the area; there was no interception.

When Oakland next got the football, they held onto it slightly over 1:30. That's one minute and thirty seconds. Then Tampa Bay regained possession, and Johnson threw his worst pass thus far, a ruptured duck twenty yards downfield right into the teeth of Oakland's middle. The Raider defender had a bead on it, stepped in front of the receiver, put up his hands and the football caromed off his fingers and fell for an incompletion rather than an interception. The Silver and Black defense could not know: they would never get another chance like the three they had just seen pass them by.

After Oakland got the ball back at midfield due to an outstanding punt return, Tampa Bay made its first interception. The Bucs' offense put together a decent drive resulting in a 39-yard field goal, making the score 6–3. Then the same Buc made another interception when the pump fake worked about as well as any of the "Seinfeld" character spin-offs. When the Silver and Black offense got the ball again, their drive again lasted three plays and 47 seconds. Tampa Bay then took a short field off a good punt return and scored the game's first touchdown to go up 13–3. By this time, Oakland had run 22 plays for 39 yards (1.8 yard average) while Tampa Bay had executed 34 plays for 136 yards (4.0 yard average).

The Raiders did get a first down the next possession before punting. At 2:26, that may have been their longest possession of the day. Tampa Bay took over at their own 22-yard line and—when they marched the length of the field to go up 20–3 at halftime—it was clear that Brad Johnson was now completely in rhythm. At this time, the game was officially on its way to becoming more embarrassing than *City Slickers II*.

But hey, the Raider offense had scored on their first possession in 10 of 16 regular-season games; let's see how they do here after receiving the second half kickoff. First down: a four-yard pass; second down, also a four-yard pass. Then, on the all-important third-and-two in an attempt to build a heartbeat of offense: an out pattern to a receiver who handled fewer passes this season than a Raiderette on game day. The pass was incomplete, and I suddenly had déjà vu: the Raiders tried the same, lame play in Kansas City. That play, also on third-and-two and also to a non-starter, was—as you might guess—also incomplete. It was at this time, as the Raider punting unit came on yet again, that I experienced another intense emotion: hopelessness.

The reason for the hopelessly lopsided loss: Oakland simply ran into the No Fly Zone. Their quarterback was hurried, harried, sacked, and intercepted more times than we remind our children to brush their teeth before they go to bed. Receivers could not get open and, when they did, they dropped passes. The offensive line was overwhelmed by a superior Tampa Bay defense, and the Raider defensive line was embarrassed by an unknown Buccaneer running back. After the debacle—faced with questions for which they had no answers—the Raider players replied to reporters, made excuses, and generally looked as if they would rather be somewhere (anywhere) else—someplace far, far away.

Half a world away, the F-15E Strike Eagle was cruising along in a North-Northwest direction at 25,000 feet, having left the Ali Al Salem air base in Kuwait some twenty minutes earlier. With a speed of 600 miles per hour and the ability to accelerate to twice that speed in a matter of seconds, the two Air Force officers strapped into the cockpit were proud of their $30 million dollar chariot of fire. The weapon systems officer (WSO) in the rear seat spoke through the radio to the pilot seated directly in front.

"Major, how's that book-on-tape you've been making for your little girl?"

"The Big Friendly Giant just blew a dream into Dreamland," answered the pilot. "But Sophie was awake and the BFG heard her heartbeat with his big, floppy ears."

"Kinda like us," interjected the WSO.

"Yeah, kinda. In time, the BFG will protect Sophie from the Big Bad Giant."

"Which one are we?" asked the WSO.

"We're the friendly giant." answered the pilot.

"Yeah, with a bad-ass plane."

Suddenly, a call came over the radio from the AWACS plane circling to the north. *"Raider Leader One, Raider Leader One, this is Mother Hen. I've got the final score."*

Mother Hen's next words were so disturbing and depressing that the pilot was struck silent. The WSO in the rear seat, having suffered through the pilot's non-stop, obsessive rants about a certain type of mystique during the previous several weeks, knew why the pilot had been rendered speechless. The long-suffering WSO simply could not resist his opportunity.

"Whoooeeee!" he hollered. *"48–21. What-a-wipeout. What happened to your team, Major? Where was that so-called mystique?"*

This well-intentioned, jocular goad touched a nerve in the pilot, and he responded in uncharacteristic fashion by pulling rank on his WSO. Harsh words shot out of him like a .50 caliber machine gun.

"You just remember who you are, lieutenant," the pilot ordered. *"You remember where we are, why we're here, and the sacrifices we endure to defend our country."*

He felt bad as soon as he said it. It wasn't the kid's fault that the Silver and Black didn't show up for the biggest game of their lives.

"Yes sir," came the chagrined reply from behind. Then, after a respectful silence, the WSO spoke again—this time in a sincere and deliberate cadence.

"You just tell me the problem you want solved, sir, and I'll do my best to tackle it."

The pilot snorted a laugh. *"Very funny,"* he said.

But the ice was broken. The heck with the Raiders. If they didn't want to be heroes, at least the two of them could conduct themselves admirably in the execution of their mission. Besides, they had bigger problems than a football game right about now.

"Heads up, Wizzo," the pilot spoke. *"32nd parallel's dead ahead."*

Both of them knew what this meant. Though their immediate

environment stayed the same—engines whining in their ears, instrument display lights blinking on and off—the rules had just changed. For the next ninety minutes, they would be a little more aware, a little more intense—and a lot more prepared. They were in hostile territory now.

They had entered the No Fly Zone.

REFERENCES

1. "Dominating Win for L.A."; Helene Elliott; *Los Angeles Times;* January 26, 2003.
2. "49ers Need to Win More Than Raiders"; Carl Steward; *Oakland Tribune;* December 15, 2002.
3. 129 plays X 16 games per Sunday X 16 Sundays X 22 players = 726,528.

CHAPTER NINE

Prologue

PROLOGUE

They're out there. Everybody knows they're out there.

It is Opening Day of the Oakland Raiders home football season. The sun is shining brightly on a perfect September day. A mild breeze caresses the inhabitants of Network Associates Coliseum. Season ticket holders greet each other warmly as they bustle in and take their seats. The excitement is palpable and the confidence brimming. This is the year the Raiders go all the way.

It is any year. Any season. Every season. Every team. And yet there is something unique to the Raiders. Back in the early '60s, before they had played a game—when the American Football League, the first outlaw organization in modern American sports was also a mystery—someone wrote this piece of pre-counterculture graffiti on a warehouse wall in downtown Oakland: "Who are the Oakland Raiders and where are they going?" This could have been said equally then of Bob Dylan, JFK, MLK, or the Univac computer. No one had heard of the Oakland Raiders. Forty-three years later, it has all become clear. We know where the Raiders were going then. We also know why MLK is now a holiday and what fate befell JFK, Stacey Toran, and Bob Chandler. We even know why a coliseum is named after a network security software company. But the real question remains: "Who are we and where are we going?" That is the one inquiry we keep begging to address, or ask the Raiders each year to answer for us—because we are loyal and pretentious and football is generally far simpler and safer than war. Or life.

Amid the affection, anticipation, and heat, the activities roll in one after another like waves of positive energy. First, there is the obligatory moment of silence for those who have died defending our country and in attacks on American soil. During this time, on every level and in every other section, there are at least two guys yelling in each other's faces "Shaddup. We're s'pposed to be quiet"—and then laughing. Next, five parachutists jump from the airplane far above and begin their serpentine descent into the awaiting bowl known as House of Thrills. Each is greeted by a roar of approval from the appreciative crowd as they land on or near the bulls-eye located around the forty-yard line, but the crescendo of vocal praise is heaped upon the last individual carrying the American flag.

Suddenly, the tell-tale gong signifies that the bell tolls for us all, and the Oakland Raiders football team walks and runs onto the field, making their ritual turn toward the Black Hole to the blaring strains of AC/DC's "Hell's Bells." The crowd is screaming now, stomping, clapping, and cheering their beloved black pirates as they go through warm-ups. An equal number of boos greets the opposing team when they show up, but you can tell the crowd doesn't really mean it and it's all in fun.

A young woman emerges onto the field and sings a soulful and stirring rendition of our national anthem, The Star-Spangled Banner. Everybody standing, hats off, people singing along as they watch the giant horizontal American flag unfurled on the playing area, pulsating just above the ground. Then, as the singer reaches the crescendo of the song, they come—the planes everybody knew were out there. Four F-16s, moving north to south at 600 miles an hour, crossing over the fifty-yard line just as she belts out "home-of-the-brave"— and that quickly, they're gone, back to Afghanistan, Iraq, or simply their home at Nellis Air Force base in Nevada.

The ceremonial coin toss is held at the middle of the field and, of course, Oakland wins. The Raiders elect to kick off, and the Silver and Black special team trots out onto the field to begin the new quest. No. 11 tees it up and, with clamorous and boisterous accompaniment, puts his foot into the ball. The season is underway. The opposing player catches the kickoff five yards deep in his end zone and places a knee down, signifying a touchback and ending the play. All movement on the field slows to a trot, except for one player. At the end of the play, after kicking it and guarding against a breakaway return, No. 11 takes off at a sprint toward the opposite end zone. Without breaking stride, he throws himself into the stands, knocking a grandmother to the ground in the process. The crowd loves it as the kicker rests serenely on the ledge, filled with gratitude and surrounded by love. There, amid the hugs, handshakes, and back-slaps, he feels strangely at home.

At home in football's blackest hole.

APPENDIX: PLAY OF THE GAME

Week 1, Seattle at Oakland: Zack Crockett sustains a first-quarter injury while delivering tackle on punt coverage, awakening Raider team effort enroute to 31 to 17 win over the Seahawks.

Week 2, Oakland at Pittsburgh: Terry Kirby returns fourth-quarter kick-off 96 yards to propel Raiders past the Steelers, 30–17.

Week 3, Bye

Week 4, Tennessee at Oakland: Phillip Buchanon's 83-yard punt return in first quarter ignites Raiders' 52–25 rout of the Titans.

Week 5, Oakland at Buffalo: Phillip Buchanon's fourth-quarter interception and 81-yard touchdown return preserves 49–31 win over the Bills.

Week 6, Oakland at St. Louis: Loss

Week 7, San Diego at Oakland: Loss

Week 8, Oakland at Kansas City: Loss

Week 9, San Francisco at Oakland: Loss

Week 10, Oakland at Denver: Rod Woodson returns a first-quarter interception 98 yards for a touchdown as the Raiders trounce the Broncos, 34–10.

Week 11, New England at Oakland: Chris Cooper and Trace Armstrong team up in the second quarter to strip and recover the football as the Raiders defeat the Patriots, 27–20.

Week 12, Oakland at Arizona: Jerry Rice catches a 37-yard, post-pattern pass from Rich Gannon in third quarter enroute to 41–20 Raider victory over the Cardinals.

Week 13, New York Jets at Oakland: Jerry Rice splits the New York Jets' seam and scores on a 26-yard touchdown pass from Rich Gannon in the third quarter as the Raiders win 26–20.

Week 14, Oakland at San Diego: Anthony Dorsett leads a third-quarter phalanx of Raider defenders to deny Charger running back on fourth down as Silver and Black dominate 27–7.

Week 15, Oakland at Miami: Loss

Week 16, Denver at Oakland: In the second quarter, Charlie Garner adjusts route and gathers in 8-yard pass from Rich Gannon as Raiders throttle the Broncos, 28–16.

Week 17, Kansas City at Oakland: In the fourth quarter, Zack Crockett motors for a 33-yard gain as Raiders shut out the Chiefs for the first time, 24–0.

Week 18, Bye

Week 19, New York Jets at Oakland (Round 2, Playoffs): Jerry Porter halls in a 29-yard third- quarter pass from Rich Gannon in a 30–10 Raider thumping of the Jets.

Week 20, Tennessee at Oakland (AFC Championship): Jerry Rice catches a 15-yard second-quarter pass, is hit hard and fumbles at the one-yard line but recovers the football as the Raiders prevail 41–24.

Week 21, Oakland vs. Tampa Bay (Super Bowl XXXVII): Loss (and while you're at it, take this Super Bowl and shove it).

INDEX

ABOUT THE AUTHOR

Craig Parker was born in Forks, Washington, raised in Aberdeen, and graduated from the University of Washington. He lives in Olympia, Washington, with his wife and daughter. This is his first book.